"With compassion, empathy, and an unwavering commitment to Scripture, Ferrer and Davison equip parents and children to defend the biblical sexual worldview. And they do not mince words when it comes to the political agenda that is pushing sexuality on kids. Through Christlike love, this book is a call to arms to defend those held captive to sex-education curricula and its damaging ideas."

Josh D. McDowell,
bestselling author and speaker

"As is typical for the Mama Bear team, the *Mama Bear Apologetics® Guide to Sexuality* transforms confusion into clarity, anxiety into action steps, and polarization into Christ-centered partnership. This book is a must-read for anyone seeking to equip kids to biblically navigate gender, sexuality, and the cost of discipleship."

Elizabeth Urbanowicz,
founder of Foundation Worldview

"The *Mama Bear Apologetics® Guide to Sexuality* is a timely and helpful book. Hillary tackles some of the thorniest issues of sex and identity today, and yet she does so with compassion, insight, and biblical clarity. And she also offers some practical steps for communicating these ideas to kids. I hope you will get a copy and start implementing these ideas today."

Sean McDowell, PhD,
associate professor of apologetics at Biola University
and the author of *Chasing Love*

"Sex is never just about sex. Teens and young adults often cite biblical sexuality for the reason behind their rejection of Christianity. That is why *Mama Bear Apologetics® Guide to Sexuality* is a crucial resource for every parent. Hillary and Amy address the most relevant and confusing aspects of parenting in the shifting sands of sexual morality in our culture, giving examples from research, media, and education. They present foundational and complicated truths in a format that is easy to understand and apply. This book will equip you to navigate the discipleship journey with your kids with grace and truth."

Dr. Juli Slattery,
author of *Rethinking Sexuality* and founder of sexualdiscipleship.com

"As mothers and avid readers, we can't recommend this book enough. The culture is poisoning the hearts and minds of our children with a twisted vision of human sexuality and identity. Ferrer and Davison not only expose these lies, but they also replace them with a wonderful vision of the beautiful and breathtaking design God intends for human sexuality. This book will help you become the wise and trusted guide your kids need, leading them to the life-giving truths about love, sex, and identity that God has for His image bearers."

Erin Kunkle and Sarah Stonestreet,
cohosts of *The Strong Women Podcast* by the Colson Center

"Hillary's book is an important parent resource to identify, deconstruct, and offer clarity to today's distorted views of sexuality. God has already created an ideal for humanity and sexual integrity, and this book reminds us to stay faithful to His truth."

Monica Leal Cline,
founder of It Takes a Family

MAMA BEAR

Apologetics®

GUIDE
— *to* —
SEXUALITY

HILLARY MORGAN FERRER
WITH AMY DAVISON

HARVEST HOUSE PUBLISHERS
EUGENE, OREGON

This book is dedicated to all those who have been willing to take up their sexual crosses and still follow Christ, even when it hurts.

All Scripture quotations are taken from the Holy Bible, New International Version®, NIV®. Copyright © 1973, 1978, 1984, 2011 by Biblica, Inc.® Used by permission. All rights reserved worldwide.

Cover design and illustration by Amanda Hudson, Faceout Studio

Interior design by KUHN Design Group

The image of the taproot in chapter 5 is © Annas_Kurniawan, Shutterstock # 1736201042; the Genderbread Person image in chapter 7 is in the public domain.

For bulk, special sales, or ministry purchases, please call 1-800-547-8979.
Email: Customerservice@hhpbooks.com

MAMA BEAR APOLOGETICS is a registered trademark of Hillary Morgan Ferrer. Harvest House Publishers, Inc., is the exclusive licensee of the trademark MAMA BEAR APOLOGETICS.

是 is a federally registered trademark of the Hawkins Children's LLC. Harvest House Publishers, Inc., is the exclusive licensee of the trademark.

Italics in quoted Scriptures indicates emphasis added by the author.

Mama Bear Apologetics® Guide to Sexuality
Copyright © 2021 by Hillary Morgan Ferrer with Amy Davison
Published by Harvest House Publishers
Eugene, Oregon 97408
www.harvesthousepublishers.com

ISBN 978-0-7369-8381-5 (pbk.)
ISBN 978-0-7369-8382-2 (eBook)

Library of Congress Control Number: 2021935208

Printed in the United States of America

20 21 22 23 24 25 26 27 28 29 / BP / 10 9 8 7 6 5 4 3 2 1

Contents

My Kid's Cartoon Showed *What*?

Why I Needed This Book Yesterday

HILLARY AND AMY

Once upon a time, the sex talk was simple. It was still mortifying for both parties, but it was simple. For the little ones, you talked about the anatomical differences between boys and girls. Where do babies come from? I'm so ~~horrified~~ glad you asked! You discussed how those anatomical differences allowed the mommy and the daddy to make a baby, praying that the kids didn't ask for more details. As they got older, you discussed God's design for marriage and God's purpose for sex within a marriage. You read some verses from Ephesians, gave a very (very) light study from Song of Solomon about the goodness of sex (but only within marriage—DON'T DO IT OUTSIDE OF MARRIAGE!!!!). And then you turned these fully prepared (*cough*) youngsters over to the youth pastor, who taught them who-knows-what out of a study guide on purity. Phew! Glad that's over.

One question though: How's that been working out for us? How'd that work out for *you*? Does it feel like we're winning the culture war on this one? Because it doesn't to us. We are losing so badly that many people have just given up and opted for the "safe sex" talk because any discussion of abstinence is just laughed at. Like, *How cute! As if you can convince teenagers not to have sex…you're funny!*

To paraphrase legendary fighter Mike Tyson, everyone has a plan until they've been hit. The church, unfortunately, is no different. Between hyper-fundamentalism, the fallout of purity culture, and the at-times graceless response to LGBTQ issues, the church has taken more than its share of hits. As Dr. Juli Slattery points out, the problem isn't that the spiritual battle defending biblical sexuality isn't worth having. The problem is that the church *doesn't know how to fight*.[1] And the fallout isn't pretty.

Pew Research Journal conducted a survey on views regarding sexuality and found that 57 percent of Christians believed premarital sex in a committed relationship was fine, while 50 percent said that hookups (sleeping with someone you aren't committed to) were no biggie![2] According to one study, upward of 80 percent of unmarried evangelicals between the ages of 18 and 29 have had sex.[3]

We parents aren't doing much better. Many of us grew up in a "don't ask–don't tell" household when it came to discussing sex, and we've happily carried on the tradition with our kids. For some of us, the silence is rooted in fear. We're afraid that if we talk about sex, then our kids will want sex. Or perhaps you are only now shaking off the weight of toxic sexual messages that were piled upon your teenage shoulders. The last thing you want is to make your children feel the same guilt and shame you did. And others just don't know what to say. Heck, we don't even understand how the biblical sexual worldview is a critical aspect in our own walk with Jesus, let alone how to explain it to our kids.[4] Instead, we rely on middle school health class, our kids' friends, and social apps to do the legwork for us.

Church, can we come together for a moment and acknowledge a hard truth? This isn't working. Our kids *want* us to talk to them about sex. No really, they do. When the Power to Decide campaign surveyed thousands of students, do you know who teens ages 12 to 15 overwhelmingly said had the most influence on their sexual decisions? *Parents.* Do you know who also won the influence race with teens ages 16 to 19? *Parents.*[5] Don't let their perpetual AirPod use or eye rolls fool you: Our kids are listening. Let's start talking.

That is why you have this book, Mama Bears. You (and your husband) are your child's primary teachers. *You* are the youth pastors of your home. And God has given you everything you need to shepherd your family in the truth while holding fast to loving like Christ. The enemy has come in and tried to confuse these categories, but that's where we at Mama Bear Apologetics come in. The area of sexuality is like one giant knot—its knots even have knots. Our hopes are that, through this book, we can slowly unravel the threads of confusion surrounding the area of sexuality.

Naturally, there is a lot to unpack here. As much as our nerdy selves would love to do an in-depth study of each and every topic, we realize we are competing with naptime, busy schedules, and an acceptable word-count for popular-level books. (You mean not everyone wants 800-page, multivolume books? Pshaw.)

What we aim to present here is a biblical perspective, to backtrack how the enemy has broken God's good design, to emphasize a loving attitude toward real, hurting people behind each of these issues, but to also tackle the topics in a way that you can start reinforcing biblical sexuality for your children. Are you up for it?

Amy's Story

I was recently hiding from the Texas heat and watching TV with my kids. With three prepubescent boys, my vote for *Call the Midwife* was (unsurprisingly) outvoted, so we cuddled up to catch the latest episode of *The Loud House.* This show follows a preteen boy, Lincoln Loud, as he navigates life with ten sisters.

That day, the Loud family was trying to figure out which sibling had been the recipient of a love letter. It had been addressed only to *L,* which presented a challenge—everyone in the family had a name beginning with L! As the show progressed, each sister confronted her Valentine crush with a love note, hoping her beloved was the secret admirer. Each sister, that is, except budding rock star, Luna.

Luna was too nervous to talk to her crush, but she spent a majority of the show casting dreamy looks toward a group of kids whose ringleader was a guitar-toting heartthrob. (Boys and guitars—am I right?) With some last-minute encouragement from the Loud tribe, Luna slipped a love note into her crush's locker and ducked around the corner just as the group came down the hall. It looked like dream-boy was about to discover Luna's note...but he walked right past the locker. In the last few moments, however, my boys and I watched as guitar-boy's bandmate, *a girl*, opened the locker instead. The credits rolled as the two girls shared a googly-eyed stare.

The whole scene lasted only a few seconds, and if I had been scrolling through Pinterest I would have missed it. I glanced at my kids, and thankfully the younger two had been distracted by Legos. My ten-year-old, however, had not. He turned to me with a confused look and said, "Wait, what just happened? Does she like girls?"

And just like that, my son was introduced to the LGBTQ world. Through a cartoon.

We're Not in Kansas Anymore

I (Hillary) sometimes joke about how the Lord teaches twice—in the lecture and the lab. The "lecture" is the actual biblical teaching—right theology, wisdom gleaned from the Word. Amy's story reflects what I jokingly refer to as the "lab" portion of learning. The lab portion is where the Lord brings opportunities for you to put into practice what you've learned. Anyone who's ever prayed for patience knows what I mean. The lecture portion is fine; it's the lab portion that knocks you to your knees. Upon embarking on this book, Amy immediately realized how real and imminent the sexual agenda was—all the way down to cartoons.

We wish we could say that this was an isolated incident, but it's not. When we crowdsourced the question on social media, asking Mama Bears to share stories of LGBTQ characters in kids' shows, we had more than 150 comments *within the first hour*. With increasing frequency, television characters are involved in same-sex relationships. Children frequently have two mommies or two dads. Why this influx all of a sudden? Simple: our culture has shifted.

Back in our day (and yes, we realize how old that makes us sound), kids' programming typically matched the biblical model, with heterosexual couples and romances. But now that our culture has redefined the family, we've seen that cartoons, music, and programming in general have shifted to follow suit. This makes sense when we remember that art mimics life… but that doesn't mean that it'll always reflect truth.

Art mimics life, but that doesn't mean it reflects truth.

Amy's not the only parent who's been thrown for a loop here. You could tell your own stories about how you've seen the corruption of sexuality in our culture. Many parents have no idea what a worldview is, let alone that their children's cartoons are projecting one which isn't biblical. (We'll address that in chapter 2.) It snuck up on us while we were busy trying to figure out how this new math worked. (Why can't we just carry the tens anymore?!?!) It invaded our homes while our radar systems were focused on decoys. We missed the warning signs, and now we're in damage-control mode.

And that's why we are glad you've come here—to this safe place where we totally understand that worries often stem from uncertainty, and uncertainty comes from not understanding. In this book, we want to help you know and understand what is going on in our culture. We want to help you to define what's happening and empower your kids to live counterculturally while standing up for truth…without becoming the playground morality police.

Our kids need to be equipped so that they can refuse to call evil good, good evil, and lies truth. And make no mistake—that is what is being demanded of them. While some people like to compare this situation to Shadrach, Meshach, and Abednego being forced to bow before a statue or be thrown into the fiery furnace, I find that our kids have difficulty drawing the comparison. There's no physical statue and no actual furnace. But we do have evidence of Christians being required to pay lip service to another god or else face the consequences.

Say It or Else!

The Roman Empire was considered a bastion of tolerance according to ancient standards. All religions were generally accepted, and their adherents could worship whoever, whatever, and however they wanted—provided their worship didn't disturb the peace or create loyalty conflicts between them and Caesar. To weed out the troublemakers, there was basically one rule: once a year, everyone—no matter their religion—was required to offer a pinch of incense and say the phrase "Caesar is Lord." The temple dudes didn't care if you believed it or not. As long as you *said it,* then you were given a certificate that allowed you to buy, sell, and trade in the marketplace. No certificate, no business. Most people were willing to do this because they were already pluralistic. Why not? What's one more god? Sure, Caesar is Lord. Whatevs.

The Christians and the Jews, on the other hand, had difficulties with this. According to both the Old Testament and the New Testament, our words matter. They could not speak this lie while maintaining a clear conscience before God.

Some within the faith tried to cut corners, thinking they could just obey Caesar in body and worship God privately in their hearts. These people (the ones who were willing to compromise on this technicality) were the first to crumble once real persecution came. Pliny the Younger noted these "Christians" in a letter he wrote to Trajan. Once arrested, not only would they worship the statue of Trajan, but they could be persuaded to "utter imprecations against the name of Christ." (An imprecation is basically a curse.) On the flip side, he notes that "there is no forcing, it is said, those who are *really Christians* into any of these compliances...I judged it necessary to try to get at the real truth by putting to the torture two female slaves, who were said to officiate in their religious rites; but all I could discover was evidence of an absurd and extravagant superstition."[6] (This superstition was that Jesus was resurrected.)

Summary: once you start compromising in the little things, it's easy to compromise in the big things. The ones who refused to compromise at the temple when things were easy were the ones to stand firm in the jail once things got hard.

While nobody is getting tortured yet, we are facing a looming crisis where we Christians will be required to pay lip service to the god of our age—sex. Our kids are being desensitized, song by song, cartoon by cartoon, numbed to the point where immorality feels like no big deal. We want them to be able to dispense with the false ideas about sexuality that our culture sends their way, which means we need to start discipling them yesterday.

Instead of pointing us to God, sexual pleasure has become a god in itself. Sexuality is our ruler, one who must be obeyed and to whom we must pay homage in word and in deed. Cloaked in the language of morality, our children are being fed lies that could lead them to kneel at the altar of pleasure. The call to open their eyes to these lies is a godly conviction.

All of that starts with calling out cultural lies for what they are. After reading the first *Mama Bear Apologetics* book, a reader told me, "These lies were all around me in culture, and I just didn't see them. But now I do. And now that I see them, I can't not see them." That's our goal for this book as well—to shed some light on the lies so you'll know them when you see them. As we discuss each one of these messages, we'll hold it up to the Word and let godly wisdom inform our thinking.

Here's What to Expect

Part 1 focuses on the biblical view of sexuality. We look at how the way we view sexuality is actually a make-it-or-break-it issue for being a disciple of Jesus (chapter 1). Sexuality isn't just some side aspect of Christianity; what we believe about what's done in the bedroom reveals what we *really* believe about God, others, reality, and ourselves (chapter 2). While people might think that the core of the sexual revolution is pleasure (and that is a big part of it), an even bigger issue is the idea of *authority*, meaning who has the right to determine what we do with our bodies (chapter 3). And we'll frame how all of these topics should be approached—with love for people who are held captive to bad ideas (chapter 4).

In Part 2, we dig into the actual standards and curricula that are being taught to your kids. Chapter 5 introduces us to the New Sex Education Standards and the worldview behind them. Chapter 6 discusses two incredibly powerful tactics—moralization and repetition—that are causing our kids to be confused about what is true. Next, we discuss how words are being changed, stolen, and smuggled, leading our society to adopt new standards of morality, all the while thinking these new morals are supported by Scripture. Chapter 7, "The Genderbread Person," is an *actual* curriculum that is being used in elementary schools across the country and will give you a cursory understanding of the new sex and gender terminology that your kids are coming home with. Chapter 8 addresses the sacred cow that undergirds everything: sex-positivity. This philosophy teaches your kids that the *only* things that matter with sex are mutual consent and physical pleasure.

In Part 3, we go over the specific things that are tripping everyone up. Chapter 9 describes how our bodies are created to chemically bond with our sexual partners, and how the porn industry has hijacked our kids' brains and started grooming them to consume and perform sexually explicit material. Chapter 10 helps elucidate the same-sex debate from a compassionate yet scientific, psychological, and theological perspective—tackling the biggest arguments that revisionist and gay-affirming advocates have used to cause the church to embrace a revised view of sexuality. Chapter 11 dives deep into the gender ideology that seems to be steering all our upcoming legislation, while providing practical tips so that your kids don't get confused about their identity in Christ. Chapter 12 takes a look at how we as a church attempted to address all these issues back in the '90s…and how it totally blew up in our faces. For these chapters, you'll recognize the popular ROAR format (*recognize* the message, *offer* discernment, *argue* for a healthier approach, and *reinforce* through discussion, discipleship, and prayer). The final chapter reminds us where the real battle is—encouraging us to take up our crosses daily to follow Christ and have compassion on one another.

As an added bonus in the Afterword, we go over things you'll want to repeat to your kids until they want to gag because, as we note in chapter 6, the human brain has difficulty distinguishing between truth and familiarity. There's power in good maxims to reinforce a biblical worldview, and we're not ashamed of using them! Our kids need good, bite-sized pieces of wisdom to combat the colorfully glittered bad philosophy that parades across their Instagram feeds.

Three Type of Readers

One of the things I (Hillary) have been convicted of from the moment I started speaking in public was recognizing the variety of personalities within my audience. What feels like a refreshing new idea to one parent feels like overload to another. So before we start on this book, I want to acknowledge three very different mom-types who might be reading this book.

Group 1: It's All My Responsibility

Some of you reading this book feel that everything is your responsibility—from organic meals and Baby Beethoven to homeschooling and driving your kids to AWANA. If it will benefit your child, you'll give it a try. These are all good things! The care and thought you give is why you are holding this book. You understand the gravity of raising kids in this secular world. You are doing your absolute best, and it feels like if anyone puts one more straw on your back you will finally collapse under the weight. If this is you, please sit for a moment and acknowledge that. Praise God for the ways you take responsibility for shepherding your children! However, there is also a time to rest. Consider saying the following prayer before embarking on this book:

> *Father God, I know Your yoke is easy and Your burden is light.*
> *I desire to please You by being faithful with my children. Lord,*
> *please teach me how to release that which is out of my control.*
> *As I read this book, I pray that the enemy's voice of condemnation would be silenced. Lord, convict me of things where I need*
> *to improve, but please protect me from feelings of guilt or inadequacy as I learn this new information. Show me the things You*

*would have me do to raise faithful, godly children, and help me
to release them back to You, knowing that You are a good, good,
Father.*

Group 2: It's All God's Responsibility

Another group reading this book has mastered the art of resting in
Christ's sovereignty, which is a good thing. However, it can sometimes lead
to assumptions that a good Christian school, a flourishing youth group,
and a few dinnertime conversations will suffice for raising their children
in the faith. This group may be less aware of the seriousness of the lies that
culture is peddling to our kids, and might need a swift kick in the pants
to realize that this world is entirely different from the world in which they
grew up. We can't raise our children the way we were raised because the
world in which we were raised is gone. If this is you, then be prepared for
a wakeup call! It will be tempting to feel like there is too much to be done,
and you might want to stick your fingers in your ears and sing, "La la la la!"

Please don't. It's not too late, and it's not too hard. There is grace for
not being a perfect parent. Don't give up! My prayer is that the Holy Spirit
would be with you in this book, convicting and motivating you to be the
warrior your kids need to raise them up in a robust Christian faith, understanding sex as a beautiful gift of God. And here's a prayer you can offer:

*Lord God, I thank You for the rest I have in You. I praise You
because You are sovereign. There is not a single bird that falls from
the sky without Your knowledge. Lord, I confess the times when I
have used my faith in Your providence as an excuse to not engage
the culture. Lord, I pray You would open my eyes to ways that I can
be actively training my kids. I pray You would reveal my blind spots.
I pray for wisdom, and I pray for discernment against the enemy's
lying tongue, bringing condemnation where You are trying to bring
conviction. Give me the strength, Lord, to face these issues head-on,
so that I might be a parent who purposely shepherds my kids to resist
cultural lies. I do all things knowing that You are with me.*

Group 3: I've Already Blown It

It is naive to think that all the readers of this book have squeaky-clean pasts. We have a God who came to remove our shame and bring beauty from ashes. That being said, I believe many of us are still walking in sexual shame and don't even know it.

Dealing with shame is not a process we can rush, any more than we can rush the process of grief. Grief is not fun, but it is *healthy*. It is *necessary*. It is practically a *requirement* for emotional healing. We cannot repress grief; it will come out in some other way. Similarly, there is no fast-tracking the repentance and healing process.

And here's where I want to make a bold thesis. It is not until we have come to terms with our own sin—fully acknowledging, fully confessing, fully grieving, and fully receiving God's forgiveness—that we can finally walk in freedom. And freedom is what I want for you and your children, friends! *Experiencing God's freedom from our sexual past is key to being able to talk to our kids about sex in a healthy way.*

Some of you have experienced sexual abuse or trauma and are still walking in bondage to a burden placed on you by another. For these Mama Bears, let me speak from experience that the Lord is faithful. Some healing comes quickly and some slowly. Never give up! Praise Jesus for the amazing counselors who are out there. He has given us His Word, and He has also given us His medical and counseling ambassadors who can help walk us through the damage that comes from sexual trauma. For you, I pray the Lord would bring healing to the parts that have been broken so that you can walk in freedom from a burden you should never have had to carry.

For other Mama Bears, freedom means receiving the forgiveness that God offers *and then forgiving yourself*. I have known amazing women, godly wives and mothers, who live in fear that someone will discover their past. For you, I want to pray peace and hope. The Lord has removed your sins as far as the east is from the west. You are *free*, Mama Bear. Don't let the enemy tether you to what the Lord has freed you from.

Now, we might have some Mama Bears who are currently in sexual sin. To you, I implore: please realize your worth. My prayer for you is that you would see yourself the way the Lord sees you. He wants freedom for you. Sexual sin is the only sin Scripture calls "sinning against your own body" (see 1 Corinthians 6:18). In Romans 1, sexual sin is referred to as people "degrading themselves with one another" (see verse 24). *Do not believe the enemy's lie that degrading yourself is empowering.*

Each one of these types of bondage can lead to difficulties in talking with our children about sex. Slavery to shame can result in fear-based teaching, confusing kids as to the innate goodness of sex within marriage. Slavery to sin results in a "do as I say, not as I do" type teaching of sex, or even a tacit permission to sin because deep down you don't believe young people are capable of controlling their urges. Whatever your bondage, it will likely be passed on to your kids when you talk about sex. It's not an insurmountable issue. But it's something to keep in mind and something to pray about as we go through this journey together.

A Final Word

We are going to address a lot of topics in this book—both from a biblical perspective and from the secular perspective, which is trying to rewrite God's commands regarding sexuality. My prayer for you is that you don't let the pervasiveness of the secular worldview overwhelm you. We need to be aware of the adversary's schemes so that we can properly defend against them. *We can't defend against that which we don't understand.* There is power in understanding the enemy's playbook. There is power in preparing to meet these schemes head-on, and we can empower our children to do the same—with grace, love, and truth.

You'll find problems here of which you might have been blissfully unaware, but ignorance isn't safety. Think of this book as if you'd discovered the enemy's manual and now, for the first time, you can actually prepare your kids for what is coming.

Get ready, Mama Bears. It's time to ROAR.

Part One

Things I Probably Already Knew...But Kinda Forgot

PRAYER OF LAMENT[1]

Turn to God

LAMENTATIONS 1:5; 3:19

Our young children have gone into captivity before the enemy. We pour out our hearts like water before You, Lord, for the lives of our children. O Lord, earnestly remember what has come upon us! Look down and see our reproach, our national disgrace!

———————

Lord, hear our prayers. We are desperate. Who else can we turn to? Where else can we go? You are our only help and refuge from the onslaught of the sexualization of everything, from the normalization of all things contrary to Your will. Our kids are in a world of trouble.

Chapter 1

Sexually Set Apart

How Sexual Holiness Is a
Nonnegotiable for Disciples of Jesus

Hillary

I n the year 2000, Hollywood graced us with the poignant and moving cinematic masterpiece *Dude, Where's My Car?* The film follows two dim-witted deadbeats who, after a night of binge drinking, cannot find their car and have unexpectedly acquired an otherworldly device about which they know nothing. Well, not nothing. They know exactly two things: It's a mysterious and powerful device, and its mystery is only exceeded by its power.

A mysterious and powerful device, you say? Of which its mystery is only exceeded by its power?!?! *That*, my friends, is sexuality. *Selah.* (That's Christianese for "meditate on that for a hot second.")

While I am joking about the movie being a masterpiece, the mystery and power of sex are no laughing matter. You might even call sex the first command. God was like, "Here's your garden; be fruitful and multiply (wink!)." As Clay Jones explains, "All Adam and Eve had to do all day long was to garden and play with creation's *only* physically perfect and com-pletely naked member of the opposite sex."[1]

The idea that sexuality should be guarded is not very popular. Our soci-ety sees it as just a prudish phase we went through back in the Victorian era. Thanks to Freud, we are now supposedly enlightened, understanding that sexual repression is basically the gateway to all mental illnesses. Be free, little birdies! It's for your own good! Don't listen to those religious nutjobs. They all craaaaaazy.

Christians are often accused of being obsessed with sex or afraid of sex because we uphold the biblical teaching that sex is intended for husband and wife...and because we speak up when abstinence is excluded from the options laid before today's teens. We believe that far from portraying sex as a dirty act, Scripture teaches that sex is good! God created it! There's even a whole book of the Bible celebrating it. As my old pastor used to say—from the pulpit, no less—"God is not a killjoy. We serve the God who *created* the orgasm." Unfortunately, our live-and-let-live world can't understand why such an awesome gift shouldn't be shared with as many partners as possible.

But let's take things back a bit...or a lot. If we are to understand sexuality, we must go back to the very beginning. As we will show later in the chapter, sex is intended to be a *sign* of the covenant between husband and wife. Every time a married couple makes love, they are—in bodily form— *repeating their marital vows*. God doesn't place limits on sex because He wants to downplay the goodness of sex. He places limits on it because sex has *meaning*, meaning that our culture has lost.

To be fair, our culture hasn't just lost the meaning of sex; we've actually lost the meaning of *meaning*! Postmodernism teaches that there is no such thing as inherent meaning. Meaning is now a social construct, *imposed* upon things by us humans. We determine meaning. We determine truth. We're fashioned into little gods who can speak truth into existence...or change it on a whim.

If you read the first *Mama Bear Apologetics* book, you know how prevalent the postmodern ideology is. Which brings me to a sad truth: if our kids can't understand the concept of unchangeable, inherent meaning, then they will never understand that *sex* has unchangeable, inherent, meaning. They will not understand that sex carries a message, and that we do not have the authority to tamper with that message. When we tamper with God's plan for sex, we miscommunicate the truths that God had intended to be seen through the marital union.

The message the world is telling our kids is that one's preference for sex is no longer even a preference; *it is a person's very identity*—a foundational aspect which can neither be questioned by others nor restricted.

Our world treats sex as the inviolable truth on which everything rests. It's the big kahuna of human experience to which everyone has a right. Secular culture sees itself as the champion of the most powerful and important aspect in the world, and we Christians as the great buzzkill, trying to downplay the awesomeness of sex.

Okay, fine. We'll play that game for a second. Let's just grant briefly (for the sake of argument) that sex *is* the most important thing in the world. Shouldn't we then ask, "Doesn't *every* important and powerful thing involve boundaries and protection from misuse?" Seriously. Name one other thing that is super important and super powerful that isn't carefully guarded or meticulously controlled (nuclear warheads, controlled substance prescriptions). In fact, the *more* important and powerful something is, the *more* it is usually safeguarded. Why wouldn't we expect the same to be true about sex?

Since God created sex, He is the only one who truly knows what it means, what it communicates, and how powerful it really is—and how destructive it is when misused.

Set Apart from the Beginning

God's commands regarding sex are not just a side issue. They are a prominent theme spanning the Old and New Testaments, especially in terms of holiness. The word "holy" literally means "set apart for a special purpose." As Christians, our sexual ethic is a major way in which we are called to be set apart from the world because sexual holiness is, in essence, a *sign of our knowledge of and commitment to God*. It has always been this way.

Throughout Scripture, we see how God's people have been called to sexual holiness—how they are to be sexually set apart. Let's take a cursory overview through the Old and New Testaments to see exactly how serious the Lord is regarding this topic.

The Old Testament: Whoring After Other Gods...
Oddly Not a Metaphor

I recommend reading through Deuteronomy 22:13-25 and Leviticus 18 and 20 to get a thorough overview of what God defines as sexual immorality and how seriously He takes it. One might notice that He's *really* thorough in these passages. His commands regarding sex aren't just revealing sexual boundaries; God is actually describing the culture that the Israelites were coming out of and the culture they were told to conquer.

Yahweh prefaces the Levitical sex laws by saying, "I am the LORD your God. You must not do as they do in Egypt, where you used to live, and you must not do as they do in the land of Canaan, where I am bringing you" (Leviticus 18:2-3). God then proceeds to list everyone (family members) and everything (animals) with whom to *not* have sex. After this extensive list, He restates His original purpose for sexual holiness: "Do not defile yourselves in any of these ways, because this is how the nations that I am going to drive out before you became defiled" (Leviticus 18:24). In other words, *This is how I am calling you to be set apart from the rest of the world! Don't mess it up, or I'll remove you just like I did them.* (And if you keep reading through Judges and Chronicles, you'll see that that's exactly what happens.)

Israel struggled with sexual idolatry from the start—and kept returning to it throughout the course of its history. There are a few pockets here and there where they are faithful to God. But more often than not, they fell right back into the practices of the nations whom they were told to drive out of the land.

The Canaanites were not—as some people might think—just a poor, unsuspecting people who were just trying to live their lives in peace. (Admit it...you've thought this before, haven't you? It's okay. I did too, once upon a time.) But if you really dive into Canaanite history and culture, at some point—after you've recovered from your nausea—you start to think that maybe, *just maybe,* this was a culture that needed to be wiped out.[2]

I cannot even begin to describe the kind of sexual debauchery that was going on in Canaan before the Israelites got there. I've never played a drinking game before, but if I were going to, I'd use Mountain Dew, and I'd do a word study of the usage of the word "whore" in the Old Testament. I remember a pastor reading through Ezekiel 16–20 and thinking "Holy schnikes, I've never heard someone say *whore* this many times in a row." It's also prevalent in the book of Hosea. When I was younger, I assumed that "whoring after other gods" language was merely metaphorical, symbolic of Israel's spiritual adultery. (And yes, it's true that the Lord uses the word this way. After all, we the church are also called the "bride of Christ" throughout the New Testament. The picture of marriage is a common theme with God and His people.) But after studying ancient Near East practices, I came to the horrifying realization that whoring after other gods was not—I repeat, *not*—purely a metaphor. People were literally worshipping other gods by having temple orgies.

The Asherah poles and the "high places" described in Scripture were giant phallic symbols. According to pagan worship, the gods needed to be stimulated into giving up the goodies—fertility, rain, and crops. So how do you stimulate the gods? By basically providing a veritable smorgasbord of live religious porn—complete with incest, child abuse, homosexuality, and...things that should never be done with a goat.[3] In this culture, sex with the temple prostitutes was the height of religious piety. I suspect there were lots of "very religious men" in this culture. "Honey, I'm going to church...again."

And what would they do with all the babies that were born from these sex-capades? They'd burn them on the altar to Molech.[4] Child sacrifice is just one more of the detestable practices of Canaan from which God called His people to separate. And before you ask (like a woman did in a lecture that my husband John and I gave on the Canaanites), "How could anyone allow such a thing to happen in their community?" remember this: *It's still happening.* Our culture serves its own Molech. It's called Planned

Parenthood. Children always have been and always will be the victims of our sexual immorality. We have not changed. We have not progressed. We've just gotten better at hiding (and renaming) our child sacrifices.

And just in case you are *still* wondering how seriously God takes sexual sin, hop over for a moment to Numbers 25. This is one of those Bible stories that will *never* be reenacted on a felt board in Sunday school, but it's an important read. Moses is giving a verbal smackdown to the entire nation of Israelite men for sleeping around with the Midianite women. In the middle of his rant, some moron traipses through the crowd with a Midianite woman on his arm and disappears with her into his tent. Aaron's grandson Phinehas sees this, follows them in, and skewers them with a spear...*in the middle of the deed.* How does God respond? He gives Phinehas and his descendants an eternal priesthood for being so zealous for the Lord. Our sexual faithfulness *really* matters to God.

The New Testament: Pointing Back to God's Design

The New Testament also has quite a bit to say on the topic, though not necessarily by Jesus Himself. And some people find that to be a problem. Since Jesus didn't explicitly condemn all the same sexual practices prohibited in the Old Testament (like homosexuality), some feel that His silence is tacit approval for all sexual unions. But this is just a logical fallacy called "the argument from silence." When Jesus came, He didn't spend much time reexplaining God's sexual law because He was speaking to Jews, and the Jews *already knew how God defined sexual immorality.* They had studied the Jewish law for centuries. If we were to take Christ's silence on topics as permission, then we could justify almost anything—sex with animals, sleeping with your mom, harvesting people's organs for profit, you name it. Don't get sucked into this bad argument.

When Jesus *did* speak on sexual morality and marriage, He stuck with the K.I.S.S. method ("Keep It Simple, Stupid") and simply pointed His Jewish audience back to their own Scriptures, back to God's original design—"A man will leave his father and mother and be united to his wife, and the two will become one flesh" (Matthew 19:5, quoting Genesis 2:24).

Later, in Romans 1, the apostle Paul describes the descent of a culture down into oblivion. The passage begins with people who know God but don't really care about worshipping Him (verse 21). Then their minds and their hearts go stupid (verse 22). They start worshipping something else (verse 23), and God gives them over to what they think they want: lots and lots of sex (verse 24). A few orgies later, their sexuality goes from depraved to unnatural (verse 26). At the end of the whole process you are left with a group that doesn't even know what good looks like anymore. Take a peek at verses 29-32, friends. This is our society's future if things continue as they are.

> They have become filled with every kind of wickedness, evil, greed and depravity. They are full of envy, murder, strife, deceit and malice. They are gossips, slanderers, God-haters, insolent, arrogant and boastful; they invent ways of doing evil; they disobey their parents; they have no understanding, no fidelity, no love, no mercy. Although they know God's righteous decree that those who do such things deserve death, they not only continue to do these very things but also approve of those who practice them.

Sexual morality is emphasized in almost every New Testament epistle, especially the ones aimed at Gentiles, who didn't have the benefit of centuries of Jewish law. Sexual immorality is not only mentioned, but it's usually mentioned first in the long lists of sins that a Christ-follower *must* forsake—no ifs, ands, or buts.

- 1 Corinthians 5:9-13: Paul is so emphatic on sexual holiness that he commands church members *not to associate with those who call themselves Christians but engage in sexual immorality.*

- Ephesians 5:3: Paul says that there shouldn't even be a hint of sexual immorality among believers—not even in jest.

- Colossians 3:5: Believers are told to put sexual immorality to death.

- Galatians 5:16-19: Sexual immorality is contrasted with the fruit of the Spirit.

- Revelation 2:13-16: A lax attitude regarding sexual immorality is a deal breaker, even in a church that is faithful in almost every other way.

- 1 Thessalonians 4:3-8: This might be the most convicting passage of all! It is God's will that we avoid sexual immorality, and "anyone who rejects this instruction does not reject a human being but God."

This is just a small sampling of verses which explicitly tell us that being set apart as a Christian is synonymous with sexual holiness. The number of references expands considerably once you include all the passages that condemn umbrella categories like "deeds of the flesh" or "unrighteousness" or "wickedness," since elsewhere sexual immorality is included under these umbrella terms. I'm not sure how much more explicit we need the Bible to be. How are professing Christians getting this so wrong?

Maybe your teenager is asking, "Where *exactly* does the Bible *specifically* say sex outside of marriage is wrong?" Read 1 Corinthians 7:9 together: "If they cannot control themselves, they should marry, for it is better to marry than to burn with passion." Paul is not offering marriage as the only and ultimate remedy for dealing with sexual desire (he sings big praises for staying chastely single as well). Nor is he saying the *only* reason to get married is so you can have sex. What he is saying is that marriage is the proper alternative for the sinning already going on. Ask your teen this: If Paul's *solution* to sexual immorality was to get married, then what do you think the Corinthians' original *problem* was? (Hint: People having sex outside of marriage!)

To which your child then tries to justify, "But they didn't have a category for long-term, monogamous, committed relationships." Stop it. Yes, they did. It was called betrothal, and it was like our engagements but more binding. (Note how Joseph was betrothed to Mary, and he couldn't just take the ring back. To break it off, he had to divorce her—and that's before they ever got married and consummated the relationship. Jewish committed relationships were even more committed than ours!) Paul closes this loophole when he addresses those who are betrothed. If their passions are too strong—meaning they're going to go crazy if they don't have sex—then by all means get married! A person looking for loopholes will always make things sound more complicated than they are in the hope that the text doesn't say what it clearly says.

> A person looking for loopholes will always make things sound more complicated than they are in the hope that the text doesn't say what it clearly says.

It should be clear by now what God says about sexuality. But the question on every teen's mind is *why? Why* does God define sexual morality in such a narrow way? It seems like an arbitrary rule. If sex is so wonderful and a gift from God, why would He try to limit it so much? The answer is simple, but it won't make sense if you don't understand the power and purpose of sex.

The Purpose of Sex

All conversations with our kids about sex need to include a very important concept: *Sex is a married couple repeating their marital vows in bodily form.* Now I don't normally point to Hollywood for transcendent truths about sex, but there is a line from one movie that has always stuck out to me. In the movie *Vanilla Sky*—not one I'd recommend for casual viewing—two characters, Julie and David, have a lot (and I mean a *lot*) of what we would consider "friends with benefits" sex. Later in the movie, when David meets a woman with whom he actually falls in love, Julie goes absolutely psycho. She screams at him, "Don't you know that when you sleep with someone, your body makes a promise whether you do or not?"

It's a surprisingly accurate (though incomplete) statement for a Hollywood movie. The act of sex is not just a promise: it is a reference *back* to a promise that was already made. As Tim Keller says in his article "The Gospel and Sex," "Sex is a covenant renewal ceremony for marriage, the physical reenactment of the inseparable oneness in all other areas—economic, legal, personal, physiological—created by the marriage covenant."[5] It is the bodily recitation of "the self-forgetting, self-transcending, self-giving" promise that was made on the couple's wedding day.[6]

What are you doing when you engage in the act of sex before committing to the covenant of marriage? Lying. You are lying. You are repeating a promise that you never made. Our bodies though, unfortunately, cannot tell the difference. Which brings us to the power of sex.

Things That Are Powerful Enough to Be Guarded

If we are to talk to our kids about sex in a way that makes sense to them, we must first establish a few categories in their heads. First is, "Things that are so powerful that they need to be guarded with boundaries," and the second is, "Things that are good or bad depending on how they are used." Fire gives a useful analogy for both categories.

Ask your kids, "Is fire good or bad?" Some might say good because they are thinking about roasting marshmallows or soaking in a bathtub surrounded by scented candles (yes, please!). Some might say bad because they are picturing forest fires or explosions. The truth is, fire as a concept is neutral; it can be good or bad depending on how it's used.

Here's another question for your kids: how powerful is fire? If they were already picturing a forest fire, then they're on the right track. Not only is fire powerful, but it can be used to accomplish great feats of strength that we'd never be able to do on our own.

Using fire, we can blow holes through solid rock on a mountainside, cook food, provide light, purify metal…you name it! Or we can burn down half of California. Fire is most beneficial when it is contained within proper boundaries and most dangerous when removed from its proper place. A fire within a fireplace can create a warm and inviting home. Take it outside the fireplace, and it can destroy everyone and everything you love in the blink of an eye. *Long story short, fire can help create and fire can help destroy. That it can do both is our first clue that it should be handled with caution.*

Enough About Fire, You Pyro...

The same line of thinking can be applied to sex. Is sex good or bad? Well, it depends on how it's used. Sexual intimacy can be used to forge bonds of intimacy between man and woman that not even Hades can separate. It can literally create a human being—from scratch I might add! Sexual energy is *really* powerful. Sexual desire—when channeled toward one's spouse—reemphasizes the vows that they made to love, honor, cherish, and protect till death do they part. When a couple takes their marriage vows seriously, they fortify their marriage, stabilize their home, and create strong families in which children can thrive. Strong families create strong communities, which lead to a strong society.

But just like fire, sex can be used to destroy as well. The sexual impulse, without restraint, can devastate an individual and destroy a marriage. If sex is—as we've stated—a recommitment to the marital vows, then even sex within a marriage can be misused. As Christopher West says in his book *Our Bodies Tell God's Story,*

> Treating a spouse merely as an object for one's selfish indulgence is never an act of love. Few Christian men understand this critical point. The books and programs that have flooded the Christian market to help in our "pornified" culture rarely get this either. The main goal of these programs is to help husbands direct their sexual desires toward their wives—a good first step, of course. But rarely, if ever, do these programs invite men to examine *what kind of desires* they're directing toward their wives.[7]

I have known far too many women who have been at the receiving end of this misuse of sex. Just because he put a ring on it, he feels that he can come to his wife and demand sexual gratification as much as he wants or in any way he chooses. Such demands in no way reflect a Christlike *agape* love which honors and cherishes his wife as a person. These demands, even if made within the confines of marriage, can undo what sex was intended to do. Rather than reinforcing, these selfish acts of lust *nullify* in bodily form the promises he made on their wedding day. And this is not just for men. Ladies, we are not off the hook. The way we initiate or respond to our husbands sexually should also reflect the vows we made to him.

So as you have probably noticed by looking around at our culture, sex misused outside of marriage—without reaffirming a lifetime commitment—often produces broken hearts, broken families, unwanted or aborted babies, and way more venereal diseases than should ever exist. Sex misused within a marriage—without the self-giving *agape* love promised on the wedding day—can hinder a marriage. Like fire, sex can create and sex can destroy. That it can do both is our first clue that it, too, should be handled with caution.

Who Are Really the Ones Obsessed with Sex — Christians or Secularists?

We have established that sex can be good or bad depending on whether it is properly channeled or contained. We have established that sex is extremely powerful. Let's go one step further in our analogy and discuss the ways that one can interact with something that is extremely powerful and potentially dangerous. Back to our fire analogy!

There are two extreme ways one might interact with fire: as an arsonist or as a fireman. Question: who of these two do you think is more obsessed with fires? I'd say they are equally obsessed, just in different ways. One is obsessed with creating as much fire as possible, and one is obsessed with containing fire to prevent destruction. The arsonist doesn't care about the consequence; he only cares about the flame. The fireman doesn't hate fire—I'm sure he loves a good campfire just as much as the next person. But he takes great pains to make sure that a flame doesn't turn into a raging inferno. Firemen put their lives on the line to help curtail the negative impact of fires gone wild. Arsonists just stand back and enjoy the show.

Our world treats sex like an arsonist treats fire. Who cares about consequences? Sex, sex, and more sex! As the arsonist hates anyone who tries to put out his fires, so our world hates anyone who rains on their sex parades. They look at the church and assume we are a bunch of dumpy, frigid, sexually repressed schoolmarms sitting atop our moral high horses, wagging our fingers and chastising people for having too much fun.

Like it or not, we as Christians are called by God to be set apart, and one of the defining characteristics of His followers is sexual holiness. And now we can understand why! He didn't make boundaries because He wanted to control us or stomp on our fun, but because He wanted sex to retain its original meaning. God desires for us to experience real, lasting, flourishing fellowship with Him and with others. As we'll see in chapter 3, we flourish best when we stick to the beautiful design He created.

Discussion Questions

1. **Icebreaker:** Has there ever been a time when you underestimated the power or danger of something and got hurt? What happened?

2. **Main theme:** *Sex is a very powerful bodily recitation of our marital vows; anything powerful enough to create or destroy can and should be carefully guarded.* What's the most powerful thing you can think of? Are there any kind of controls or regulations that govern it? What do you think would happen if there were no guidelines for it?

3. **Self-evaluation:** What were you taught about sex growing up? Was it treated as something good? Something dirty? Did your family even talk about sex? Have you ever been tempted to think that sex was "no big deal"? What are your thoughts on it after reading this chapter? How seriously does God take sex? Why do you think that is?

4. **Brainstorm:** As a group, compile a list of powerful and dangerous things in the world that should be treated with caution. Nuclear bombs? A rabid raccoon? You name it. Make sure you have a clear category in your head of "things that are so powerful that they need boundaries." (Because you're going to do this with your kids next!)

5. **Release the bear:** Here's a fun discipleship idea! Create a secret handshake with your child and give it a meaning that involves a

promise. It could be something like, "I'll love you forever and ever," or even, "I'm sorry, and I'll try to do better." Use it often in place of the words, showing your child how they can *use their bodies to restate a promise that was already made with their words*. Ask them frequently if they remember what it means and have them recite it to you. Later, when they are old enough for "the talk," you can tell them how sex is the way adults use their bodies to restate their wedding vows to their spouse.

6. **Pray:** Have you treated sex with the gravity God describes in Scripture? Pray and ask the Lord to work in your heart to understand sex the way He does. Pray that He would show you when to start having these conversations with your kids so that they can understand the goodness and power of sex.

Chapter 2

Sex Is Spelled
W-O-R-L-D-V-I-E-W

Wait, What's a Worldview?

HILLARY AND AMY

(Hillary) remember the exact moment when I understood the *why* behind the Bible's teaching about saving sex for marriage. My husband and I started dating in 2006, and for my birthday he got me a book titled *Sex and the Supremacy of Christ.* (Because that's what nerds in love give each other as gifts.) I underlined a portion of the book that made two life-changing points which transformed my outlook on sex forever.

> The first is that *sexuality is designed by God as a way to know God in Christ more fully.* And the second is that *knowing God in Christ more fully is designed as a way of guarding and guiding our sexuality...*
>
> Now to state the two points again, this time negatively, in the first place *all misuses of our sexuality distort the true knowledge of Christ.* And, in the second place, *all misuses of our sexuality derive from not having the true knowledge of Christ.*[1]

Boom. Mic drop. Mind blown.

My world changed in that moment. A misuse of my sexuality could distort my perception of God? Whoa! I don't want that to happen. Or wait…when someone has a distorted view of God, His mandates regarding sex won't even make sense to them? That actually kinda makes sense now that I think about it…

I've had few worldview shifts of this magnitude in my life. All of them can be summarized by a quote from C.S. Lewis: "I believe in Christianity as I believe that the Sun has risen, not only because I see it but because by it, I see everything else."[2] Those two little statements made so many other things in my life make sense—especially God's biblical commands.

All of God's super detailed laws about sex? I think I get it now. *Of course! You put boundaries around anything that is powerful enough to change the way a person sees God!* The New Testament epistles telling us to flee sexual immorality used to sound all preachy. Now they sounded super practical. *Of course! These new Christians were just getting to know God, and they were supposed to be representing God to the pagans around them. If having a distorted sexual life resulted in their representing a distorted view of God, then they needed to get that nonsense out of the church. God was trying to warn them that they were misrepresenting Him to the people He was trying to save! Duh! How had I missed this?*

When I finally understood how sex and the image of God were intertwined, it was like a million other lightbulbs went on. I didn't believe Piper's statement because he was "an expert." I believed Piper's statement because it made sense of things I'd already observed.

I have actually witnessed firsthand the distorting impact that sexual immorality can have on one's view of God. I've had friends who, once their commitment to sexual holiness went out the window, so did their theology. One friend whom I had been in youth leadership with just walked away from the church altogether after becoming sexually involved with a non-Christian man whom she eventually married. Another friend—a girl whom I had been in leadership with at Cru—eventually turned not only away from God but *toward goddess worship.* She now teaches classes on how sex is at the "core of our vitality," whatever that means. It was a slow process, and it didn't happen all at once. But when she changed her views (and her actions) to match a worldly view of sex, her heart didn't just reject God, it went full pagan, just like God warned the Israelites in the wilderness. Similarly, another girl I knew (through mutual friends) now teaches classes involving chanting to the moon and the volcano while a group of women masturbate together in the woods. I wish I were joking!

All this to say, I have seen Piper's warning in action, and I did *not* want to go down that road. I really, really, value truth, logic, sound thinking, and being able to see things correctly. I was horrified at the thought of *anything* messing with my ability to perceive reality accurately—especially the reality of God. And overnight, my motivation to save sex for marriage changed from external (I'm not supposed to) to internal (I want something else more). It almost wasn't even a temptation anymore.

That is what a worldview shift can do. We no longer operate as children who are told what to do and what not to do. As mature adults, we learn to value that which is true, good, and meaningful more than that which is fun and pleasurable but ultimately degrading. And we value these things on their own terms, not because some pastor somewhere said so. Our kids can learn this too. Although I am sorry to report that if a person really doesn't *care* if they see God correctly or not, this revelation will not be nearly as compelling.

How to Understand a Worldview

While most people think of sexual morality as only a moral issue, the implications are much more complex. At its core, a person's view of sexuality isn't just tied to their view of God, but to their entire *worldview*. The word *worldview* may be an ambiguous concept for some. The following are helpful analogies to better understand how a worldview functions.

A Worldview Is Like Rules to a Game

You can't really play a board game unless everyone knows what the goal is and what you can and can't do. When it comes to life on this earth, there are metaphysical rules that we play by. What constitutes reality?

Does truth exist, and if so, how do we find it? What counts as good? What counts as evil? Where do we come from, and where are we going? What does it mean to be human, and what is our purpose here on this planet?

Our worldview answers every one of those fundamental questions, influencing how we see the world, humanity, and our role in both. Conflicts happen when people are not in agreement as to how these fundamental questions should be answered.

A Worldview Is Like a Lens

A lens determines how accurately we perceive reality. If you've ever gotten glasses, you know the difference it makes to look through a good pair of lenses. The wrong lenses can lead to a fuzzy picture of the world around you. Or the prescription might be totally wonky, distorting your view like a carnival mirror. The right lenses, on the other hand, sharpen your vision, giving you a clear picture of reality. (Everyone who's ever gotten glasses knows the "Holy cow! Trees have leaves!" moment.) Likewise, a well-oriented worldview allows our perceptions of purpose, suffering, and human nature to snap into focus.

A Worldview Is Like a Filter

A filter separates things, allowing certain materials to pass through and other materials to remain. A good worldview should allow truth in while keeping lies out.

The quality and function of a filter is determined by the size of its holes. If the holes are too big (in our analogy, being too tolerant of bad ideas and sin), then lies slip in, and we start looking like the rest of the world. Make the holes too small (that is, "majoring in the minors"), and we create unnecessary division where there should be unity.

A Worldview Is Like a Puzzle Box Top

Think of a puzzle box top as an accurate representation of reality. Our goal as humans is to piece our lives together in a way that reflects that reality. All our beliefs (the things we think are true) are like pieces to the puzzle. Our actions are like us piecing together the puzzle, showing others what picture we are building and what we believe to be true about the world.

First, this analogy really illustrates the difficulty we find ourselves in today. It would be great if there were only *one* puzzle, *one* complete box of pieces. But the moment sin entered our world, another puzzle—Satan's puzzle—began vying for dominance.

Second, it would be great if we got all the pieces at once, and we could just dump them out and put them together in a single sitting. But that's not the way life works. We don't get all the pieces at once. We collect them as we grow and learn about the world.

One by one, little puzzle pieces (ideologies) are being handed to our children. As they're confronted with ideas, they have to decide which pieces to reject and which to accept. They have to ask, *Does this piece belong to God's worldview puzzle or the enemy's?* Sometimes the beliefs (puzzle pieces) look very similar—as in the case of love and tolerance.

Some people may claim to be Christians, but the picture portrayed by their actions looks nothing like what Scripture describes (i.e., God's box top). Knowing what a biblical worldview is *supposed* to look like helps our kids to not only order their own lives, but also recognize which influences in their life are actually Christlike and which are just paying lip service.

Your children's grip on Christianity will only be as strong as their confidence in its truth. So to disciple our kids into a biblical sexual worldview, they first need to know God's original design. We can't be content with giving our kids bits and pieces of the picture. They need to see the whole enchilada—the full picture created by the Christian worldview—so they can begin piecing their worldview together as they grow and learn.

> Your children's grip on Christianity
> will only be as strong as their
> confidence that it reflects reality.

An Overview of the Christian Worldview

This world will not sit idly by while your child pieces together their biblical worldview. Our culture is hell-bent on ripping away anything that smacks of historic Christianity. We need to understand what the culture is telling our kids about truth in order to help them understand why the secular worldview falls flat. If we have done our jobs well, they can confidently commit to the Christian worldview, even when the culture calls them hateful, hurtful, intolerant, abusive monsters for doing so. (And, by the way, that's what they are being called now. Not Jesus freaks or goody-goodies. That assumes people agree on the definition of "good." No. Our kids are facing much harsher names—names that are meant to shame them out of their Christian beliefs.)

To stand against the harsh criticism, our kids need to understand how what the Bible teaches makes sense of the world they see. The Christian worldview is a beautifully coherent story which centers around the relationship between God and humans. It starts at creation, explains sin and separation, and ends with redemption. Let's take a look now at the puzzle pieces that make up the Christian worldview.

1. God Himself Is the Foundation of Reality and Truth

According to the Bible, God created all things. And while there are many differing views within Christendom on exactly how this creation took place, we should all stand united around the knowledge that *God alone created,* through Christ, out of nothing (John 1:1-3). If out of God all things came to be, then God *Himself* is the foundation of reality and truth. There is nothing in existence that does not derive from His attributes. God is good, and so everything He created was good. And then sin entered the world, and Satan had a field day. But we must remember that all Satan can do is pervert something that was originally good. There is no independent entity which is evil. Any kind of evil you try and conceive of is really just one of God's good gifts that has been twisted, used in the wrong way, or in the wrong amount. (Except maybe scorpions. I have a hard time picturing those *ever* being good.)

2. Ultimate Truth Is Discovered, Not Created

Since God *is* truth and God *is* eternal, then there exist eternal truths that we can discover. God embedded these eternal truths within us in the form of the moral law written on our hearts.[3] Eternal truths are also present...

- *in creation.* "The heavens declare the glory of God; the skies proclaim the work of his hands. Day after day they pour forth speech; night after night they reveal knowledge" (Psalm 19:1-2). And "since the creation of the world God's invisible qualities—his eternal power and divine nature—have been clearly seen, being understood from what has been made, so that people are without excuse" (Romans 1:20).

- *in God's revealed Word.* "All Scripture is God-breathed and is useful for teaching, rebuking, correcting and training in righteousness" (2 Timothy 3:16).

- *in relationship with God Himself through the Holy Spirit.* "The Advocate, the Holy Spirit, whom the Father will send in my name, will teach you all things and will remind you of everything I have said to you" (John 14:26).

There are even abstract truths that we discover, like the laws of logic and mathematics. And since humans were created in the image of God, our minds reflect a hunger and ability to discern these truths—truths which lie *outside* of ourselves. Since truth is ultimately traced back to God, it isn't subject to our desires or opinions.

3. Humans Are Uniquely Created in the Image of God

God created all things, but humans are unique in that we are created *in the image of God.* Theologians and philosophers have debated for millennia what exactly this statement means. It may refer to 1) the way we co-exercise dominion over the earth, 2) how the marital relationship mirrors God's internal relationship within the Trinity, or 3) our creative faculties and cognitive abilities which allow us to partake in the creative process to a degree unparalleled within the animal kingdom. Regardless of how *imago dei* is defined, the point is that we reflect God to the world in a unique way, and that's both a privilege and a responsibility.

4. God Created with a Purpose

Embedded within God's creative act is the concept of *teleology*. Teleology implies that a designer designed something for a purpose. We might say the purpose, or *telos*, of a printer is to print stuff—that's what it was designed to do, and that's what we use it for. Since the Christian worldview teaches that God not only created but *designed* us, then we, too, have a teleological purpose, a *telos*, a reason for which we were created.

Within this teleological view, our bodies have a purpose. Our minds have a purpose. Sex has a purpose. Gender has a purpose. Everything about being human has a purpose, an end goal, a reason for being. (We'll dig deeper into this concept in chapter 3.) Built into us as humans is a need to fulfill our purpose. Everything goes screwy when people don't understand the purpose for which they were created. The most satisfying life we can live is one in which we fulfill our *telos*—in worship and in relationship to God, in relationship with others, and in stewarding His creation.

5. God's Moral Law Is Part of Our Telos

Walking within God's boundaries allows us to live in harmony with Him. And since Christians believe that the eternal moral laws stem from an eternal, moral law giver, then we believe that following His commands will lead us to a life of flourishing. Failure to do so will have disadvantageous outcomes.

It's actually pretty simple when you think about it. Don't use the curling iron while sleeping. Don't put water in a gas tank. Use things the way they were intended, and things tend to run more smoothly.

But that was before sin came into the world and things got all janky.

6. Sin Got Us All Confused

Living according to God's moral law is no longer natural or easy. Humans instinctively know that there is something wrong with the world.

Where most worldviews differ is in defining what is wrong with the world and how to fix it.

The Christian worldview has a simple yet very effective answer for what is wrong with the world: the doctrine of sin. Sin changed our inclinations away from obedience to God—away from our intended design—to obedience to the sinful self.

Don't get too literal with this analogy, but picture a connection like a blood vessel between God and our hearts, providing spiritual life to our souls. (I realize that this analogy leaves out the doctrine of God's wrath, a huge piece of the puzzle. But it's still helpful for the littles to understand that there is an objective reality of separation from God that we can't change on our own, where we need a Savior's help.) When Adam and Eve chose to disobey, it's like they took a pair of scissors and severed the connection, resulting in an immediate spiritual death and, eventually, physical decay and death. We, who are descendants of Adam and Eve, are born without that connection. It's not God being unfair. It's just reality; Adam and Eve couldn't reproduce what they didn't have. Without that perfect connection to God intact, we were born with our souls inclined to sin and our bodies prone to decay. This wasn't a surprise to God. He knew the end from the beginning. So before the world ever came to be, God had already figured out a way to solve the problem created by our foreparents (Ephesians 1:4-5).

7. We Cannot Be Reconciled to Our Telos Until We Are Reconciled to God

Just like every worldview has its own version of original sin (i.e., what's ultimately wrong with the world), so every worldview has its own version of redemption (how to fix what's wrong in the world). The Christian worldview teaches that our main problem is that we are separated from God by our sin. And we can't exactly reach up to heaven, so God had to come down to us. He did so in the person of Christ. Thus the solution, in order to fully live out our intended purpose (our *telos*), is a savior who will restore the part of us that was lost in the garden. Jesus is the one who made this possible. Through faith in Him, our sins are removed so that we can once again be in right relationship with our Creator. God's Spirit in us gives us the ability to fully live out our *telos*—which is where our ultimate satisfaction and flourishing occurs.

8. Not Everything Is Redeemed...Yet

You'd think that all we had to do was restore the connection between us and God and everything would go back the way it was. Not quite. Our redemption is not completed on this earth. Instead, as Paul puts it, we "groan inwardly as we wait eagerly for our adoption to sonship, *the redemption of our bodies*" (Romans 8:23). "Though outwardly we are wasting away, yet inwardly we are being renewed day by day" (2 Corinthians 4:16).

God has restored our spiritual life, and we can pray for physical healing—which God can and does provide sometimes here on this earth, but not every time. Even in good health, our bodies still carry the scars of sin and the reality of living in a sinful world. Since our fleshly bodies are not yet redeemed, we will continue struggling when our fleshly desires wage war against our souls (1 Peter 2:11). Knowing this, we can *expect* that obedience to God will sometimes feel like a battle within ourselves. (Read Paul's Hamlet-esque soliloquy on the battle between the flesh and the spirit in Romans 7:7-24.)

> Obedience to God will sometimes feel like a battle within ourselves.

9. We Will One Day Be Fully Redeemed

But there is even more good news! Our struggle with sin is not in vain, and neither will it be eternal. The best news is that we will one day be *fully* redeemed! No more cancer, no more anxiety. For all you Mama Bears who pee a little when you sneeze, I'm pretty sure that'll be gone too. This world will pass away, and the Lord will make all things new (Revelation 21:5). And though we don't understand what it all means now, God has told us that the way we live here will affect our eternal afterlife. I like to think of it as the ultimate 401(k). I can live large here (in comfort, security, and indulgence) and have a smaller retirement, or I can live small here (in obedience, generosity, and humility) and save up for an eternity which will far surpass my years on this earth.

How Does This Worldview Affect the Way We View Sex?

As you can see, the Christian worldview is comprehensive. The good, the bad, and everything in our lived experiences can be explained by understanding God's original design and how that design has been warped. This worldview also helps us to determine whether or not we are living according to our intended purpose, our *telos*. Like the rules to the game, a biblical worldview helps us spot truth, know our ultimate goal, play fairly, and determine what to expect and how to live. These beliefs about ultimate truth radically affect the way we view ourselves, our gender, and our sexuality.

Since God says He can be known through His creation, and God created sex, a correct or incorrect view of sex can therefore give us a correct or incorrect picture of God (just as it was stated in *Sex and the Supremacy of Christ* on page 35).

We also know, according to the Christian worldview, that what we do with our bodies matters, because our bodies were created for a purpose. Since we are sinners with a fallen human nature, we expect that we will have desires (including sexual desires) that go against God's revealed truth.

Our desires don't change the truth; they just reveal our fallenness. There are people who have sexual proclivities *they did not ask for*. But even if those desires come naturally through no immediate fault of one's own, it does not make the desires moral, or in accordance with God's design or intended purposes.

According to the Christian worldview, we also expect that living out God's design (that is, being sexually set apart) will be difficult and will not make us popular with the world. First Peter 4:3-4 notes that pagans live in "debauchery, lust, drunkenness, orgies, carousing and detestable idolatry. They are surprised that you do not join them in their reckless, wild living, and they heap abuse on you." But this doesn't surprise us. We can expect those who have not chosen to place their faith in Jesus will likely live according to their own desires. Why wouldn't they? We must also remember that *their problem is not their sexuality. Their problem is that they have not been made alive by Jesus.* If we focus on sex and gender but miss their souls, we miss the heart of the gospel. Period.

There are churches that promise God's freedom *apart from His sexual telos.* Such teachings are false. We know they are false because God has provided us His thoughts on the matter. We read about them in chapter 1. We cannot fall into the trap of saying that God hasn't spoken (or spoken clearly) when He has. But on the flip side, we also have churches with members who sit on their moral high horses, preaching love but failing to truly minister to those who are in bondage to sexual sin and gender confusion. That is not how a faithful disciple of Jesus behaves either.

Mama Bears, I realize this is a narrow road to walk, but such is the road that God has laid out for us. When we teach our children the intellectual tenets of the Christian worldview, we should couple that teaching with an intense love for people. In this way, we truly fulfill both the first and second greatest commandments—to love the Lord our God with everything in us, and to love our neighbor as ourselves. Don't let anyone tell you that these two commands are mutually exclusive, or that the second greatest commandment can redefine the first. Through faith in Christ, we can now obey God's sexual mandates because we trust that He alone, as Creator, fully understands the purpose of sex and knows how His good gift is to be best enjoyed.

Discussion Questions

1. **Icebreaker:** Who wears glasses? What was it like the first time you put them on? See if someone in the group can procure a pair of wacky glasses that distorts everything. Pass them around and try to read a paragraph of this book. How much harder was it with the distortion glasses?

2. **Main theme:** *The Christian worldview is complete and coherent. It describes a good original design, what happened to mess it up, how God provided Jesus to redeem what was broken, and how He plans to continue to redeem us in the midst of a broken world.* How does the Christian worldview affect our view of sexuality? According to the secular worldview, what is the purpose of sex?

3. **Self-evaluation:** What aspects of the Christian worldview do you find hardest to apply to your everyday life?

4. **Brainstorm:** How does the Christian worldview change the way we view sex, gender, and our bodies? How might a person's world-view be different if they think that they weren't created, that what they do with their bodies doesn't matter, or that physical pleasure is the main goal for this life?

5. **Release the bear:** Our kids need to understand that the Christian worldview explains both the *good* things in life as well as the *bad* things in life. Make a game out of identifying original design, brokenness, and redemption in everyday life. A day with family enjoying food and fellowship? Original design. Getting a stomach flu? Brokenness. Forgiving each other when we say mean things? Redemption.

6. **Pray:** Pray that the Lord would begin showing you areas where your worldview lens might be askew, and thank Him for how beautiful and cohesive the Christian worldview is. If you can't see it, ask for Him to reveal to you the beauty of His ordered design.

Chapter 3

A Pretty Great Design, When Followed

How Gender, Marriage, Sex, and
Family Show Us the God We Can't See

HILLARY

Coherent and beautiful: those are my two favorite adjectives for the Christian worldview. And I say that because I've studied the other worldviews. I know this is a book on sexuality. That's the dumpster fire *du jour*. If we start with sexuality, however, it's like opening a book right in the middle of the story. We cannot understand what is going on in the middle until we know what came before. And we cannot fully appreciate the significance of the middle unless we know how it weaves into a glorious ending—the *telos*, the purpose, the end goal of the rest of the story.

In order to address how gender, marriage, sex, and family show us the God we can't see, we must first address the giant elephant in the room. I truly believe that much of the distortion surrounding gender, sex, and marriage can be traced back to a fundamental principle: the principle of authority. Who has the authority to say what we do with our bodies? Who has the authority to define sexual morality and immorality? Who has the authority to define marriage? What does authority even mean? What does good authority look like? Can it even exist? Doesn't absolute power corrupt absolutely? How do we prevent people from abusing their authority? (Because when you think about it, it's the systems in which power is abused that create the worst fallout.)

Right off the bat, I want to acknowledge those of you who have experienced unhealthy authority, especially those who have been sexually abused at the hands of someone you trusted. Sexual abuse messes with a person's ability to trust or interact with authority in a way that most people will never understand. I hear you. I grieve with you. (I am one of you.) And at the same time, I want to encourage you to never let a bad representative define what God has called good. Our God is the great Restorer, the Healer, the One who makes all things new.

In reading the biographies of people who have gone from sexual brokenness to freedom in Christ, I have noticed a theme. They were never convinced of God's sexual *telos* (His purpose for sex) for intellectual reasons. Their submission to God's design was only possible when they finally understood the goodness of God Himself, submitting to Him out of love and not out of fear.[1] I do not expect that I can talk anyone into what the Bible describes as a good design if they've never seen it. So let me try and draw you a picture from my own lived experiences.

But first a disclaimer: Though my circumstances may appear picture-perfect in comparison to others, let me assure you that I had my fair share of struggles. In and out of the hospital for most of my life, I felt ostracized by my peers and frequently jealous of all the things that they could do with their healthy bodies that I could not. Most people would not want to take on the number of medications I have to take on a regular basis, or deal with cancer that keeps peeking its ugly head into my life. The Lord gives us each our own burdens. My purpose in this section is to present one area of my life that has been easier to paint a picture in your minds of how awesome God's plan was for marriage and family…when it is followed.

My Story

I never had a hard time submitting to my father's authority because my father is the pinnacle of provider and protector. He didn't use his authority to get his way. He used his authority to serve us. He served our family by providing for us materially. He served our family by leading us spiritually. He served (and still serves) our family by loving my mom fiercely and faithfully. In turn, I saw her honor my father by joyfully submitting to his leadership. And as she submitted to him, he laid down his life (metaphorically speaking) for her. He looked to his own needs and wants as well, because that's what a healthy human does. But my mother's, my sister's, and my needs and wants were always at the forefront of his mind.

I rarely ever saw my parents fight; they discussed—sometimes at length—but never with raised voices. They seldom made a decision without making it together, and they made sure my sister and I couldn't play them off each other. When my dad put his foot down (which happened occasionally), none of us questioned it because my dad is such a gentle man and we trusted him. If there was something within his power and means that would benefit us or bless us, he did what he could to provide it. If he didn't think it was a benefit or necessary, he said no.

My father also gave me (and still gives me) the most important thing a father can give: time and attention. What was important to me, my mom, and my sister was important to him. I don't think I ever had a hobby in which he didn't participate in some way. When my sister became a teacher, he found ways to involve himself by taking her out to buy decorations for her classroom. When I was an athletic trainer at Texas Christian University, he got himself and my mom season tickets to the football games, just to watch me do my thing. When I was a photographer, he went to photo conferences with me. And now that I'm a writer, he and my mom read most everything I write before it goes to press. If it is important for my work, it is important to him to support it.

I'm sure we still had power struggles as I grew up. That's part of learning obedience and submission. And despite what the media is trying to make us believe, our kids are *not* the best authorities on what is good and right for them. Their brains aren't fully formed, and we should rightfully refuse parenting advice from a demographic who encourages each other to eat Tide Pods. (And no, Gen Z, you will never live that down.)

The legacy my parents left for me is one in which authority means that you *cultivate those under your care the way God made them, not the way you wish they were.* I never mistook my parents for my friends growing up. If I spoke to either of them with a disrespectful tone, it was addressed *immediately.* They made sure I knew I was not their top priority—their relationship was. Through healthy boundaries, we developed such mutual respect that now, as an adult, I *can* say that they are my best friends. It is still a joy to honor my parents because of the way they honored God's authority structure in our home. My foundation is ultimately in Christ. But a pretty big part of my emotional stability still derives from having grown up in a home with parents who modeled servant-leadership and healthy submission toward one another.

I looked forward to marriage because of how my father and mother modeled it for me. Anyone who knows me knows I can have a strong personality. I have a will of my own, and plenty of thoughts on most every matter. And now, wonder of wonders, I get to write about them for a living. (Holla!) A shrinking violet I am not. So how could I not bristle at the idea of a man, my peer, being "in authority" over me? Simply put, because authority always meant security to me, not subjugation.

When it came time to form my own family, I found a man who is very different from my dad in looks and personality but still very like him in essence. I can say with no hesitation that it is a joy to submit to John D. Ferrer. A major part of that is because the submission issue very rarely comes into play. My husband literally calls me "his garden" and muses about how his role as my husband is to cultivate me in the Lord. And at the same time, he knows that the active pruning role belongs to the Holy Spirit. Every now and then when we are at an impasse, he'll come straight out and ask me to submit. It is always couched with, "Will you please submit to me on this one? I answer to God for our family. I think this is the right course of action, and you have full 'I told you so' privileges if I'm wrong." He pulls this card so rarely that I know he's not just saying stuff to get his way. And he doesn't demand my submission. He requests, and I have yet to refuse—*because he has earned my trust in a million ways.*

When it comes to providing for me, my husband passed up many jobs which would have helped him in his career in order to make sure that I had health insurance—since my cancer and other health issues put me in the high-risk population. Even now, he has a PhD and works ten-hour days at a window factory because he missed a lot of the job opportunities to advance in academia when he had the chance. My current career as an apologetics writer is actually the job that my husband labored in grad school *for 12 years* to do. But when he saw God blessing Mama Bear Apologetics, he put his credentials aside and said, "I see the Lord blessing this, and I will do whatever I need to do to make sure that you are able to flourish in this role. Far be it from me to get in the way when the Lord is moving." That is the kind of man I married and why I will never begrudge him the honor and respect and submission that Scripture says I should pay him (Ephesians 5:22-24). I rarely think about it, it's such a nonissue.

And why shouldn't it be? What woman in her right mind wouldn't jump at the opportunity to be under a man who provides physical and emotional security? Where is the downside? I can't see it. When my husband leads with such gentle and sacrificial love, I gladly allow him to be the tiebreaker at times when we can't quite reach an agreement, which isn't that often. I gladly defer to him as the head of our family. And as a ministry leader, I understand the gravity of leadership. It's not a position for the faint of heart. I answer to God for what happens at Mama Bear Apologetics, and John answers to God for what happens in our family. I will gladly be #2 to not have that level of responsibility. Honestly, if leadership doesn't scare the pants off you, you're probably not ready to lead.

Putting This in Perspective

I don't go into all this to brag about what a great family I have. What have I been given that wasn't a gift? Nothing. Rather, I go into this because I want to emphasize that God did, in fact, create a really great system *when it is followed*! My family and I are by no means perfect. But I think we get the gist of what God was going for, and our lives have been easier for it because we purposely chose to submit to His good design.

I know there are people out there who may have never seen what it looks like to have really healthy authority structures. The word *authority* may have meant that you weren't allowed to ask questions, or that trying to understand a decision was interpreted as insubordination. Is it any surprise that people reject God's teachings on sex when the only reason behind them is that "God says so"? If the authorities in their life never loved them or served them, then why should they trust God as an authority on any subject? In their experience, authority was reduced to blind obedience—*or else*. And yes, authority does imply obedience. But it's not obedience out of fear of punishment. It is obedience that is *rooted in gratitude for the provision and protection offered by the leader.*

Leading through service and cultivation is the way God designed it to be. And speaking from my own personal experience, it doesn't just work. It rocks! Every Father's Day, I thank my dad for helping me understand what God the Father is like. And every anniversary, I thank my husband for showing me what Jesus looks like through the way he serves me. After all, Jesus was the original and ultimate servant-leader.

Authority Within the Godhead

Authority implies a hierarchy, and some people misunderstand hierarchy. They have rarely seen power and authority used for good, so any kind of authority structure sounds like sinful humans creating systems to oppress one another. One of the reasons I know authority was part of God's original plan is because we see a hierarchical authority structure within the Godhead. Before we discuss this, however, we must first understand the difference between ontological hierarchy and functional hierarchy.

Ontology refers to the nature or essence of a being. We as humans are ontologically different from the rest of creation. We have a different essence and a different level of authority. We are, however, ontologically equal to all other humans—no matter the gender, ethnicity, or developmental level.

Functional hierarchy refers to a hierarchy of roles between ontologically equal parties. A conductor and a violinist are ontologically equal—of equal worth and value. Functionally, they have different roles. We see this functional submission at work in the Godhead. Jesus submits to the Father over and over again. Jesus says, "I do exactly what my Father has commanded me," and "I have come...not to do my will but to do the will of him who sent me" (John 14:31; 6:38). He even says, "the Father is greater than I" (John 14:28). While Jesus submits to the Father, this doesn't mean He's less important or less-God than the Father. It's a functional submission, since ontologically Jesus is also our Lord and our God (John 20:28), "God with us" (Matthew 1:23), and the "exact representation of [God's] being" (Hebrews 1:3). The church fathers explained this by saying Jesus is "fully God and fully man," being the "same substance" as the Father.

The main message about the Godhead from Genesis to Revelation is one of *unity*, not division. Obedience and submission are not an issue within the Godhead because there is unity of purpose. In John 6:37-40 Jesus says,

> All those the Father gives me will come to me, and whoever comes to me I will never drive away. For I have come down from heaven *not to do my will but to do the will of him who sent me.* And this is the will of him who sent me, that I shall lose none of all those he has given me, but raise them up at the last day. For my Father's will is that everyone who looks to the Son and believes in him shall have eternal life, and I will raise them up at the last day.

Likewise, the Spirit is unified with the Father and the Son in purpose as seen in John 16:13-14:

> When he, the Spirit of truth, comes, he will guide you into all the truth. *He will not speak on his own; he will speak only what he hears,* and he will tell you what is yet to come. He will glorify me because it is from me that he will receive what he will make known to you.

Within the Trinity, there is a sharing of responsibility and authority. It is the unity and love among them that makes this work so flawlessly. *This is what Christian marriage and family were meant to represent to the world.* We are raising little men and little women who may one day form their own families. The way they see us *serving* in leadership and honoring in submission affects how they will one day view authority as well. And this isn't just authority when it comes to family, but also the police, the president, their teachers, their bosses, and especially how they view the authority of God. Is God a cosmic killjoy out to command His minions, or is He a loving father who wants the best for His children? *Their experience at home will either help or hinder the way they view God because family was intended to show us the unity and love and submission within the Godhead.*

Can you see what an amazing civilization we would have if this model of authority and submission were followed in the family, in the church, in the workplace, and in government? It is health that breeds health, life that breeds life. Done well, it is a beautiful, harmonic order where all are elevated in value.

Why Is It So Important That We Get the Concept of Authority Right?

Some might be thinking, "This is a book on sex, not a book on marriage. Why are we going so deep into authority?" Understanding authority is imperative for understanding sex because sex—as we discussed—is a bodily recitation of the marriage vows that were already spoken. But there's a really important second aspect, one that makes some people uncomfortable and that's this: Marriage itself was intended to be a picture of Christ's relationship with the church.

As Christopher West points out in his book *Our Bodies Tell God's Story,* Scripture is bookended by two marriages: the first marriage between man and woman, and the final marriage between Christ and His bride. In the epistle to the Ephesians, Paul is explicit about the purpose and meaning of marriage: "For this reason a man will leave his father and mother and be united to his wife, and the two will become one flesh. This is a profound mystery—but I am talking about Christ and the church" (Ephesians 5:31-32).

Our very sexuality, the unity of two different genders united in an embrace of love, is meant to be a picture of what is to come. And if we feel awkward about that, it only serves to point out how far our understanding of sex and marriage has degraded from God's original design. It is a beautiful picture of oneness in the midst of diversity. And without the two sexes, without the marriage, and without the coming together of two—who literally create one flesh through their union—we do not understand the purpose of our lives, the purpose of marriage, the purpose of sex, or even the purpose of our bodies.

No one explains this better than Rachel Gilson in her book *Born Again This Way:*

> When God speaks of himself and his people being "married," God is *always* the male, and his people are always the female… Why does sex difference matter for the metaphor? First, the relationship by definition can't exist without both parties. So if you lack one of the parties you destroy the picture. Lose the male from the marriage, and you lose the picture of Christ. Lose the female, and you lose the picture of the church…Second, the members are not interchangeable—Christ is not the church and the church is not Christ…Third, the male and female are different from each other yet able to be united because of shared humanity. So too, God and his people are essentially vastly different…The gospel is about an uncrossable chasm shockingly bridged.[2]

As I stated in chapter 1, we have lost the deeper meanings of God's creation. We have been carefully trained by culture to think that meaning is a human construct, but it is not. Within marriage is a picture of God Himself—which is why, if we get it wrong, we see God incorrectly too.

The Fashion Analogy

I want you to picture for a moment that you are a clothing designer who is about to present at fashion week. You have worked tirelessly for months creating a clothing line that is beautiful, functional, and that tells a very personal story. In fact, as the models walk down the catwalk, pieces of a poem you have written are shown on the screen behind them, and each line is only understandable by viewing the garment coming down the aisle. You have created poetry in word and in form. It's an artistic masterpiece!

Now picture the night before the fashion show, someone comes in and cuts all your pieces up and resews them together in some odd fashion that is neither beautiful nor coherent, and that makes the poem you carefully crafted sound like utter nonsense. Your name is still on the fashion show, but it is no longer your work. And every person in the audience is judging you, your skill, and your message by this chopped up, incoherent mess they see in front of them. Based on what they see, they don't understand you, they now reject you, your reputation is in tatters, and your message is lost.

Friends, this is what humanity has done to God.

God is the designer. Gender, marriage, and sex are the clothes, and the poetic message that united them is now incomprehensible because it has been separated from God's original design. We have separated gender from sex, and sex from marriage. Then we redefined marriage and now are in the process of redefining gender. If we are having a hard time understanding who we are, who God is, and where our ultimate destinies lie, it is not because God hasn't communicated it; it's because we have destroyed His picture.

The Message of Gender: A Picture of the Image of God (Imago Dei)

In Genesis 1:27, Moses writes: "God created mankind in his own image, in the image of God he created them; male and female he created them." In case we missed it the first time, he restates it in Genesis 5:1-2. And in case we *still* missed it, it is repeated by Jesus in Mark 10:6.

God made humankind in His image, male and female. Who is made in God's image? Not man alone. Not woman alone. Male and female together reflect the image of God.

Does this mean that a single person cannot carry the image of God? By no means! Scripture gives great dignity to those who are single—whether by choice or not (Matthew 19:12). "All people are called to prepare themselves for eternal union with God. Christian celibacy, as 'the self-giving' of a human person wedded to God himself, expressly anticipates this eternal union with God and points the way to it," writes Christopher West.[3] Keeping oneself wholly united to Christ and His work here on earth in no way destroys this picture.

The Message of Marriage: A Picture of Christ and the Church

Marriage was intended to point us to our ultimate destiny as members of the church body, and the church being joined eternally to Christ. Marriage is a tiny little microcosm of that reality. But this picture has been distorted by the way some have twisted authority and submission. Some men love to quote the Ephesians passage about wives submitting to their husbands as unto the Lord and use it as carte blanche permission to treat their wives like a lesser vessel instead of *with care* as the weaker vessel (1 Peter 3:7). But if husbands are to be a picture of Christ, then their authority is not one of power, but one of service. Just look at how God defines the husband's role in Ephesians.

> Husbands, love your wives, just as Christ loved the church and gave himself up for her to make her holy, cleansing her by the washing with water through the word, and to present her to himself as a radiant church, without stain or wrinkle or any other blemish, but holy and blameless.
>
> In this same way, husbands ought to love their wives as their own bodies. He who loves his wife loves himself. After all, no one ever hated their own body, but they feed and cherish it, just as Christ does the church—for we are members of his

body. "For this reason a man will leave his father and mother and be united to his wife, and the two will become one flesh" (Ephesians 5:25-31).

The command to the husband is one of *dying to his own desires* in order to serve his wife just like Christ died on the cross to serve His bride. *That* is what biblical authority is to look like. That is what my father modeled to me, and that is how I recognized the kind of character that I wanted in a husband.

The Message of Sex: A Picture of Our Eternal Destiny

This is where I find most people get the most uncomfortable with the analogy of Christ with His bride. It's sounds like a kind of cult where all the women are to have sex with the leader. But this fails to acknowledge that it is with *the church*, not individuals, with whom Christ is being wed. There is no cell of my human body that interacts with my soul apart from all the other cells. It's not some bizarre cellular orgy. Together, they form one body. It is a perfect example of diversity and oneness—all the cells, all the muscles, all the organs working together to form one whole person— me. Similarly, we as the bride will be made up of a diverse union of "every tongue, tribe, and nation." It is we together who are the bride of Christ. There is a reason why Paul calls this one-flesh union a "profound mystery." How does one understand a spiritual version of sex?

Again, we have to look at our bodies as the language of God's mystery. Our sexuality is carved into the very bodies of male and female— the man coming into the woman, and the woman willingly receiving the man. The joy, the ecstasy of oneness. There is a feeling of belonging, of being whole—almost a feeling of *worship*. There is tension, there is release, there is rest. Through this process, the man as the figure of Christ deposits part of himself into the woman, and she then unites a part of herself with the man's—resulting in a bodily form of this one-flesh union. It is a *physical* representation of the Lord's *Spirit* working in us and through us—bringing us new life and multiplying that life around us. And all of this takes place within the context of two people who have pledged themselves to each other forever, forsaking all others, fully and without reservation. If sex is pointing to the greater reality of what's to come, and if it is a *lesser* version of the eternal reality to which it points, then can you imagine what awaits for us, for those who love God and have been called according to His purpose? If you can't, it's only because the picture on earth has become so perverted and distorted.

The act of sex itself is a beautiful picture of what we will one day experience for eternity: oneness, belonging, joy, euphoria, the utter giving of self, the receiving of God in holiness, in communion, forever and ever.

The Message of Family: A Picture of Servant Leadership

The bearing of children is literally the result of *two* people becoming *one* flesh. God's original command to Adam and Eve was to "be fruitful and increase in number" (Genesis 1:28). Spiritually speaking, this is the same command Jesus gave the disciples: "Go and make disciples" (Matthew 28:19). The physical act of sex creates new physical life just like the spiritual act of oneness with Christ creates new spiritual life.

And just as we talked about how authority was to be exercised between husband and wife, so this is how our authority as Mama Bears is to be exercised with our children. Our children will learn to love or despise authority based on the model we have in the home. As we exercise leadership over our children, we do so by serving them. This doesn't mean we are at their beck and call. Rather, our job as parents, grandparents, aunts, and uncles is to assist them in whatever way they need for becoming mature adults.

And as we joyfully exercise our authority over them through service, we help them understand how to submit to the authority—a skill set required for any job they'll ever have. Granted, most of the time they don't understand that we really are "doing things for their own good." Our "service" probably won't be recognized till later, but that's okay.

Part of this service is encouraging them to exercise authority in their own sphere of influence. Do your kids know that they, too, have a sphere of authority? They do. They are in authority as stewards over their bodies.

They can exercise that authority to benefit their bodies or to harm their bodies. All humans, even tiny humans, also have authority over the earth, the creatures on the earth, and whatever resources we provide them (like crayons and toys). How are they learning to steward that authority?

If you have pets, this is a great way to get your kids to understand the service aspect of authority. Feed Fido on time and in the correct amounts. Take him for a walk, even if you don't feel like it. And one of the most important aspects for cat owners is asking our kids, "Are you petting the cat the way *you* want to pet the cat, or how the *cat* likes to be petted?"

> ## Our children will learn to love or despise authority based on the model we have in the home.

Now Back to Reality...

The sad reality is that many of us have not gotten a very clear picture of God from marriage, sex, and family. In the real world, there are people who use their authority for their own benefit—advancing their own agenda and lining their own pockets. They don't give a thought to the people beneath them. They demand unwavering obedience while exercising their power with an iron fist and for the purpose of glorifying themselves, pretending that the buck stops with them. I won't pretend that this kind of authority doesn't exist. Abusers abuse, people cover for them, and there's really no end to how badly authority structures can break down due to the sin nature that lies within each of our hearts.

On the home front, moms and dads leave or fight. Marriages are broken. "Till death do us part" has become "until it stops working." (What is the mysterious "it," and why are our marriages contingent upon whether "it" works or not?) The entire system is in shambles due to human selfishness and brokenness, with only the smallest wisp every now and again of what God's original design actually looks like. And, consequently, our perception of God becomes just as ugly. What do we do?

On the one hand, if we keep emphasizing God's good design, those who have already fallen short feel like we're heaping judgment and shame on their backs. Or the ones who worked tirelessly to make the marriage work (while the other party sabotaged their efforts) feel like they should have done more, more, MORE! That's not the picture of Christ and His church either. I'm so thankful that God gives us grace when we cannot attain His perfect design. There is no situation so damaged that He can't redeem it, no ashes so ashy that He can't create beauty. I acknowledge and celebrate this with no ifs, ands, or buts. Well…maybe one but…

Without letting go of the above truths, there can be a problem on the flip side if redemption is the *only* thing we focus on. When we stop lifting up God's original design, sometimes our kids get the message that God's ideal is unattainable or irrelevant. They subsequently don't go into marriage expecting forever. They go into marriage(s) expecting that it might take a try or two before they get it right. There's always a chance for a do-over—at least that's what they've always heard. And, sure enough, failing to plan for marriage, they plan a failed marriage. Like all things, we need balance. We cannot elevate God's good design to the point where people who have missed it feel like they are forever on the outs. And we cannot elevate God's redemption to the point where people feel like there's a get-out-of-jail-free card whenever things get tough. I know this is a difficult balance to convey, so I hope y'all hear my heart on this.

Living Within the Tension

I really want to emphasize this balance for us as a community of Mama Bears. We cannot stop lifting up God's design as the ideal, even if we haven't attained it. And I recognize that it hurts a lot when we realize how far we are from God's original design. I want you to have permission to feel that pain. I don't think healing means that the pain always goes away, and I'll tell you why: we will always experience the pain of living in a fallen world, but it's coupled by hope as we look ahead to the ultimate marriage to the lamb! We have a God who wants to pledge Himself, in love and faithfulness, *forever*. Patiently enduring a painful present while living for that future hope has always been and always will be a major part of the Christian life!

Are you divorced? Point your children to the goodness of marriage anyway. Are you in a blended family? It's okay to tell your kids, "This isn't the way it was supposed to be…but I'm so glad we still have a chance to be family." Death and divorce were not in the original plan. But even in the grafting in of families we can remind our children how we were grafted into God's family alongside of Israel! Jew and Gentile—the original blended family!

Are you married to a person who doesn't serve sacrificially? Praise them in front of your children whenever you do see them lead well. You can also look for other examples of good authorities in your community and point your kids in their direction. Whatever you have to do, let your kids see healthy, loving authority in action. How in the world will they ever mimic what they've never seen?

There is beauty in sacrificial love, and there is beauty in joyful submission. And that is precisely the point about gender, sex, marriage, and family. When done well, it helps us understand God better. We can have all the apologetics arguments in the world. We can be the smartest people in the room. But I will maintain till my dying day that the most effective apologetic (rational defense) for God is *family*. Family is the first institution created by God. Almost everything that can be known about God was *intended* to be known within the context of family.

Marriage and family done well are glimpses into heaven itself, how the kingdom was intended to function. And every aspect that was intended to be a picture of God is currently being perverted and ruined by an enemy who hates the very image of God. Gender matters because within gender is the image of God Himself. Sex matters because it bodily reinforces the marital vows. Marriage matters because it points us to our eternal unity in Christ. Family matters because it teaches us all how to serve *in* authority and how to joyfully submit ourselves *to* authority. It all matters because gender, sex, marriage, and family were intended to show us the God we can't see. And even more that, *they point the world to the God whom they cannot see in hopes that what is invisible can become more understandable.* Any movement which seeks to destroy gender, sex, marriage, or family is destroying the message God intended, the picture He gave us in order to understand Him. And that picture is a pretty great design… *when followed.*

Discussion Questions

1. **Icebreaker:** What is a time when you have experienced really good authority? When is a time you experienced really awful authority? How hard was it for you to obey the bad authority? Was it easier to obey the good authority?

2. **Main theme:** *Gender, sex, marriage, and family are intended to represent an invisible God in a visible way, and our understanding of authority can help or hinder this picture.* Which message and picture (gender, marriage, sex, or family) have you seen done best in your life? How have they helped you to understand God better?

3. **Self-evaluation:** How did you react to Hillary's story about her experience with authority in her life? Did it sound beautiful? Did it make you feel angry? Are there authorities in your life that you have a difficult time submitting to? Why?

4. **Brainstorm:** We cannot be responsible for how other people treat us, but we are responsible for how we respond. Ask each person to pick an area where they are under authority, and brainstorm ways that they can bless their leader by their actions. Now pick an area over which you have authority. Brainstorm all the ways you can cultivate the people under your care.

5. **Release the bear:** Our kids need to know that they aren't just under authority, but that they also *have their own sphere of authority.* They are in authority over their bodies, the earth, and their pets. Talk to them about how good authority treats those underneath them. If you have pets, talk about the ways they can be good authorities over the pets.

6. **Pray:** Thank the Lord for the amazing way He structured authority. Pray over the ways that you can exercise your authority to His glory. Is there anyone in the group who has been or is under cruel, selfish, or abusive authority? Grieve together. Have the whole group pray over those hurting among you.

Chapter 4

Demolishing Arguments, Not People

Releasing Ideological Captives

HILLARY

I grew up on 90 acres of land. The land was heavily wooded, and I remember seeing my parents come home all scratched up and bloody from clearing away the brambles. Why the blood? They weren't just clearing away ordinary vines and bushes; they were clearing *thorny* vines and bushes. Regular bushes and vines just need a quick hack with a machete or a snip of the shears. Catch and release. Thorn bushes are a different beast altogether.

Thorn bushes hold you hostage. All the thorns go in different directions. The more you try to free yourself, the more the thorns dig in until the whole vine wraps around you. The only way to free yourself is to have someone else help to pull out each thorn individually while holding the vine away from you—otherwise the vine will snap right back onto you. One does not simply grab hold of thorn bushes; thorn bushes grab hold of you. No matter which direction you move, there's pain. There's blood. Helping someone with thorny problems in their life can be a similar experience. And often in the process of helping someone, you get tangled up yourself.

The secular worldview is all over the place. It cries out: *There's no ultimate truth! Everyone has a right to their own truth. We'll fight anyone who disagrees that everything comes down to power and oppression!* (We'll get to that in chapter 6.) There's only one word for someone who adheres to such contradicting claims: bondage. And the more the ideas sink in, the less able a person is to separate herself from this worldview. Eventually the bad ideas are not just beliefs; they become that person's very identity.

This is the difficulty we find ourselves in today. We cannot merely tell people to let go of the lies. Like that thorn bush, the lies are holding on to the person. And when it comes to sexual sin, we're often not dealing with rebels; we're dealing with *captives*. And captives need to be freed.

A captive will rarely be able to hear your rejection of his or her ideas without feeling like you are rejecting him or her as a person. It's a bit of a tricky process. But we will do our best to explain how it can be accomplished. To do so, we will break down our approach into a few important categories.

First, we will explain the difference between *people* and *ideologies* and why distinguishing between the two is imperative. If you confuse the two, you'll end up either compromising truth or coming off as a clanging cymbal (1 Corinthians 13:1).

Second, we will grapple with what it means to love God and love others.

Third, we are going to learn the anatomy of an argument. Every single idea has a flow of logic, whether it be good logic or bad logic. To break down the lies in our culture, we need to understand what reasoning is being used to justify the beliefs. (And trust me when I say that when your kids learn how to do this, "empowered" will be an understatement.) We will compare and contrast emotional reasoning and deductive reasoning. Much of what passes for sound argumentation these days is really just emotional reasoning. It is important to understand how emotional reasoning works so that we can best love the person. But it's also important to be able to translate that faulty reasoning into a logical form. This is how we break down the strongholds of bad ideas.

Finally, we will end our discussion by looking at how Jesus loved. He treated ideas (agendas) and people very differently.

Is This a Person or an Idea?

In 2 Corinthians 10:5, the apostle Paul tells us, "We demolish arguments and every pretension that sets itself up against the knowledge of God, and we take captive every thought to make it obedient to Christ." Notice that believers are to demolish *arguments*—not people. Later, in Colossians 2:8, Paul writes, "See to it that no one takes you captive through hollow and deceptive philosophy, which depends on human tradition and the elemental spiritual forces of this world rather than on Christ." Read these two verses together, and it becomes clear that we are dealing with two separate issues: an idea and a captive.

The polarization of our culture has made it difficult to see past labels. But we as Christians are called to distinguish the person from the ideology—*no matter our political persuasion*. Protestors rioting in the streets are people made in the image of God, every one of them. Those talking heads on the news, hollering about the downfall of America? Jesus died for them too. My husband reminds me every time we get in a fight: "Hill, remember who the real enemy is. You and I are on the same team."

An Enemy with No Scruples

No war is pleasant, but the Vietnam War was particularly heinous. Very few who went to Vietnam came back unchanged. No side was innocent in that war; each committed its own atrocities. Americans spent a decade dropping Agent Orange on the Vietnamese, exposing millions of noncombatants to toxic chemicals. Over a million people today remain disabled as a result of their exposure. At the same time, the Viet Cong were developing their own deadly tactics. They used the most vulnerable population as human shields and suicide bombers. They hid out in hospitals so that the Americans wouldn't bomb them. Little kids were given live grenades and told to walk into groups of US soldiers. Kids who were barely ten would suddenly pop up with machine guns. And the worst one of all, toddlers had their diapers or teddy bears stuffed with explosives and were then abandoned, left for the US troops to find. You only make that mistake once. Every piece of humanity our poor military boys had was stripped from them. They could either keep their sense of humanity by comforting the crying child but risk killing their entire platoon. Or—as usually happened—they had to silence their most basic human instinct, and treat the kids for what they were: a weapon of the enemy. Nobody can gun down a bunch of children and return home unchanged—even if they knew that the children would have killed them first.

I find us in a very similar situation when it comes to the sexual agenda. We, too, have an enemy with no scruples. Satan is the father of lies, and he has no problem targeting the hurting, the vulnerable, and the broken— the ones who are most in need of love—and then strapping an ideological bomb onto their backs. What do we do? *We cannot accept the ideologies into our fellowship*; upon detonation, churches are rewriting God's commands thinking they are "loving others." *Kablooey* goes the gospel. But neither can we turn a blind eye to these broken and hurting people. That profanes the *purpose* of the gospel. *Kablooey* goes our witness.

> Satan is the father of lies, and he has no problem targeting the hurting, the vulnerable, and the broken— the ones who are most in need of love—and then strapping an ideological bomb onto their backs.

I think many of us in the church have recognized this catch-22. It's an impossible position we have been put in. We just haven't been able to articulate it. Loving God and loving others sounds so simple…until an unbiblical agenda attaches itself onto the very people we are called to love. The enemy has convinced them that the agenda is their identity, and our refusal to embrace the agenda feels like a rejection of their very selves. Like the soldiers, some of us may have even grown numb because it feels like a lose-lose situation. Why even try anymore? Our love has grown cold because to love has become deadly, from a spiritual perspective.

There was no way to disarm the children in Vietnam, but we can do our best here with the sexual agenda. Like those soldiers, we have to balance our compassion with our commitment to truth. We can encourage our sweet and compassionate kids to love the vulnerable, the broken, the marginalized, and the misfits—just like Jesus did. *But unless we teach them how to diffuse the ideological bomb first, they run the risk of having their Christian worldview blown to smithereens, all because they desired to show love.*

Agendas are often promoted through media and education until they become so ingrained that they define the new normal. We *must* resist agendas which rewrite the rules of truth and morality and teach our kids to do the same. Remember that "our struggle is not against flesh and blood, but against the rulers, against the authorities, against the powers of this dark world and against the spiritual forces of evil in the heavenly realms" (Ephesians 6:12). These enemy forces have *no* scruples.

When Jesus was asked what the greatest commandment was, He replied with the Jewish Shema: Love the Lord with all your heart, soul, mind, and strength, and *secondly* love your neighbor as yourself. [1] The problem we are seeing is that people are switching the order of these two commands. Within progressive Christian circles, loving God is reinterpreted in light of a new definition of love—one which elevates feelings over truth. One popular progressive Christian author described a conversation with another Christian leader about their "different teaching styles." She told the other teacher, "In Jesus' awesome summary of life's main work—love God and love people—you lean into the 'love God' part best and I lean into the 'love people' part best." She writes that "When 'loving God' results in pain, exclusion, harm, or trauma to people…then we are absolutely doing the first part wrong." [2] (Guess the early church didn't get the memo?) This is nonsense. We can't do one without doing the other. Done right, they will never be in competition…unless a person has redefined love…which is what I suspect has happened here.

Loving God means we do what pleases Him. We love people the

same way—*by doing what pleases God.* Scripture famously defines what love is in 1 Corinthians 13. Most everyone on the #loveislove train is totally fine with all the "patient" and "kind" stuff. It's verse 6 that often gets left out of the equation: "Love does not delight in evil, but rejoices *with the truth.*" Truth is included in the definition of love. And as Christians, we do not believe that truth comes from within. It is eternally grounded in God and in the person of Jesus. By Scriptural definition, we cannot love people if we succumb to lies; it ceases to be biblical love. Love and truth are probably the two most primary virtues to which we as Christians must cling.

Our task, then? We need to maintain our Christian worldview while loving those living in or struggling with sin. This fulfills the greatest commandment *and* the second...*in the right order.* We balance truth with grace, never sacrificing either. Let's dig into each in turn.

Loving God by Loving Truth

If we see an ideology pushing people away from God's precepts, we should fight that ideology on its own turf. As parents, we need to show our kids that we understand and can refute the assumptions on which the ideology is based. Refuting poor reasoning is a requirement for elders who are leading the church, so it should be a requirement for us as we help train up our kids (Titus 1:5-9). As we saw from the Romans 1 passage, when people suppress truth, their ability to reason is the first thing to go.

The Anatomy of a Logical Argument

Logical or deductive reasoning starts with assumptions and facts from which a conclusion can be drawn. If we are to teach our kids how to identify lies for what they are, we need to show them how to form a cogent argument. For the purposes of this book, I will use the following formula:

Statement 1:   Assumption
Statement 2:   Fact claim
Statement 3:   Conclusion

Let's use the cosmological argument for God as an example.

> Assumption: Everything that begins to exist has a cause.
> Fact claim: The universe began to exist.
> Conclusion: Therefore, the universe had a cause.

Just who or what *caused* the universe? That can be discussed, and that's what our goal is: productive conversation.

Let's take a crack at some of the assumptions in the Christian worldview and those of the secular worldview and see how they compare.

> Assumption: If human beings were created by God, then they were designed with a purpose.
> Fact claim: Human beings were created by God.
> Conclusion: Therefore, human beings are designed with a purpose.

Let's contrast this with the secular worldview:

> Assumption: If human beings evolved, then they were not designed with a purpose.
> Fact claim: Human beings evolved.
> Conclusion: Therefore, human beings were not designed with a purpose.

The funny-not-funny thing is that many people who believe that human beings evolved also believe that human beings have purpose. But purpose implies an original intention. An intention can only come from a mind. Evolution is, by definition, *without purpose, without intention, and without a mind*. This is where we identify what it means for a worldview to be *incoherent*—meaning the desired conclusion does not follow from its foundational premises. Evolution can never tell us what *ought* to be or what *ought not* to be. At best, evolution gives us what survived over time. It can never give us purpose.

Trying to discover the "purpose" of a purposeless process is a waste of time. Thinking that you *can get purpose* through a purposeless process is illogical. Believing that one can reject the creator God and still have purpose reflects what philosophers call "the grounding problem." A person may believe the sentiment "My life has purpose," but may lack the worldview foundation on which to build that conclusion. They may decide that their "purpose" is to love their neighbor, but they could just as easily have decided that their "purpose" was to *eat* their neighbor. You cannot judge these two "purposes" from an evolutionary perspective because it provides no outside standard by which to judge which purpose is better. You can't do it, friends. It's a losing battle.

As you start to familiarize yourself with the assumptions, fact claims, and conclusions of an argument, the incoherence of the secular worldview becomes more apparent. As Christians, our worldview allows for truth and morality because we have an objective standard *outside of ourselves,* a personal God who intentionally created us and who endowed us with purpose. A moral law requires a law giver. The only other option is for everyone to become "a law unto themselves." Indeed, the Bible is full of such experiments (Judges 17:6). They didn't usually work very well.

When we teach our kids to recognize bad reasoning, it helps them to stand even firmer with truth. When they stand with truth, their faith's roots go even deeper. Why? Because "faith is confidence in what we hope for and assurance about what we do not see" (Hebrews 11:1). The more confident and assured your kids can be of the truth, the more their faith grows. God does not ask us to check our brains at the door!

A well-trained mind is one of our biggest spiritual protections against the enemy's schemes. This is why Romans 12:2 commands us to renew our minds—because that renewal will prevent us from being conformed to the world, and we will be able to "test and approve what God's will is— his good, pleasing and perfect will" (Romans 12:2).

Emotional Reasoning

When dealing with people versus an agenda, we need to understand a completely different type of reasoning—emotional reasoning. Emotional reasoning usually starts with the conclusion (a feeling) and then finds facts to support it. In its most basic form, the underlying assumption for emotional reasoning is, "If I feel it, it's true." Emotional reasoning works in the exact opposite direction of deductive reasoning. The feelings determine the facts in a self-fulfilling prophecy kind of way. And then the person turns around and states those facts as if they came first, and not the emotion. Confusing feelings with facts is where our culture is tripping up our kids.

For example, oppression is still an issue in our world, and we need to know how to combat injustice when we encounter it. So how can we tread on this topic wisely? Here's an example of how emotional reasoning might cloud the issue.

> Assumption: If I feel oppressed, it's because I am being oppressed by someone or something.
> Fact: I feel oppressed.
> Conclusion: Therefore, I am being oppressed by someone or something.

Based on this emotional argument, the next "logical" step is to identify the oppressor. This is what we see happening within identity politics. But notice how this reasoning does not start with facts. If we were to use proper deductive reasoning, it would look like this:

> Assumption: If someone does [X] to me, they are oppressing me.
> Fact: Someone did [X] to me.
> Conclusion: Therefore, I am being oppressed by someone.

This is a legitimate argument. This is how we identify when a real wrong has been committed. However, if someone wants to engage with this argument, they cannot start with whether or not someone feels oppressed. They must start with whether or not [X] constitutes oppression.

Now I am not trying to make any kind of political statement as to whether certain groups are being oppressed or not. What I am trying to do is to show how confusing feelings with facts carries weighty implications for us as Christians. For example, what if culture changes the rules as to what constitutes oppression? What happens when teaching about biblical sexuality, by law, becomes oppressive hate speech? Those who define the terms determine who is the oppressor and who is the victim. They can paint anyone they want as an "oppressor," and according to our culture, *oppressors must be silenced at all costs*. In the case of gender and sexuality, things like binary language (male and female), the definition of marriage (between a man and a woman), or skepticism regarding the health benefits of sex change operations—these are all now considered "oppressive." But just because someone *feels* that being called female is oppressive does not make it oppressive. That is an assumption, and one that we should be preparing our kids to question.

Embracing Our Inner Warrior Bear and Nurturing Bear

While it's important to understand how logic and reasoning work, we cannot be content with winning an intellectual argument. Logic-ing someone to death has rarely a disciple made. Ideas are nothing outside the mind of a person—a person made in the image of God, who should be treated with kindness and compassion.

So we need two hats, Mama Bears. When we combat ideas, we are Warrior Bears. A Warrior Bear stands firm against ideas and agendas raised against the knowledge of God (2 Corinthians 10:5). We cannot sacrifice truth no matter how much that truth may offend.

When we address the *people* who espouse these ideas, we are Nurturing Bears. A Nurturing Bear tends to the wounded captive, loving them tenderly back to health and always pointing them toward the Healer. We don't have to compromise conviction to show compassion (and vice versa).

One of these hats (warrior or nurturer) probably comes more naturally to you than the other. But if we want to be like Jesus, if we want to be "conformed to the image of [God's] Son" (Romans 8:29), we must embrace both roles. Let's look at how Jesus did this.

> We don't have to compromise
> conviction to show compassion.

Modeling Our Speech After Jesus

When you read the Gospels, you'll notice that when Jesus speaks to crowds, He doesn't mince words. Take a few minutes to read the Sermon on the Mount—you'll find it in Matthew 5–7. In that sermon, Jesus unapologetically gives the smackdown of all smackdowns. He doesn't just condemn acts of sin. He includes the attitudes of the heart and the mind as well.

When speaking to the masses, He addresses the ideas for what they are. Look, for example, at Matthew 5:28-29. To the crowds, Jesus says, "Anyone who looks at a woman lustfully has already committed adultery with her in his heart. If your right eye causes you to stumble, gouge it out and throw it away." (Well, that escalated quickly.) Jesus's message to the public was not intended to remove shame. It was intended to convict and to convey truth. It was about destroying every single loophole people were using to excuse their sin.

Compare the force of that message with the way Jesus dealt with individuals. To the woman caught in adultery, Jesus spoke differently (John 8:2-11). He did not shame her into obedience. He first removed her shame and *then* called her to a life of obedience. She was hurting. She was embarrassed. She expected judgment. He didn't need anyone to tell her that what she was doing was wrong; she already knew. What she needed to know was that there was redemption and healing and a new chance to get it right.

For the sake of argument, does Jesus ever speak harshly with individuals? Actually, He does. But guess who it is toward? Jesus dealt very harshly with the Pharisees. The Pharisees were dead positive that they were doing everything right. Their own self-righteous confidence (and their scorn for the little guy who didn't compare) effectively prevented hurting and broken people from experiencing the living God. The Pharisees made people think that they were disqualified from approaching God. We have these same kinds of Pharisees in the church today—hyper critical, hyper legalistic, super confident that they are God's chosen mouthpiece to condemn all the dirty rotten sinners. These people warrant open rebuke.

I'd like to point out a second type of Phariseeism I have noticed cropping up lately. These Christian leaders are also dead positive that they are doing everything right—except their confidence lies in their reinterpretation of God's Word. They appeal "to the lustful desires of the flesh" and "entice people who are just escaping from those who live in error. They promise them freedom, while they themselves are slaves of depravity" (2 Peter 2:18-19). These types of modern Pharisees often rail against the traditional type of Pharisees. What they don't realize is that *they too* are preventing hurting and needy people from encountering the living God. Traditional Pharisees block people by making them feel too dirty to approach God. The modern pharisees block people by making them feel that their sin is not something that needs to be repented from.

So is there ever a time to be harsh? Yup. There sure is. But it's usually when you're dealing with a person who is puffed up with self-righteousness, not a person struggling with brokenness. It's okay to be confident as long as your confidence lies in God's Word. Everywhere else, we need to exercise humility.

> ## The time to be harsh is when you're dealing with a person who is puffed up with self-righteousness, not a person struggling with brokenness.

Jesus dealt with ideas forcefully and without apology. He also dealt with individuals according to their need: what was keeping the person from unifying with the heart and mind of God? We should model our approach after Jesus. We don't just answer questions, we answer *people*. There is a time to demolish arguments and a time to love a person tangled in a thorn bush of bad ideas. Ultimately, we need to teach our kids how to do both.

> ## We don't just answer questions, we answer *people*.

Discussion Questions

1. **Icebreaker:** Have you ever had to help an animal who was in pain? How did it act toward you?

2. **Main theme:** *Biblical love means demolishing bad arguments while showing compassion to those held captive to the lies.* What do you think it means to demolish the argument while loving the person? What does that look like in a practical way?

3. **Self-evaluation:** Have you ever been trapped in emotional reasoning, starting with a feeling and then trying to find people or events around you that justify the feeling? How can this become a self-fulfilling prophecy?

4. **Brainstorm:** My friend Elizabeth Urbanowicz, founder of Foundation Worldview, has created a great worksheet to practice your argument mapping skills. Head over to www.mamabearapologetics.com/logic-worksheet to download the worksheet and map out the arguments.

5. **Release the bear:** Look for an opportunity this week to discuss emotional versus logical reasoning with your children. You'd be surprised at how much they can understand at a young age. For inspiration, see Natasha Crain's article "How I'm Teaching My 6-Year-Olds to Be Critical Thinkers" located at natashacrain.com.

6. **Pray:** Our world is filled with so many hurting people who are held captive to bad ideas. Pray that God would begin letting the scales fall from their eyes (Acts 9:18) when it comes to the lies so that they can finally come to the God who loves them so much.

Part Two

Wait, My Kids Are Being Taught What?!

PRAYER OF LAMENT

Bring Your Complaint

LAMENTATIONS 1:9; 1:16; 2:14

Look at our affliction, Lord, for the enemy has magnified himself in triumph. For these things we weep; our eyes overflow with tears…our children are desolate and perishing, for the enemy has prevailed.

Lord, we are sickened by the lies our children are being raised to believe are truth. Our children are enticed to follow their hearts, do what makes them happy, and let feelings be their god. They're taught a foreign language of promiscuous activities that distort Your image and Your message. We have been blindsided by all the portals to filth, debauchery, confusion, lies, and deception. Our insecurities pile up like dirty laundry because when we try to speak the truth, others look at us like we are soiled by lack of "compassion."

Biblical marriage is mocked. What is evil is called good. What is wrong is called right. What is truth is called an opinion. The nonsense makes us nauseous. We too often go silent for fear of being misunderstood, of our disagreement being labeled hate. We feel unequipped. Overwhelmed. Uninformed. Defeated before we toe the starting line. Afraid of not finishing the course. Even family members, close friends, and fellow believers aren't necessarily running the race beside us. We feel alone and want to quit. Do You see this? Do You care?

Chapter 5

Are You Sex Smarter than a Fifth Grader?

Understanding the New National Sexual Education Standards

HILLARY

When I was in fifth grade, I was obsessed with *The Little Mermaid*, and my biggest ambition was to win the Jump Rope for the Heart competition with the ragtag group of misfits I had managed to assemble. (And yes, we crushed the competition, thanks to my choreography.) My sister and I had just moved from a private Christian school to a public school, and I was shocked to hear what one of the guys did to a girl in the movie theater on a date. (A date? In fifth grade? Who were these kids' parents?!?!) Of course, it could have all been gossip. I only heard it through the grapevine, not from the health teacher.

Fast-forward to the fall of 2020. According to the National Sex Education Standards (NSES), by the end of fifth grade, your children should be able to explain the following:[1]

- "Distinguish between sex assigned at birth and gender identity and explain how they may or may not differ.

- "Define and explain differences between cisgender, transgender, gender nonbinary, gender expansive, and gender identity. (I was tracking up until gender expansive...)

- "Describe the role hormones play in the physical, social, cognitive, and emotional changes during adolescence and the potential role of hormone blockers on young people who identify as transgender.

- "Explain common human sexual development and the role of hormones (e.g., romantic and sexual feelings, masturbation, mood swings, timing of pubertal onset)."

Oh, and by the way, this is how "common human sexual development" is defined earlier in the NSES document: "The developmental process for young people often involves *experimenting with many different identities...* and sexual identity is not exempt from this type of exploration" (emphasis mine). Yes, you heard that right. Experimenting with different genders and different sexual orientations is apparently a "normal" part of sexual development. To this I have to ask, "How did *we* all turn out okay? Were we all doing it wrong up until now?" In this chapter, we'll get an understanding of what the NSES is, its ramifications for your child's education, and its guiding mission and vision.

The New National Sex Education Standards?

The NSES were written by a group called SIECUS—Sexuality Information and Education Council of the United States—in conjunction with several other advocacy groups. SIECUS was founded in 1964 by Mary Calderone, former medical director at Planned Parenthood. And where did she get the seed money to form this organization? Hugh Hefner.[2]

These standards are used to create the many comprehensive sex education programs—and those curricula are making their way to a school near you (sooner rather than later if you are in the Northeast or the West Coast). And while they sound super official, they're not an official government group. That's the first thing you need to know. If you go to the

Department of Education, there are no curriculum standards for sex education (for now).

This doesn't mean schools aren't fooled by the name, though. The standards have already been adopted by more than 40 percent of school districts in the United States.[3]

What Are Your Rights as a Parent?

First off, I'd like to reiterate that, as of writing this book, there are no national sex education standards on the Department of Education's website. This might change soon, though, as sexual orientation and gender identity (SOGI) laws become more prevalent. Currently, sexual health education is still up to the states, and it's the responsibility of individual school boards to comply.

So what's your first step? Gather information. Contact your local school district to find out what sex education standards and curricula will be used in your children's classrooms. You can also contact the teacher to find out when the curriculum will be taught, who will teach it, and what class time will be used. Will the girls and boys be separated? How will questions be handled? (This one is important because if questions are a free-for-all, there's no telling what topics will be covered.) Find out who wrote the curriculum. Do they have ties to the abortion industry?

Finally, ask if the curriculum teaches sexual risk *avoidance* or sexual risk *reduction*. *Avoidance* means the curriculum teaches unwanted pregnancy and STDs can be prevented by abstinence. *Reduction* means the curriculum assumes kids will be having sex and teaches them how to suffer fewer consequences. This is a critical difference. Technically—according to research partially funded by Planned Parenthood—the "risk reduction" programs correlate with the lowest number of teen pregnancies—the only real metric that they care about. It's worth noting that it also correlates with higher abortion rates.[4]

If, after researching, you want to object to your school's sex education curriculum, you must file a notice first with the instructor, then the principal, then the schoolboard, and then up to the state level. But you need that paper trail. It is important (and helpful for your cause) to honor the chain of command and the prescribed process for making a formal complaint as dictated by the school district. Also, it's extremely helpful to document any conversation in person or on the phone with the date, the time, the name of the person you spoke with, and the most important points of the conversation. You might even email the person you spoke with, thanking them for talking with you, and then describing the important points of your conversation. If that person replies without challenging what you wrote, you now have a reliable document for future reference. But make sure your conversation or email doesn't feel adversarial.

And keep in mind that, though your primary job is to protect and educate your children, you also have the opportunity to be salt and light to teachers and administrators in the way you conduct yourself during these conversations. Don't let your objection to the curriculum be the only contact they have with you, reinforcing the stereotype of the neurotic Christian parent. The more you engage your child's teacher with a helpful attitude, and the longer your track record of service grows, the more likely they are to give you a gracious reading if you object to the sexuality unit. And remember, sometimes the teacher is someone who shares your values but doesn't know how to implement a Christian worldview in the classroom while still protecting her job. It's a tough position to be in. Our conversations need to be seasoned with grace and discernment.

What's New About These Standards?

Six main topics are covered in the NSES. These topics repeat every year, from kindergarten through twelfth grade, with more details and descriptions added at each successive grade level.

If your school district is using these standards to develop their curricula, they're likely complying with the second edition, published in 2020. This edition contains notable changes from the first edition, published in 2012. And, unfortunately, these changes reflect a worldview that doesn't even come close to reflecting the one we discussed in chapter 2. Here's a small sampling.

Consent

Previously called "Healthy Relationships," this section has been retitled "*Consent* and Healthy Relationships." Every single grade level now focuses on *consent* being the new moral standard for sexuality. The message our kids will be getting every year, for 13 years, is that if someone consents to a sexual activity, then it's okay—*healthy* even. And just in case they aren't sure what consent is, Planned Parenthood has made a super awkward little video explaining allllll the ways your child can get consent. Check it out.[5] It's basically a voice-over on videos with same-sex couples making out. There's like two seconds of a heterosexual couple, but that's it. Oh, and FYI, it has dozens of comments from kids who were *required to watch it for health class.*

Emphasizing consent isn't necessarily bad. Rape is still rampant in our society. So is childhood sexual abuse. Your kids should know that they have control over their own bodies. (That's part of their sphere of authority, remember?) Nobody should have the right to touch them without their explicit permission. But the type of consent the standards are emphasizing is more about sexual autonomy—meaning that all kids at any age should have the right to decide when they want to have sex, and nobody else's input matters. What the standards are pushing for is sex-positivity, a topic upon which we will expand in chapter 8.

And What Exactly Do They Mean by Healthy Relationships?

Healthy is a sneaky little word. You can only know what's healthy if you know what is good for someone. And you can only know what is good for someone when you have properly defined *good* to begin with. You don't quite see what the standards mean by healthy until twelfth grade, where they finally define it as consent, communication, and freedom from gender stereotypes. I gotta say, that's a pretty low bar for "healthy."

From the perspective of sex-positivity, the goal is to help kids become familiar with their own sexual wants and needs so that they know what they do and don't want to consent to. (And as we saw on page 84, healthy sexual development is now defined as exploring all these options.) Under this definition, not being able to explore these options is "unhealthy." Progressive pastor Nadia Bolz-Weber totally agrees. She muses in her book *Shameless* (after talking to a girl who felt awkward during her first sexual encounter), "*You were robbed.* The church took away over a decade of [this girl's] sexual development. All this time, she could have been gaining the kind of wisdom that comes from making her own choices, from having lovers, from making mistakes, from falling in love."[6]

That's basically the mindset behind these standards. Under the new definition, "healthy" means experimenting, and consequences are merely "mistakes." This definition of health has nothing to do with what is actually good for your kids. If your 12-year-old decides that being choked sounds like fun, then a "healthy relationship" is one in which he or she and their partner can weigh the pros and cons of that decision together and learn how to choke without anyone getting injured. That technically meets the standard's criteria of "healthy."

Sexual Orientation and Identity

Instead of sex education being about bodies and reproduction, it is now about exploring *who* you want to have sex with. And only you can decide that for yourself. As mentioned above, experimenting with different orientations is being taught as a normal part of sexual development. Children are introduced to this concept as early as kindergarten when they start learning about the "different kinds of families"—same-sex parents being one of the categories. By eighth grade, students should be able to define the whole range of sexual orientations, including heterosexuality, homosexuality, bisexuality...and even being queer, two-spirit, asexual, and pansexual. (We'll define some of these in chapter 7.)

Gender Identity and Expression

According to gender identity and expression, a person's biological sex can be different from their self-perceived gender, and both can be different from the person's gender expression (that is, which societal gender norms they adopt). Chapter 7 will go through an actual sample curriculum (The

Genderbread Person) that is teaching these views of gender and sexual identity in public schools to kids as young as kindergarten. While writing this chapter, one of my Texas Mama Bears confirmed that this curriculum has made its way into the San Antonio school district. If it's in Texas, y'all, it can be anywhere.

The Guiding Principles and Values of the NSES

We must remember that practices and procedures don't just come out of thin air. They come from an ideological background which, in turn, stems from a worldview—how a person perceives reality and what they think needs to happen in order to improve the world. There is an end goal in mind—a worldly *telos* that is competing with the *telos* of God. *If you don't understand the worldview behind the policies, you'll find yourself unable to see the pattern that is emerging*, the picture that is created from putting all these little puzzle pieces together. So let's break these down, bit by bit.

I will here give an overview of each guiding principle of the NSES. For the sake of brevity, I'll treat each like a mini-ROAR, briefly describing what it is and discerning the truth from the lies.

Equity and Reproductive Justice

Equity is another word like *tolerance* and *inclusion*, which sounds biblical. When the standards say *equity*, what they mean is that people should all have equal opportunities to everything. That sounds good, right? But there's a catch. Smuggled into the definition of "equity" is that idea that equal opportunities will necessarily produce equal outcomes, so if we don't see equal outcomes, there must not have been equal opportunity. Commitment to equity rightly acknowledges that society should not prevent people from pursuing life, liberty, and happiness. But this definition removes any causal connection between personal agency and final results. Anytime there are unequal outcomes between various demographics, it is assumed that there is a *structural impediment* (i.e., a "system") preventing people from achieving the same amount of success. To have true social justice, it is said, we need to root out whatever "system" is holding people back. The problem with this is that it teaches our kids that we are just helpless pawns in the hands of fate. It downplays personal responsibility.

Also, our politically correct culture dictates what factors we are allowed to look at. There are multiple studies which show that religiosity and family structure have a much larger impact on the future success (especially academic) of individuals than do school or government interventions.[7] Under equity, however, we are not allowed to discuss this impact out of fear of "stigmatizing" anyone for their family structure or religion (or lack thereof).[8]

Reproductive justice is a fancy way of saying "right to abortion." The argument is that since a man is never forced to carry a baby to term in his body, then a woman should never be forced to carry a baby to term in her body. Equal outcomes, therefore, necessitate allowing a woman to choose whether or not she wants to be pregnant, even if conception has already occurred. While facing an unwanted pregnancy is indeed very scary, we shouldn't be so quick to lump *biological differences* into "human rights." It opens a virtual Pandora's box of bad ideas.[9]

Language Inclusivity (i.e., Queer Theory)

As mentioned above, the new standards state, "The developmental process for young people often involves experimenting with many different identities, forms of expression, and behaviors, and sexual identity is not exempt from this type of exploration."[10] Facebook famously allows users to select one of 58 genders for their profiles—with an additional "fill in the blank" option in case their gender still isn't recognized.[11] I'm hoping this section will shed some light on why there are so many options.

According to postmodern Queer Theory—and specifically philosophers Judith Butler and Michel Foucault—words are not just information. They are a means of actually *creating and regulating reality*. (Let that sink in for a second…) In postmodern babble, words are a socially constructed power used by the oppressor class to "regulate and police sex," thereby controlling sexual minorities and women.[12] When I say "socially constructed," I mean like how the meaning of red and green lights are social constructs which tell us "stop" and "go." There's nothing universal or inherent about these colors which would define them this way. It's something we made up—a socially constructed system.

According to Queer Theory, words—more commonly called "the discourses"—work by arbitrarily defining *normal* and then marginalizing anyone who doesn't fit in. (By *marginalizing*, they mean stripping away that person or group's power.) A person steeped in Queer Theory will argue, for example, that the words male and female are a human-made binary (meaning only two options) which wrongly assumes that there are only two genders.[13] After establishing these two genders as the only options, this language can now marginalize (strip away the power of) those who fall outside traditional gender norms or gender stereotypes. Therefore, in order to have a fair and just society, we need to expand our language so that all feel included and nobody is marginalized.[14] So like I said, people can create whatever reality they want with the words that they use. It's almost like a secular "name it and claim it" philosophy.

Furthermore, since Queer Theorists believe that words have created an unfair power differential, then the way to correct this unequal distribution of power is by changing the language we use. Norms are redefined so all variations are considered viable—thus the 58 labels for gender. But expanding biological categories to encompass psychological categories feels backward; why should the genders expand? Have we, perhaps, been too rigid in our understanding of appropriate ways to express one's masculinity or femininity?

The answer is that Queer theorists firmly believe that gender is a social construct independent of biology. And if society made the two-gender rule, they can make the 58-gender rule. No harm, no foul.

The Marxist Taproot

The rest of the "guiding mission and values" section cannot be understood without first understanding their parent category: Marxism. The social justice movement is basically neo-Marxism in skinny jeans. It is identical to Marx's views, except that it defines the "haves" and the "have nots" in terms of social power instead of money and capitalism. If that

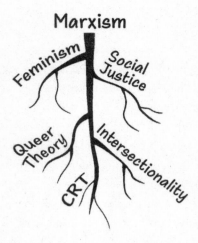

sounded like gobbledygook, then let's take a step backward…

Picture a plant. The roots of a plant start with one large taproot from which numerous smaller roots branch out into the soil. If we want to uproot the whole root, we need to get both the taproot and the secondary roots. The taproot is Postmodernism and Marxism, and from them flow all the other ideologies like Intersectionality, Social Justice, Queer Theory, Critical Theory, and Critical Race Theory—most of which are explicitly mentioned in the standards. But Marxism is the lifeline of the whole shebang.

Marxism rarely shows up the same way twice. Once people discover how it destroys a society, they are loath to allow the same thing to happen again. So it keeps cropping up in new and inventive ways meant to disguise and distance itself from past failures. (Even Encyclopedia Britannica is getting on the rebranding bandwagon by renaming communism "Command Economy.")[15] But when push comes to shove, it's the same circus, same monkeys.

There are three main assumptions within Marxism from which all other theories derive. The first is that *all of society can be divided into the haves and have nots*. In Marx's day, he defined these groups in terms of who owned the businesses and who worked the businesses. The owning class was unfairly reaping the benefit of the workers' toil. To have a fair and just society, resources should be distributed equally.

This same ideology is at play today, except instead of business owners and workers, everything is about power differentials—who has social power (the haves) and who does not (the have nots). Social justice teaches that those in the privileged class have a duty to champion the cause of the oppressed. As we'll see in the next section, Christians are considered privileged, and the LGBTQ community is considered the oppressed minority that needs protecting.

The second assumption is that *in order to have a fair and just society, the have nots must overthrow the haves.* According to Marxism, the oppressed (have nots) will only take their oppression for so long before revolting. When the revolution comes, the have nots will reclaim ownership of all the resources and then everyone will work together, each according to their ability and receiving according to their need. Only then can a society be stable and fair to all.

The final assumption? *The ends justify the means.* The end goal is to have a fair, just, peaceful, and stable society. This in itself is not a bad goal. Who doesn't want this? The Marxist, however, believes that the route to achieving this utopia can only come by forcefully disrupting the current structure of society—family, government, all of it. And since the assumed final outcome is so wonderful, one must be willing to do whatever it takes to bring about this transformation. The only moral imperative is progress toward utopia. As long as you are pushing society in that direction, then no action you take to accomplish it can be considered unethical or wrong. As C.S. Lewis said in *God in the Dock,* "Of all tyrannies, a tyranny sincerely exercised for the good of its victims may be the most oppressive. It would be better to live under robber barons than under omnipotent moral busybodies. The robber baron's cruelty may sometimes sleep, his cupidity may at some point be satiated; *but those who torment us for our own good will torment us without end for they do so with the approval of their own conscience*"[16] (emphasis mine). In other words, a person will go to any lengths they deem necessary when they are convinced that they are acting for the greater good. This is what we saw happen during the Holocaust. Cruelty had no bounds because those in power *thought* that what they were doing was for the benefit of their society, even if it meant getting rid of a few "undesirables." Survival of the fittest turned into social dogma.

All in all, as a worldview, Marxism answers many of the same questions the Christian worldview answers, albeit very differently.

Why are we here? *To create a fair and just society where everyone is equal.*

What is morality? *Anything that is done to bring about this fair and just society.*

What is wrong with the world? *Unequal distribution of resources and power.*

How are we redeemed from what is wrong with the world? *Through the redistribution of resources and power so that they are equally shared among all.*

It must be noted that the end goals of Marxism are not bad goals. The difference between them and Christianity is that we differ on how (and when) we think these goals will be accomplished. Christianity doesn't promise a perfectly fair and just society; at least not before God intervenes to make it all right. But that is another story for another time.

> A person will go to any lengths they
> deem necessary when they are convinced that
> they are acting for the greater good.

Social Justice and Intersectionality

Now that we understand the taproot (Marxism), we can examine the secondary roots—social justice and intersectionality. According to social justice theory, society is made up of systems of power. In our case, these systems benefit those who are white, male, Protestant, and heterosexual. Those who belong to these groups have—whether they realize it or not—played a part in marginalizing those who don't belong to these categories. In order to have a fair and just society, these systems of power need to be dismantled. This comes by first recognizing that the systems of power exist and, second, by identifying where you are within the system of power.

If you are in the privileged class, you must repent of your privilege and ally yourself with an oppressed group. If you are not sure how privileged you are, take a handy-dandy online quiz to see where you fall on the "Matrix of Oppression."[17]

Social Identity Categories	Privileged Social Groups	Borderline Social Groups	Oppressed/ Targeted Social Groups	"ism"
Sex	Biological Men	Intersex and Transgender	Biological Women	Sexism
Gender	Gender conforming bio men and women	Gender ambiguous bio men and women	Transgender, Genderqueer, Intersex	Transgender Oppression
Sexual Orientation	Heterosexuals	Bisexuals	Lesbians, Gay men	Heterosexism
Religion	Protestant Christians	Roman Catholics	Jews, Muslims, Hindus	Religious Oppression

There are a whole lot more categories if you Google "matrix of oppression," but these are the most relevant ones for the purposes of this book. These categories are intended to help individuals identify who is part of the privileged "system of power" and who is the oppressed minority class who has historically been robbed of social equality.

Intersectionality comes from an observation that a person may have intersecting identities—some of which are classified as privileged and some as oppressed. Pay close attention to the categories here involving gender, sexual orientation, and religion. In this new framework, a Protestant man or woman who is content in the body God gave them and who is living out God's design for sex and marriage is in the oppressor category. This would be a person who would need to acknowledge their privilege and stand in solidarity with oppressed groups. Not doing so will earn a person the label of hateful, homophobic, transphobic, Islamophobic, and hater of all underdogs. Our kids aren't just being called "goody-goodies" anymore. They are being shamed out of their Christian beliefs and brainwashed into defending actions the Lord has called sin.

To be fair, are there groups in our country who have less power than others? Yes. Do we need to correct *actual* injustices when and where they occur? Absolutely! But again, when we take action, we should make sure that we are doing so on the basis of real information, not someone else's categorical terms. (We'll explore the relationship and differences between categories and actual information in the next chapter.)

With instruction in social justice and intersectionality, our kids are having a category hammered into their brains from kindergarten through their senior year of high school. The category consists of "oppressed people whom I should defend." This is a great category when teaching our kids to defend individuals who are experiencing mistreatment of some kind. This is *not* a great category in teaching our kids to defend entire classes of people. Why? Because doing so teaches our kids that guilt and innocence are derived from one's demographic, not from one's actions. That is definitely not a part of the biblical worldview!

> Guilt and innocence are derived from
> one's actions, not one's demographic.

What Is the Outcome of These Ideas?

Part of being an ally to a marginalized group means that you step aside and elevate the minority's voice, experiences, and opinions. This, too, hits our kids where they are most vulnerable. Who doesn't want to be cheered on for their identity? Who doesn't want to be celebrated as a hero just by adopting a label? Who doesn't want their words to carry more weight?

As a result, we are witnessing an alarming number (one in six) of Gen Z'ers self-identifying as LGBTQ. This is almost *double* the number of Millennials, which was itself more than *double* the number of Gen X'ers.[18] And these are all adults we're talking about! If this trend continues, we should expect *one-third* of our kids under 18 to soon self-identify under the LGBTQ banner.

Many of these cases are real and shouldn't be dismissed. These young adults need love and guidance to carry their unique sexual cross while still being faithful to Christ. But for some, this new identity is an experiment. Once a person starts messing with the image of God and hormones, there are certain effects that are difficult to undo.

Classically, gender dysphoria has been almost exclusively a phenomenon observed in young boys, affecting less than half a percent of the population.[19] These boys, usually from early childhood, insist that they have been born in the wrong body. Females have typically been in the minority of this small group. Suddenly, between 2016 and 2018 the numbers skyrocketed, with the UK reporting a 4,400 percent increase in girls seeking gender treatment.[20] The discomfort and anxiety are real, but our kids' inner turmoil will not be relieved by hormone treatments.

And here we are in church, still singing songs about Father Abraham while our kids march like proverbial lemmings over the cliff of bad ideas. For starters, they have allowed society to redefine truth and goodness under the banner of love, inclusion, and protection for the oppressed. *It is very difficult to remain an orthodox Christian once truth and goodness are redefined.*

It is very difficult to remain an orthodox Christian once truth and goodness are redefined.

Our kids are seeking what we all sought back when we were young—a way to fit in and be accepted. They used to want to grow up to be firefighters and astronauts because that is who our society lauded as heroes. Today, there is a virtual parade of new "heroes" whose only claim to fame is who they sleep with or what has changed between their legs. Declaring oneself to be a sexual minority is not just accepted but celebrated, and our kids are interpreting it as the fastest fast-track ever to celebrity. Kids who used to be bullied suddenly find themselves sitting with the cool kids once they declare themselves transgender. (One study showed that 60 percent of kids claimed that their transgender "announcement brought a popularity boost."[21])

The Remnant

I know this chapter was a bit of a Debbie Downer, and I don't want to end on that note. Yes, these philosophies are wreaking havoc, but think of this section like a visit from Dickens's ghost of Christmas future. *This does not have to be the fate of your kids.* Just in reading this book, you are preparing yourself and your kids to spot the lies before they ever take root.

Take a deep breath and realize that the world will do what the world is gonna do, just like it's done in every pagan society throughout the course of history. Yes, in this world we will have trouble, but our God has overcome the world (John 16:33). He has given us the power to demolish ideas raised against the knowledge of God (2 Corinthians 10:5). Remind yourself of this truth: No matter how bad things have ever gotten, *the Lord has always preserved a remnant.* There will always be a group, however small, who will not bow their knee to another god. And that remnant has a beautiful future—"They will do no wrong; they will tell no lies. A deceitful tongue will not be found in their mouths. They will eat and lie down and no one will make them afraid" (Zephaniah 3:13). No one. Not even a Marxist sex ed teacher.

Mama Bears and Papa Bears, when we are committed to Christ, to loving our neighbor, to standing for truth, and for immersing ourselves in the Word, *we are the remnant.* The Lord reserves for Himself those who have not bowed their knees to worthless idols (1 Kings 19:18). That idol right now is sex and all the agendas that go with it.

You are not alone, even though the enemy is trying to make you feel that you are. We are not responsible for the entire direction of culture. We are only responsible for what happens in our families. Daniel 12:3 says, "Those who are wise will shine like the brightness of the heavens, and those who lead many to righteousness, like the stars for ever and ever." The Lord has given us everything we need for wisdom, and the ones you are leading in righteousness are your children.

The beauty of this modern era is that we have the resources to anticipate what the world is throwing at our kids. This book is just one such tool. Now, we can't guarantee that just by knowing the right things that your kids are guaranteed protection from the seduction of bad ideas. And if your kids have already fallen for some of these lies, that doesn't make you a bad parent. Our kids are responsible for their choices, and we are responsible for ours. But you are choosing, right now, to inform yourself so that you can better shepherd your kids. You are one step closer to understanding the worldview that is being taught to your kids. Remember, *we cannot refute that which we do not understand.* When you prepare your kids to recognize the unbiblical worldview, the teachers can say whatever they like. Your kid will be empowered to see right through it.

> We cannot refute that which
> we do not understand.

Discussion Questions

1. **Icebreaker:** Which of the "by the end of fifth grade, your children should be able to explain the following…" statements was the most shocking to you? How old were you when you had to grapple with those concepts?

2. **Main theme:** *The sexual agenda is coming from a blatantly antibiblical worldview using Christian-sounding virtues.* What are some good points that social justice and equity make? What lies have they slipped in that are in conflict with the Christian worldview?

3. **Self-evaluation:** How involved have you been in what the schools are teaching your children? Does understanding these principles make you want to get more involved?

4. **Brainstorm:** Take a look at the guiding principles from the NSES document (pages 89-91). Get a white board and draw a line down the middle. Label one side "NSES Worldview" and the other "Christian Worldview." Brainstorm how you think each of these worldviews would answer the following questions: 1) Where did we (humans) come from? 2) What is original evil? 3) What do we need to do to fix the evil in the world? 4) What is the definition of

good? 5) What is the definition of bad? 6) How should we treat our bodies? 7) What is the purpose of sex?

5. **Release the bear:** It is going to take a movement of Mama Bears to stem this cultural tide in the schools. Contact your school this week to find out what curricula they are using for sex education. Go over it on your own or with a group. Do you see any of the principles from this chapter at play? While we need to speak up when we see dangerous ideologies being taught to our kids, as Christians we should *first* ask ourselves "How can we as a group *bless* the teachers and administration?" Earn some rapport...and then lovingly start to question the ideologies being presented—moving up the chain of command as necessary (as described on pages 85-86). *Why is it important as Christians for us to earn trust before we try and criticize and change the system? How might doing so make our efforts better received?*

6. **Pray:** Discuss what it means to be "the remnant." Pray for the courage for you and your children to face hostility for not going along with the cultural tide.

Chapter 6

The Enemy's New Playbook

The Language and Morality of the Sexual Agenda

HILLARY

In the previous chapter, we discussed the mission and vision behind the new sex education standards as well as some of the expectations that are being required of our fifth graders. We must remember that this didn't happen overnight. As we continue on this journey through sexuality, it would behoove us to not only understand what is going on, but *how we got here* and which of the enemy's schemes we have unknowingly fallen for. The agenda (yes, agenda!) to erase biblical sexuality is not new, nor is it an organic, grassroots movement. It is extensively funded and has been strategically planned and executed.[1] And very successfully, I might add.

A person can fall when they trip over something. The reason they trip over something is because they *didn't see it coming*. The enemy loves for us to operate in the dark, but no more, Mama Bears! It's time to shine a big ol' spotlight on his schemes. (And remember, when we say the "enemy" we are meaning the enemy—Satan and his demons who have captivated people through hollow and deceptive philosophies—and not the people he has captured.)

The first two tactics are prevalent for everything in this book, namely the power of moralizing evil and the effects of repetition. Next, we will discuss the importance of words and how our culture has hijacked language, tricking our Christian kids into affirming unbiblical principles using biblical words, concepts, and virtues. These tactics are all being used to establish a new moral code and erode our kids' ability to understand and live out God's design for sexuality. Helping our kids anticipate the secular sexual agenda is the best protection we can give them.

> Helping our kids anticipate the
> secular sexual agenda
> is the best protection we can give them.

The Power of Moralizing Evil

This is the number one tactic that we Mama Bears need to understand. The new sexual agenda is being pushed on our kids under the guise of love, tolerance, and inclusion. There is no limit to what a person will do if they are convinced they are acting for the greater good. This tactic is especially effective in manipulating our kids, whose God-bestowed giftings are in empathy and protectiveness.

Moralizing evil means that a person has taken something that would normally be considered immoral and *dressed it up to look good*. No one has codified this process more than the 1960s community organizer Saul Alinsky in his book *Rules for Radicals*. Alinsky's thesis reads as follows: "My aim here is to suggest how to organize for power: how to get it and how to use it." So let's be clear: his goal is how to get power to manipulate people to seeing and doing things his way. How does one accomplish this feat? Alinsky writes, "Do what you can with what you have and *clothe it with moral garments*," because "all effective actions require the passport of morality."[2]

Let's unpack this: Alinsky is not advocating for actual morality. He is using the *concept* of morality as a *tool*. He's exploiting the fact that people generally want to do the right thing. If you can't get them to do what you want them to do straight out, you can trick them into obedience *by using moral language to legitimize your agenda*. God's view of morality is for us to know the right thing, and then do it. Alinsky's moral rationalization means "I do what I want to do, and then I go back afterward and explain how it was the moral thing to do." That's essentially what he's teaching.

This, Mama Bears, is how the enemy is tripping up our kids—through a rewriting of the moral code. Our kids need to realize that the secular agenda is being clothed in moral arguments, *meaning it will sound Christian*. We should expect nothing less as even Satan himself masquerades as an angel of light, and his servants masquerade as workers of righteousness (2 Corinthians 11:14). The people pushing this agenda sincerely believe they are doing the right thing, but they are deceived.

The Effects of Repetition

Advertisers have long understood the effects of repetition on consumer behaviors. (How else do you think our girls got convinced that "mom jeans" were a cool fashion trend? Not from objective reasoning, that's for sure.) A slurry of scientific studies documents the effects of repetition on the brain. As psychologist Daniel Kahneman states in his book *Thinking, Fast and Slow,* "A reliable way to make people believe in falsehoods is frequent repetition, because familiarity is not easily distinguished from truth."[3]

But remember, Mama Bears, repetition in and of itself is not good or bad; it's a tool like any other tool. Repetition serves to burrow stuff deep into your brain until the thought or action becomes second nature. *What* gets burrowed in there is up to us, based on what we choose to focus on. We can be purposeful in reinforcing biblical ideas, or we can let the unbiblical ideas dominate by default. As parents, sometimes we need to be repeating the biblical worldview so many times that our kids threaten to gag if they hear it one more time. But sometimes a good eye roll is the best proof that you're doing something right. In fact, this book's Afterword is dedicated to things you should be repeating over and over until your kids want to gag.

Remember our discussion of cartoons in the introduction? The media is reinforcing their secular worldview through constant repetition. Below, we will describe many of the secular worldview components that our kids are having repeated to them *ad nauseum*. It is changing what they think is true about reality, humanity, and sexuality. And if you remember nothing else, Mama Bears, remember this: *we can't refute that which we don't understand.* So let's start understanding what's going on, shall we?

Why Words Are Worth Defending

As we discussed in the section on Queer Theory (pages 90-91), words themselves are being used as a weapon of the enemy, distorting reality by twisting words. Distorted reality leads to a distorted worldview. So if we want to protect our kids' ability to accurately perceive reality and piece together a biblical worldview, we cannot ignore what is currently taking place with words.

Defending words is a type of apologetics I never expected to have to do, and yet here we are. Some people view apologetics as a side issue to evangelism. A cool hobby, but not really *that* important; it's evangelists and pastors who do the real work. There are even some who view apologetics as if it were in *competition* to evangelism, or worse—*damaging* to evangelism! Church, we need to stop this. *We are all on the same team, and we are all working toward the same end—the spreading of the gospel to the ends of the earth.* That is what we were commissioned by Jesus to do. Apologists and evangelists are coming at it from two different angles, but it is all in service to the gospel. And here, I would like to make an argument for the purpose of this particular chapter: the apologetic importance of defending words.

The gospel is, in essence, humans and God coming back into right relationship with one another through the sacrifice of Jesus on the cross. This gospel requires that humans understand their true identities as sinful rebels in need of saving. It also requires us humans to understand the true nature and identity of God—a perfect deity whose goodness and justice demands payment for sin—a payment He was willing to accept through Christ's death. To have an effective gospel, you have to correctly identify the parties involved. Distort either of these identities, and you cannot have the true gospel.

If humans are redefined as their own little gods, without sin, under no one's authority, with no need to repent, then they will *never* end up in right relationship with God. A distortion of their true identity leads to an inability to understand why they need the gospel in the first place. Likewise, if we have a God who winks at sin, or who is not all-just or not all-good, then we don't have the God of the Bible. Try as we might to reconcile with that god, we are reconciling ourselves to a figment of our own imagination, a god of our own making. Such a god cannot save.

If the enemy wants to thwart humans and God from coming into right relationship again, he can go after their individual identities. That's what we saw happen in the garden, that's what we saw when Satan attacked Christ here on earth, and that's what we are seeing happening now.

So how is he attacking identity? Let's go back a step and think about what is required to even *have* a true identity. At minimum, you need two things: truth and words. You cannot *have* a true identity without the concept of truth, and you cannot *convey* a true identity apart from the use of words. Destroy truth and words, and you can destroy our ability to communicate true identities, which in turn impedes our ability to communicate the gospel. No one will accept the truth of Christ if they don't believe in truth. And if we can't even define what is good or evil anymore, how can we know we need a savior? So while some of these concepts we're about to discuss may seem like side issues, I assure you they are not.

Furthermore, this tactic of twisting language should come as no surprise when we remember how Jesus Himself is referred to in the Gospel of John: "In the beginning was *the Word* [the logos], and *the Word* was with God, and *the Word* was God" (John 1:1). Christ is *the logos of God.* If the enemy is to attack Christ, it makes sense he would attack words. Words are under attack because the *logos* is under attack. Words are also under attack because, by them, we understand truth about God, the truth about humans, and the saving message of the gospel. In this chapter, we're going to take a look at the ways the enemy is trying to trip our kids up—by messing with language.

The War on Words

Just as our ideologies are shaped by underlying assumptions, our worldviews are also affected to an enormous extent by the language we speak. Words are constantly evolving—that's just how language works. Take, for example, the word "nice." Five hundred years ago the word was used to describe a person who was foolish, silly, or ignorant. In the intervening centuries the word has taken on a much more positive connotation. Semantic shift, y'all; it's a real thing. But that's not what we are talking about in this chapter.

What we're talking about here is much more sinister and much more purposeful than an innocent evolution of language. In the first *Mama Bear Apologetics* book, I refer to a tactic called "linguistic theft." Linguistic theft occurs when a person purposely takes a concept, abstract virtue, or idea and *changes the definition to promote their own agenda*. Without understanding that this change has taken place, many people swallow an agenda to which they would normally object. We must teach our kids to expect that sin and secular agendas will be promoted using Christian-sounding virtues like love, tolerance, and justice.

In researching for this book, I realized that linguistic theft was just scratching the surface. There are so many weird word games going on (which we introduced in the previous chapter with Queer Theory). The second kind of wordplay I'm seeing is what I'll call linguistic smuggling.

I like to differentiate between categories and actual information. Categories (or categorical words) are umbrella terms used to describe many things. There is no single object that is good, evil, moral, or immoral, but we do know it when we see it. Using these words, we can *classify* thoughts, beliefs, or actions, but we are not providing *actual information*. Hang with me here. I promise I'll make this more understandable.

Information is very specific. It refers to a concrete thing or behavior. For example, a child might use the categorical word "mean" and say, "My friend was mean to me." At this point, we could challenge his category by asking for *information*. "What did your friend *do* that was mean?" What if your child answered, "He sat with the new kid in the class instead of with me at lunch." This statement is informative—it contains actual information. We know exactly what happened and what action was categorized as "mean." But was his friend's action mean? I would say that it was improperly categorized based on your child's perception. Maybe we could challenge him to understand that his friend was not being mean to him, but rather being "nice" to a new student. Being nice to someone else isn't the same as being mean to us. Your child thought he was providing you with information, but he didn't. He provided his perspective on the situation using a categorical term.

The secular agenda is being packaged in the same way. We are seeing actions being smuggled into the categories of moral, immoral, harmful, beneficial, inclusive, and oppressive. These are all *categorical* words. The only way to know if we are on the same page with someone is to have them provide *actual information*.

Linguistic smuggling is when someone slips an unrelated action under a well-known categorical word and hopes that nobody asks for more details (or refuses to provide any). We have seen this happen with the word "bullying." Most schools now operate under a zero-tolerance bullying rule—which I heartily agree with! We shouldn't allow kids to bully each other. (One kid bullied me mercilessly in middle school, and I still don't understand why.) The problem our kids might face, however, is when an agenda smuggles something unrelated under the banner of bullying.

When most people think of bullying, they think of teasing, taunting, name calling, pulling hair, shoving kids into lockers, and (of course) the time-honored and infamous *wedgie*. But what do we do when "using the wrong pronoun" is smuggled into the umbrella category of bullying? What about refusing to tell someone that all religions are equally valid ways to God? Or that all manners of sexual expression are equally healthy?

When things like these are put under the banner of "bullying," and there's a "zero-tolerance policy," do our kids have the language to understand what is happening? If your child has been raised to respect authority, he or she may do or say whatever their teacher or principal tells them to do when it comes to not bullying, even if that means affirming something that isn't true. Affirming things that aren't true in behavior is just a step away from our kids starting to believe the lies they are forced to affirm, all in the name of tolerance, love, and anti-bullying.

How Does Linguistic Theft Work?

Messing with language through linguistic theft or linguistic smuggling is an effective tactic of the enemy for a variety of reasons.

1. It Divides Us

Confusing the language is how the Lord divided the people at Babel, and it's what the enemy is using to divide us now. If two people are using the same word with two different meanings, they are talking past each other and productive conversation is hopeless. As Voltaire is said to have mused, "If you wish to converse with me, you must first define your terms." Similarly, when we hear someone use a familiar word but something seems "off," we should seek information by asking, "What do you mean by that?" followed by "How did you come to that conclusion?"[4] The goal is to figure out what actually happened without interpretation being smuggled in. Use these questions often in your home; they're key for productive communication, which should always be our goal. We may not always agree with one another, but at least we should aim for clarity.

2. It Can Redefine Morality

Linguistic theft and smuggling assume that our culture still has vestiges of the Judeo-Christian ethic. Thus, if secular culture can redefine biblical concepts like love and tolerance, or place our worldview under the banner of oppression and injustice, then they can literally rewrite morality. It doesn't happen all at once. This tactic is especially effective when coupled with repetition—because the human mind confuses familiarity with truth.

3. It Pits the Underdog Against the Villain

Everybody loves a good underdog story, and villains are the people we all love to hate. But these are both category words. If secular culture can redefine or smuggle stuff into words like *harm*, *damage*, and *oppression*, then they can decide who is the victim and who is the villain. This is what our culture is doing with gender identity and sexual orientation. And guess who the villain is? You got it. It's we who hold to the Christian worldview. With a few simple changes to definitions or a little smuggling of concepts, our kids might begin to believe their identity is as a privileged oppressor whose primary job is to sit down and be quiet, even when truth is being maligned.

4. It Allows Subjective Experiences to Define Reality

Many of the words we'll see require a person to experience them. In other words, someone's feelings are allowed to define what *category* an action falls under. If someone *feels* hurt, then they assume they have been harmed. If someone feels like something is unfair, then injustice has occurred, at least in their minds. And if we have learned anything, it's that you cannot reason with someone's emotions. We need to remind our kids that feelings don't always reflect reality.

Stolen Words

To get a better idea of how linguistic theft and linguistic smuggling occur, let's take a look at some of the current fan favorites. After that, we'll discuss the ideologies that are using these smuggled or redefined words to advance their agenda.

Harm

This one is big in all the LBGTQ and Progressive Christian literature. The going narrative is that advocating for biblical sexuality is not only outdated, it is *harmful* to people. Progressive pastor Nadia Bolz-Weber writes in her book *Shameless* that she wishes she could "sit down with the people who wrote the Nashville Statement" and show them how "their loyalty to a doctrine or an interpretation of a few Bible verses has created *harm* in the bodies and spirits of the people" under her care.[5] (The Nashville Statement was the multidenominational effort to define biblical gender, marriage, and sex. It's a really good document. I suggest reading it.[6])

Most of the dictionary definitions of "harm" involve two more words: injury and damage. We must remind our children that something can hurt without injuring. For example, resetting a broken bone hurts, but it is actually helping, not harming. Likewise, demolishing a bad idea causes "damage" to the idea, but bad ideas deserve to be damaged! We should not confuse it with damaging a person.

We don't want to minimize that there has been real harm within the LGBTQ community by self-righteous zealots who have treated these individuals like they are less than human. Likewise, our kids can acknowledge that when someone's feelings are hurt, that person *feels* harmed. But we must remind our children that we do not have control over other people's feelings. We can control whether we are kind, patient, and caring. We cannot control if biblical truth will cause another person distress.

Injustice

Romans 2:15 tells us that the law of God is written on our hearts. This means that everyone (psychopaths aside) has an innate sense of right and wrong. God makes Himself clear in Scripture that He is a God of justice (Psalm 50:6; Isaiah 30:18). The Greek word *dikaiosýnē* is translated as justice or righteousness. Justice, then, can be understood as righteous living— obeying the commands of God.

But let's look at how our society is using the word justice. Our world treats justice as synonymous with equal. If anything is unequal, then it is unjust. As we discussed on page 90, abortion rights are being argued for under the umbrella term of "reproductive justice." Abortion advocates use the logic that since men never have to face an unplanned pregnancy within their own bodies, then women shouldn't either. "Not being pregnant" is redefined as a *right* that women should have equal access to—even if that means killing her child-in-utero. Denying her that right is unjust. Similarly, "marriage justice" assumes that marriage itself is a right. Denying anyone equal access to that right is unjust. But, of course, this assumes a linguistically thefted definition of marriage.

Marriage

The word "marriage" is currently being redefined out of existence. In our current culture, it basically means a legally committed relationship between two (and, in some places, more) people. This relationship is predicated on the mutual satisfaction of the parties involved. If a marriage is unsatisfying, then it is no longer fulfilling its function. Time to move on.

But God is the One who created marriage, so I say He gets to define it. While different forms of marriage are *represented* in Scripture (usually multiple wives), that is not God's *definition* of marriage. Genesis 2:24 says "a man leaves his father and mother and is united to his wife, and they become one flesh." A man unites with his wife, not wives. Jesus affirms this original design when people start asking Him about divorce in Matthew 19:4-5. Later in 1 Timothy 3:2, we learn how church leaders are required to be above reproach. One of these criteria is being "faithful to his wife." Marriage, according to the Bible, is a man and a woman united for life, until death do they part. And while Jesus is clear that concessions were made by Moses because of the hardness of people's hearts, concessions do not change God's original purpose or His original design.

Power, Authority, and Oppression

Power properly defined is merely the ability to act or produce an effect, but it has been redefined as a person exerting their authority to get what they want. This bad definition of power is now being touted as synonymous with authority—both of which now have negative connotations.

As we saw in chapter 3, however, the concept of authority is biblical. We see hierarchy built into the Godhead, with Christ and the Spirit submitting to the Father. There are God-given authority structures within the family unit. God has ordained government to exercise authority on behalf of the people. And biblical authority always goes hand in hand with greater responsibility. We see this in the parable of the talents when Jesus concludes with, "From everyone who has been given much, much will be demanded" (Luke 12:48).

Just because bad authorities exist doesn't mean that authority itself is bad. As we saw in the previous chapter, the concept of oppression is getting really watered down and is now a state of being rather than an action perpetrated by someone. People who are deemed to have "social power" are automatically declared to be oppressive and privileged, and the people without power are automatically oppressed. But I'd like to point out that under this definition, our children are oppressed. And while this might sound like I'm making a silly joke, I'm not. As we write this book, transgender surgery for young children is being argued for under the guise of "children's rights"—as if the kids are now an oppressed class. If they are the oppressed, guess who is the oppressor? The woman in the mirror, my friend. You and your husband.

You Fired Up Yet?

I hope so! Because when you awaken your inner Mama Bear, I know there's almost nothing you won't do to protect your kids. Moms are the sleeping giants of our society. I'm reminded of the line from *Prince of Thieves* where Kevin Costner says, "One free man defending his home is more powerful than ten hired soldiers." To that I'd say, *one Mama Bear defending her cubs is more powerful than ten hired activists.* And when you get a whole *bunch* of Mama Bears together? Sweeeeeet heavens to Betsy, stuff is 'bout to get real!

Discussion Questions

1. **Icebreaker:** Did you ever come across a statistic or story that you thought was true because you'd heard it so many times, but then later found out that it wasn't true after all?

2. **Main theme:** *The secular agenda is being advanced through repetition and the use of Christian-sounding words, and it's tricking our kids into adopting beliefs that are contrary to the Christian worldview.* Why do you think that co-opting words is so effective?

3. **Self-evaluation:** Have you found yourself adopting any of the linguistically thefted words on pages 109-111?

4. **Brainstorm:** What is the difference between categorical words and actual information? Pull out a newspaper or online publication and find headlines that use some of these buzzwords. Read through the article. Did they provide information for what actually happened, or does the article only use the buzzwords? To figure out if they provided actual information, ask yourself, "If I were to reenact the scene, would I know what to do?" If you're not sure, then the article has not provided actual information.

5. **Release the bear:** Make a buzzwords board to put next to the television. Add words to it whenever you or your kids encounter "category words" that seem to be trying to push a narrative without giving any facts.

6. **Pray:** Jesus is the *logos,* the Word of God. Praise Him for being the true Word, and pray for the ability to discern when words are being stolen or used to promote ideas raised against the knowledge of God (2 Corinthians 10:5).

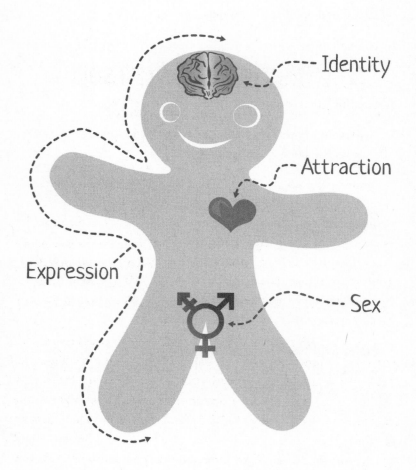

Chapter 7

The Genderbread Person

*The New Definitions of Identity,
Expression, Sex, and Attraction*

HILLARY

In the previous chapters, we've led you through the maze of what is going on in the schools. We've looked at the New Sex Education Standards and discussed the language and morality that is being used to advance an agenda. Now, let's take a look at one of the actual curricula being used with the littles.

Forget the muffin man. Do you know the Genderbread Person? The Genderbread Person is a commonly used tool for teaching kids about sexual orientation and identity. (The Gender Unicorn is a similar curriculum. They are basically the same concepts.) You need to be aware of this curriculum so you can understand and discuss the implications of it with your kids.

Hold on tight, Mama Bears. First grade just got a lot more confusing.

In a lesson plan titled *Genderbread Person and LGBT+ Umbrella*, kids as young as kindergarten are taught all about sexuality.

> LGB all represent sexual identities. And the T represents a
> gender identity, as well as an umbrella term for many gender
> identities. Queer means different things to different people,

for some it describes sexuality, for others their gender, for others both. When we say "sexual identities or sexual orientations" what we are talking about are the ways we categorize and define who we are attracted to, romantically, sexually, or otherwise. When we say "gender identities" we are talking about the ways we categorize and define our genders.

...Gender is best understood when broken up into three parts: gender identity (which is how you, in your head, define and understand your gender based on the options for gender you know to exist), gender expression (the ways you demonstrate gender through your dress, actions, and demeanor), and biological sex (the physical parts of your body that we think of as either male or female). Let's talk about these one-by-one.[1]

Yes. Let's. Starting with how they define gender identity.

Identity

I didn't know a creature known as a slow loris existed until I saw a fabulous YouTube video of one being tickled. However, my lack of awareness had *no bearing* on the slow loris's existence. Reality is independent of my knowledge.

The Genderbread curriculum teaches the opposite, saying identity is all in the head. And make no mistake, that is where this kind of curriculum is headed—to remove gender from the realm of objective reality to subjective preference or experience.

The logical law of identity states that a thing is itself and not something else. For example, an apple is an apple and not an orange. Twelve equals twelve, not twenty-four. But according to the Genderbread Person curriculum, identity is not set. It is based on an individual's current perceptions. And if those perceptions change, a person's identity changes. Essentially, an apple can turn into an orange as soon as it becomes aware that oranges exist—if fruit were conscious.

Merriam-Webster defines *identity* as "the distinguishing character or personality of an individual" or "the relation established by psychological identification."[2] Did you catch that second definition? A relation established by *psychological* identification. We have just defined the essence of a thing as contingent on a person's psychological state. What could possibly go wrong? If identity is defined by a person's psychological state, then we cannot tell people in the midst of depression that they are not worthless. They *feel* worthless, and according to this definition, they are worthless—because that is the relation that has been established by their psychological identification.

I can't tell you how many times my emotions have been hijacked to feed me lies. (You can ask my husband, though. He probably knows. He's the one who gets to hear *all* about it.) Mama Bears, if our kids think their identity is based on how they identify in the moment, then there is no security in Christ. If they don't *feel* saved, then they aren't. If they don't *feel* like God is close to them at the moment, then He's not. If they *feel* ugly, then they are. Don't try to talk them out of it: The Genderbread Person taught them all about how to determine their identity.

When it comes to identity, the Genderbread Person also relies on completely regressive gender stereotyping. The curriculum states, "Gender identity can be thought of as the aspects of man-ness and woman-ness you either do or don't align with."[3]

Hard stop right here.

Who defines this "man-ness and woman-ness"? And if there are a bunch of different definitions, how could a child possibly know which they align with? Don't worry. The Genderbread curriculum will define it for you.

> In this case, we are talking about the norms (social expectations) and roles (ways we fulfill or act out those expectations) placed upon "men" and "women" in a society. A few typical norms of man-ness might be *strong-willed, logical, athletic* and roles of *leader, builder, protector*. For woman-ness, we

might think of the norms *empathic, sensitive, caring* and roles *teacher, caretaker, supporter.*[4]

Raise your hand if you have a daughter who is strong willed, athletic, and logical, and maybe a bit scant on the sensitive caretaker role. (My mom should be raising her hand right now.) Is there a tendency for guys and girls to fit into these roles? Absolutely. Does it change their gender if they don't? No! This curriculum is *literally* telling your sensitive son who wants to be a nurse that he is actually more of a woman, and it's telling your athletic, leader-oriented daughter that she is actually more of a man. (Didn't the feminists take on this gender stereotyping back in the '80s? Have we really regressed to such one-dimensional definitions of man and woman?)

Furthermore, if gender identity conforms to society norms, then according to this definition, a person's gender can theoretically change when they travel. (I'm not saying that this is what the Genderbread Person curriculum is teaching. However, this is a logical conclusion that cannot be refuted by their definition.) If gender identity is based on norms, we cannot ignore that masculine and feminine norms are different in different countries. There are cultures where it is considered more acceptable for a man to cry. Does this mean an emotional and sensitive person is more feminine in America and more masculine in...I don't know, Italy? (Disclaimer: I am only speaking from my husband's comments while watching Italian soccer matches. Apparently, the players get a little overly dramatic when it comes to fouls.)

Again, an identity *is what something is* and not something else. Reality doesn't change, no matter what's in your head or where you are on earth. A person's psychological state might feel like reality to them, but it is just a perception. And while we should not ignore the impact that perception can have upon a person, we shouldn't give that perception the power to shape reality.

When we turn to Scripture, we see two clear genders from Genesis to Revelation. Jesus even affirms this in Matthew 19:4: "At the beginning the Creator made them 'male and female.'" Scripture doesn't include a single instance of a male or female identifying with the opposite gender. What *do* we see? We see people defying gender stereotypes all over the place. Deborah was a female judge. David played the harp and cried a lot. The Proverbs 31 woman is a complete entrepreneur. (No, seriously. Read her résumé.) And our current translation "wife of noble character" sadly misses the traditionally understood Hebrew translation "woman of *valor*." Valor was generally reserved for praising military prowess. This is the Hebrew equivalent of saying, "Here's a woman in beast-mode."

God has poured out His gifts on both men and women, and He doesn't discriminate based on gender. If you have a child who conforms to gender norms, praise them for their qualities! If you have a child who doesn't conform to gender norms, *praise them for their qualities.* Reinforce that God has made them logical or empathetic, athletic or artistic, no matter if they were born a boy or a girl. Reinforce the ways that God has created them *male and female* with these characteristics.

Expression

> Gender expression can be thought of as the aspects of masculinity and femininity you display in your clothing, grooming, speech, actions, demeanor, and more. As examples, masculine dress might be considered baggy, umprimed, or functional. Feminine dress is form-fitting, colorful, and frivolous.[5]

My first thought upon reading this part of the Genderbread Person curriculum: This is a really schizophrenic view of gender. *I mean, what happened to just being a good old-fashioned tomboy?* (A tomboy is, of course, a girl who has more traditionally masculine interests and energy levels and hates wearing dresses.) Why do we have to separate our genders based on fashion and grooming? When I was a teenage girl, we called that our "mood." What mood am I in? Am I in a cargo-pants-with-boots mood, or a slip-dress-with-sandals mood? If I had to wrestle with being told I had different *gender* expressions on different days…good grief. I would have grown up so confused.

My second thought? *Ohhh. I think I see the problem now.* Because if I'd finished my thought above, it would have sounded like, *Why can't we just have tomboys and uh…and…uhhhh…*

What about the boys? When I was growing up, what options did they have except being a Mr. T, Tyrannosaurus rex–loving, G.I. Joe–backpacking, rough-and-tumble boy? *They didn't.* Sure, there were boys who didn't fit the stereotype, but they were often relegated to the sidelines in terms of status (think band nerds). They didn't fit the mold, so they lost punches on their man-card, whether or not it was stated verbally or not. Often, it was stated physically in the form of bullying.

This was, and is, a problem. Girls could be girly girls or tomboys and were affirmed in their womanhood for both roles. We looked up to female athletes, artists, and intellectuals equally. But the boys could be rough-and-tumble boys…or sissies. Them's the options. These "tomgirls," as I've heard them called, are guys who might be a tad more on the soft-spoken, artistic, sensitive side of the spectrum. Where did they get to fit into society's gender norms while maintaining the same level of masculinity that the jocks had? They didn't—unless they created their own little subculture (which high schools are full of). I suspect the seeds of our current gender schism may have started there.

The fact is, there is a spectrum of gender expression. Not all women express their femininity in the same way, but it doesn't make them any less of a woman. Not all men express their masculinity in the same way, but it doesn't make them any less of a man. As Bible teacher Sue Bohlin writes, "Narrow gender stereotypes don't honor the creativity of the God who makes varieties of girls and boys on a femininity spectrum and a masculinity spectrum."[6]

In my parents' generation, boys were boys, men were men, girls were girls, and women were women. No ifs, ands, or buts. Even the girls' softball team wore dresses to school every day. Everyone was equally shoved into a gender-conforming stereotype. You fit in—or you became a pariah. (I think of Eugene from the first *Grease* movie.) But that all started to change in the '80s with third-wave feminism.

It was pretty awesome to be a girl in the '80s as opposed to previous decades. We girls were told early on that we could be anything we wanted to be. Dream big! Play sports! Wear pants! Wear sneakers! Home Ec is optional! (No complaining from me yet. Except for the shoulder pads in the '80s. It was like a weird mix of businesswoman and football player.) Girls had all the freedom of expression in the world. But the boys…nope. They were still shoehorned into their stereotype—or mocked mercilessly if they failed to conform.

Can we all just take a deep breath and recognize how incredibly unfair this was for little boys who loved to dance, or paint, or sing…or shower on a regular basis? To be treated like they were less of a boy, and later, less of a man?

I think we tried to fix this inequality by creating a new category, but it was too little, too late. The category I'm referring to is "metrosexual." The metrosexual movement was for guys who liked to groom themselves, shower, and wear nice clothes, but who didn't self-identify as homosexual. These guys were often artists, musicians, and philosophers who loved craft brew, specialty coffees, and beard grooming products. They put the *man* in *manicure*. The metrosexual movement made it acceptable to be refined and artistic without sacrificing one's perceived masculinity. (Just look at all the youth pastors and worship leaders who adopted the skinny jeans.) These guys can wear tight, colorful, "frivolous" clothing without anyone questioning their manhood.

This was probably a really healthy movement. It was the first step we'd ever taken in allowing guys to express themselves in a legitimately masculine way that would have otherwise been seen as feminine. But even this movement is starting to take an unhealthy turn. Instead of teaching little boys that their God-given masculinity can be expressed in a variety of different ways, we are instead telling them that these gender expressions make them girls.

When a person is backing away from some ideology—in this case, rigid gender stereotypes—they often back into something worse. In our society, people have backed into an outright denial of gender as an objective fact about a person and turned it into this messy, fluid, confusing, daily-changing spectrum of expression that will leave even the strongest of kids confused about who they really are.

Sex

Nothing summarizes our discussion more today than the famous scene from *Kindergarten Cop* where a little boy respectfully raises his hand to speak and waits to be called upon. His words of wisdom for the class that he so ardently and patiently waited to share? "Boys have a penis. Girls have a vagina."

In 1990, this was considered so obvious that it was part of the joke. Fast-forward 30 years, and a statement like this could be prosecuted as hate speech.[7] According to the Genderbread Person curriculum, the simple definition of biological sex is "the physical traits you are born with or develop that we think of as sex characteristics, as well as the sex you are assigned at birth."[8]

Sex, then, is all a matter of perception. The physical traits are those "*that we think of* as sex characteristics"—not those that objectively correspond to biological sex. Notice this shift in language—a literal, physiological, scientifically testable statement has been reduced to a perception. The Genderbread Person's shift in language—from biological sex being absolute to being subjective—is something we need to make our kids aware of.

Along these same lines, the Genderbread curriculum defines biological sex as the "sex that you are assigned at birth," as if the doctor just flipped a coin and slapped a label on you as male or female. I don't want to oversimplify this, but this really is a simple concept. For millennia, unless a baby was born with a genetic abnormality—which does happen[9]—assigning a sex was as simple as looking at their nether regions. Unless there is some sort of abnormality, this method of announcing biological sex has, historically, been extremely reliable.

But before we accuse the curriculum of only looking at body parts, I do applaud it for being more comprehensive than the kid in Kindergarten Cop.

Let's consider biological sex in the ultra-reductive way society does: being female means having a vagina, ovaries, two
X chromosomes, predominant estrogen, and the ability to
grow a baby in your abdominal area; being male means having testes, a penis, an XY chromosome configuration, predominant testosterone, and the ability to put a baby in a
female's abdominal area; and being intersex can be any combination of what I just described...In reality, biological sex,
like gender identity and expression, for most folks, is more
nuanced than that.[10]

Is this really ultra-reductive? In some ways, yes. Being female doesn't
necessarily mean that you have certain body parts. There are plenty of
women who have either had hysterectomies or cancer which required
the removal of the uterus and ovaries, and they are no less female than a
woman with ovaries and uterus. If I were to tweak this statement to be
more accurate, I'd say that a woman is "a person who possesses the genetic
programming for these characteristics, which will be manifested unless
abnormalities or tampering occur." It pains me that we have to get this
specific, but *part of (successfully) engaging in the cultural battle means that
we have to use words that cannot be refuted.* We *must* take objective arguments and create objectively true statements. Otherwise, we will be argu-
ing over nuances, technicalities, and perceptions.

And speaking of nuance, intersex individuals are worth our consider-
ation. Intersexuality and transgenderism are *not* the same thing. While a
variety of genetic abnormalities can render the simple XX/XY distinction
confusing, those situations are different from "gender dysphoria"—feeling
that you were born in the wrong body. Intersex conditions occur when
there is a genetic or physical anomaly in a person's sexual characteristics.
I think about these individuals every time I mark "female" on a survey. I
can't imagine how truly confusing and frustrating that one little question
must be for this group *every* time they fill out a form.

This group has a real, legitimate difficulty in that they are truly intersex.

And it should be noted that this particular group—the one group that has a science-based reason to question their sex—is not the group that is advocating for a redefinition of sex outside of the binary of male and female. According to the Intersex Society of North America, "We are trying to make the world a safe place for intersex kids, and we don't think labeling them with a [third] gender category that in essence doesn't exist would help them."[11] This condition is real, and confusing, and individuals who were born with it cannot be lumped into the same category as the rest of the LGBTQ camp.

Remind your children that while abnormalities exist, they do not redefine normal. Science (and especially medicine) cannot progress without a concept of "normal." For example, some people are born with six fingers, but we will never see textbooks redefining human hands as having anywhere from five to six digits. Normal human hands have five digits. And abnormalities do *not* make a person "less than."

All this talk of normality aside, the word *atypical* might be better to use with your kids than *abnormal.* While *abnormal* just describes deviation from the norm, it has the connotation of being "weird" for kids. Nobody wants to be abnormal. Like me—I have an abnormal kidney, but that doesn't make me weird. (I'm weird for a whole lot of *other* reasons.)

When you talk with your children, affirm that they can use the reality of their bodies to understand the truth about their gender. In a popular TED talk, cardiologist Paula Johnson says, "Every cell has a sex—and what that means is that men and women are different down to the cellular and molecular level. It means that we're different across all of our organs, from our brains to our hearts, our lungs, our joints."[12] In other words, no matter what your gender philosophy, when you are ill and the doctors put you on the operating table, they still need to know your original biological sex in order to give you the best possible health care.

Our physical bodies are an objective reality. If kids can't even use their bodies to tell them who they are, how can we expect them to understand themselves in any meaningful, non-transient way? We can't. Life becomes an ever-shifting reality that can't be pinned down by anything. That, friends, is a really confusing worldview to expect our kids to live in.

Attraction

> Sexual attraction can be thought of as the want, need, or desire for physical sexual contact and relationships. Romantic attraction is an affinity and love for others and the desire for emotional relationships. Some folks have both, some folks have neither, many experience more of one than the other. Sexual orientation is all about who you are physically, spiritually, and emotionally attracted to (here we've broken it out specifically into sexual and romantic attraction), and the labels tend to describe the relationships between your gender and the gender types you're attracted to.[13]

In this curriculum, sexual attraction refers to the gender with whom you want to be sexually active. Romantic attraction is the "affinity and love for others and the desire for emotional relationships." I don't mean this in a condescending way at all, but this is what *friendship* is—having an affinity toward another person with whom you would like to have an emotional relationship. We need to emphasize to our kids that desiring an emotional relationship with someone does *not* change their sexual orientation. Even loving someone does not mean that we are in love with them. You would be surprised at how confused many kids are regarding this concept.

Friends, we were created by God for relationship, and healthy relationships include an emotional component. What has happened to our understanding of healthy, platonic, same-sex friendship? If our kids are buying into the propaganda that a desire for an emotional attachment with someone of the same sex means that they have a same-sex sexual orientation, then be prepared for a lot of confusion. Healthy relationships begin with healthy same-sex friendships.[14] We cannot take a normal desire and make it a predictor of sexual identity. By this definition, everyone is romantically attracted to their best friends.

So let's figure out what romance looks like according to the Genderbread Person, getting a better idea of the terms the curriculum is using.

> If you are a man and you're attracted to women, you're straight. If you're a man who is attracted to men and another gender, you're bi-sexual. And if you're a man who is attracted to men, you're gay. These are the labels most of us know the most about. We hear the most about it, it's salient in our lives, and we can best understand where we stand with it.[15]

A quick pause here to point out that this statement can't make sense if we've already redefined what it means to be a man or a woman. According to this statement of attraction, we need to know what *we ourselves* are and what the *other* person is in order to even put a label on our sexual identity. However, as we've already seen, this curriculum has sawed off the branch it is sitting on. If one's gender is determined by subjective and mental associations that can be fluid throughout life, we have lost the ability to identify who is a man and who is a woman. And it is impossible for us to determine what someone else is apart from their informing us. We cannot even call someone gay or straight unless we are willing to commit to a definition of male and female! I think the authors of the Genderbread Person foresaw this issue because they say…

> It's pretty cut and dry, right? Maybe. There's much more to attraction and sexuality. Some folks define and experience attraction without gender as a factor; they might identify as "pansexual." If you experience romantic attraction but not sexual, you might identify as asexual or "ace," or, depending on the gender(s) you're attracted to, hetero-, homo-, or pan-romantic. If you're attracted to folks who are trans or androgynous, you might identify as skoliosexual.[16]

This is getting a bit confusing, so allow me to make a cheat sheet here:

- Homosexual—a person sexually attracted to people of the same gender.

- Lesbian—a woman sexually attracted to women.

- Bisexual—a man or woman sexually attracted to two genders, but the curriculum is careful not to state *which* two genders because that would affirm that there are two. I suspect this term will soon become passé for this very reason.

- Pansexual—being sexually attracted to all genders. This is probably the term that will replace bisexual.

- Asexual (or Ace)—not having any sexual attractions, regardless of gender.

- Heteroromantic—being romantically and emotionally attracted (but not necessarily sexually attracted) to a person of the opposite gender. (Call me old fashioned, but I used to call these my "guy friends.")

- Homoromantic—being romantically and emotionally attracted (but not necessarily sexually attracted) to a person of the same gender. (I used to just call these my friends or my girlfriends.)

- Panromantic—being romantically and emotionally attracted (but not necessarily sexually attracted) to someone regardless of the person's gender. (Isn't this good, ol'-fashioned engaging with your community and having relationships with other people?)

- Skoliosexual—being sexually and or romantically attracted to people who are trans or androgynous. If you were a woman who was attracted to a man who had transitioned to a woman, you would be skoliosexual, not hetero or homo.

Truths to Affirm

Your eyes may be swimming with all these new definitions, so let's just keep to our main question. What do we need to emphasize to our children?

1. We Were Created for Relationship

The Genderbread Person curriculum provides a range of orientations, but not one of them includes the concept of healthy, nonromantic, nonsexual friendships. Our God exists eternally in relationship within the Trinity, and He created humankind because He desired a creation with whom He could relate. Our kids need to know that as children of God, our identity is rooted in that relationship. We were created by a relational God for relationship, and our families, friendships, and communities give us a picture of the way God relates to us.

2. Not All Love Is That Kind of Love

Our society has taught children that all strong feelings of love have a sexual component (that is, eros—romantic love). This misconception can be easily fixed if we help our kids understand the different categories of love, especially platonic love (*phileo* in Greek). Let them know that sometimes their attraction for another person is really respect for traits they admire. Those traits can even be physical beauty. That doesn't make them gay. We are by nature attracted to beautiful things, but appreciation for beauty does not equal sexual attraction.

The more you talk with your kids about the distinctions between the different loves, the less they'll be confused about their own feelings of love. The different categories will already be in their minds.

3. Touch Isn't Always Romantic

We were created for physical contact. In fact, babies in the neonatal ICU are able to leave more quickly when a person engages in "touch therapy" with them.[17] And boys, in particular, face a crisis now that the category of platonic touch between men has been removed. Psychologists call it "skin hunger."

When I was a kid, we had roller-skating parties. The DJ always played a "couples only" song. It never once occurred to any of us that picking a friend to hold hands with during the couple's skate meant that we were anything other than friends. It was a couple's skate. We were two people. We fulfilled the requirement. Let's hold hands and skate!

This is a luxury our kids no longer have. I'm a really touchy person. Just ask any of my close friends or family. I've hated how my innocent instincts for snuggles and physical touch have been perverted by society. Before my sister died, we got to the age where she wouldn't hold my hand in public because she didn't want people to think we were a "couple." As her sickness got worse, I think she got over it and unashamedly held my hand in public. I have to admit that even I felt self-conscious when I could tell people were looking at us and wondering what our hand-holding meant. I just chose not to care and held her hand anyway, and I don't regret it—especially now that she's gone and I can't hold her hand anymore.

We need to reaffirm to our kids what kinds of touch are appropriate and inappropriate. This isn't just important for helping them understand themselves, but it will also help protect them against predators when they know what kinds of touch are inappropriate. In fact, the more appropriate touch your kids receive from you, the better they will be able to tell when someone is touching them inappropriately. They can say, "Mommy and Daddy don't touch me like that." Affirm and model *phileo* love and platonic touch.

4. Male and Female He Created Them

Together, we reflect the *imago dei* in a way that man and woman cannot on their own. We need words and categories to defend this *imago dei* to our kids, and we need the care, tact, and understanding to model healthy relationships to a world that is, frankly, starving for love.

Yes, the new sexual ethic is concerning. It seeks to normalize sexuality that mars the *imago dei*. We should not support an agenda raised against the knowledge of God. But *do not confuse the ideology for people.* We are called to love *all*—no matter their understanding of sexuality and gender. We are called to love people and demolish bad ideas. May we never mistake the two. Never.

Discussion Questions

1. **Icebreaker:** As a child, how did you understand gender expression? Did you feel that you fit the norm established by your peers, or did you have to change to fit in?

2. **Main theme:** *Kids are being taught to deny gender as an objective fact, leaving them confused about God's design, romantic attraction, and even their identity.* Describe ways you're already seeing the faulty logic of the Genderbread curriculum play out in culture.

3. **Self-evaluation:** Have you ever tried to urge your child into a gender stereotype? How about discouraging them from doing something that was gender atypical? How did that affect your son or daughter?

4. **Brainstorm:** Together, make a list of ways you can affirm your children in their sexuality. How can you nurture your kids' tendencies toward athleticism, leadership, or quiet contemplative work no matter their gender?

5. **Release the bear:** This week, talk with your kids about friendship. Discuss how admiration and attraction are not necessarily romantic, but simply appreciation for the way God designed one of His children.

6. **Pray:** Pray over your children's friendships this week. Ask the Lord to provide them with close, intimate, same-sex friendships so that they can grow up knowing the difference between friendship and sexual attraction.

Chapter 8

Sex-Positivity

Anything Goes if It's Consensual

HILLARY AND AMY

Sex-positivity. You might not have heard the term, but you've definitely heard the concept—and this new movement is actively shaping your child's view of sexuality. It shares a good amount of ideology with the sexual revolution of the '60s, but with fewer tambourines and more deodorant.

Its ideas can be traced back a century to a man named Wilhelm Reich, the man who popularized the phrase "sexual revolution."[1] His goal was to free sexuality from the social and religious structures that taught that sex should be limited to married adults. He encouraged open sexual boundaries for all (including young adolescents), was a champion for abortion, and taught that sex could cure mental disorders. This made even Sigmund Freud (his mentor) roll his eyes. (Good grief—If *Freud* thinks you've gone too far with the whole sex thing, *you've definitely gone too far.*)

So why would a chapter on current sexual issues reference someone that even Freud found excessive? Because the beliefs of Reich (and others like him) are now being promoted *en masse*. Today, sex-positivity websites praise Reich as the leader of sexual liberation. His views supporting promiscuity, abortion-on-demand, and comprehensive sex ed are being pushed as healthcare. His materialistic view of the universe asserted that the physical world was all there is, and it promised health and even salvation through sex.[2] In short, Reich's views advocate a sexual worldview that is still leading the charge on school campuses across the country.

I probably don't have to tell you that this sex-positive lifestyle is everywhere in mainstream media. Take Cardi B's song "WAP." When this moral dumpster fire of a song hit the airwaves, business partner Brooklyn Johnny defended the explicit lyrics as a way that women are leveling the sexual playing field. "Men can talk about whatever…they aren't getting scrutinized."[3] Women should be able to be just as confident.

Who cares that this definition of "confidence" is degrading toward women and men? Nope, let's demand the right to objectify ourselves just like the guys do because nothing says, *I'm a confident female,* like grinding in a pool of water around colorful fountains shaped like a woman's backside! What do you think, Mamas? Sound about right?

I can't begin to tell you how tantalizing this sounds to teen girls. Yes, even yours. From an early age they have absorbed the cultural message that being sexy gets you ahead in life. They see it in their toys, they see it in their clothes, and they see it dancing across their afternoon shows. Social media expands a teen's social peer group to global levels while fostering an addictive, perform-reward cycle for validation (which we'll talk about in chapter 9). By the time they are in high school, sexually explicit material barely makes a blip on the conviction radar. So when their hormones are kicked into overdrive and a cleverly titled sexual movement paints promiscuity as a positive way to know thyself, many girls will happily leave their convictions at home. And as for the guys? Well, let's just say that the guys are just happy that the girls have *finally* gotten the memo.

If our kids are to stand a chance, they have to be able to recognize the lies of progressive movements like these and, in Nancy Pearcey's words, see the "Christian worldview as a viable alternative."[4]

ROAR Like a Mother!

RECOGNIZE the Message

Activists will point to Reich for the origins of the sex-positivity movement, but much of the undertaking has been shaped by the desire to soothe past hurts and prevent future harm. Even sex-positive activists struggle to define what the movement is and isn't.[5] However, there are three key points they all agree on.

1. The Only Thing That Matters Is Consent

Like all worldviews, sex-positivity has a source of morality, and it's found in the concept of consent. (Remember the new sex ed guidelines in chapter 5?) It's like the mythical philosopher's stone, but instead of turning whatever you consent to into gold, you turn it into *good*. The label "good" can apply to anything from strict abstinence to the kinkiest kink that ever kinked. As long as you and whomever you've got tied to a bedpost have consented to what's going on, then nothing is wrong with the pleasure it brings. Whatever you mutually approve of is now considered moral, valuable, and worthy of celebration and protection.

2. Thou Shalt Not Judge

Not only has "good" been redefined as "consent," but sex-positive people would never dream of judging anyone else's decisions. (On the plus side, no one can say anything against you for being cisgender and abstinent until marriage.) In turn, however, you're not allowed to discourage someone from, say, having an anonymous tryst with some couple they met on a partner swap website.

Sex-positivity emphasizes personal agency and pleasure while minimizing any kind of moral judgment.[6] To be truly sex-positive, says one expert, you "have to genuinely believe that other people can have sex any way they want with whoever they want, so long as consent is involved."[7] If you find yourself cringing at another person's choices, then you're being sex-negative.

This anti-judgment platform means your personal convictions and sex-positivity will be at odds. Like someone being pulled out of a cult, you'll have to work to deprogram your conscience—and silence the Holy Spirit, for that matter—from reacting negatively to any sexual choice that's consensual. Only when you have been fully desensitized and support your brothers and sisters (and children too) in navigating their sexuality can you truly be sex-positive.

3. There Are No Taboos

This open-mindedness isn't going to come on its own. Nope, it has to be fostered. Any sexual stigmas that have existed in the past—whether because they were grossly immoral or just physically unhealthy—must be erased. This is accomplished through open and comprehensive discussion about alllll the things. Every question is welcome. The goal of sex-positivity is transparency, affirmation, and the nurturing of sexuality at each developmental age, from childhood on up. This is one of the objectives of the comprehensive sex education movement. What better way to get people to value sexual "diversity" than by discussing every possible sex act in all its glory through the 12 most formative years of a child's life?[8] But don't worry—it's done in an "age appropriate" (cough) manner of course. But then again, according to the NSES standards, it's "age appropriate" to ask middle schoolers to explain the difference between oral, anal, and vaginal sex.[9]

OFFER Discernment

Before we go into the lies of sex-positivity, let's look at the biblical truths we can affirm. For one, the brokenness of our fallen world is never more obvious than when we have to sit our boys and girls down and explain the importance of consent. But it's much broader than #MeToo. Sex-positivity highlights the importance of continued respect and autonomy in all relationships—something we here at Mama Bear Apologetics fully support.

Sex-positivity also makes huge leaps where some churches have traditionally fallen flat. I mean, seriously folks, have you read some of the descriptions of what the bride and groom are looking forward to doing in Song of Solomon? They weren't eating raisin cakes for the fiber. They were looking forward to getting *busy*! Sex-positivity points out what the church should have been shouting all along: Sex is good! Pleasure is good! Desire is good! As my (Amy's) son once shouted as he tore through the house naked, "My body is beautiful!" Yes, it is, but put on some pants, son. You're scaring the neighbors.

We also affirm how sex-positivity encourages better communication when it comes to sex. Frankly, the church has tiptoed around this topic far too much. Christian kids have been ridiculed as being notoriously ignorant about the human body and sometimes clueless about STDs. Treating sex as such a hush-hush topic has led to young Christian married couples either suffering in silence when things don't go smoothly, or seeking out secular resources for help because the church hasn't provided many. We don't have to affirm everything to teach both medically accurate and biblical information.

So yes, sex-positivity is highlighting some important points, but not everything that glitters is gold. Beneath the shiny surface is an entirely destructive worldview masquerading as a "healthy and positive" viewpoint.

Lie #1: If It's Consensual, It's Moral

Obviously, everyone agrees that consent is vital in any healthy relationship. It shows that we are being respectful of ourselves and others. But it makes a terrible foundation for morality. Why? Because consent doesn't actually make a moral claim about an action. It only says that you're willing to let that action occur.

The concept of pleasure suffers from the exact same problem; it cannot make any moral claims. Pleasure only says that you enjoy what you're doing. Newsflash: *Sin is usually enjoyable.*

Lie #2: Pleasure Is the Only Purpose of Sex

There is a reason pleasure takes center stage in the sex-positivity movement. Well-meaning Christians have sometimes painted *pleasure itself* as sinful. I kid you not, a relative of mine was taught that it was an affront to God for a woman to do anything but lie back, close her eyes, and think of England while she and her husband tried to conceive.

Physical pleasure without any acknowledgment of the spiritual ramifications of sex treats the body and the soul as two separate things. Do you know what an actual separation of the body and soul is called? Death. That is literally what death is—when the soul separates from the body.[10]

I (Hillary) noticed a trend while researching all the ways we humans have strayed from God's design. Almost every deviation is accompanied by an *increased risk of suicide and suicide attempts.* As we'll see later in this chapter (and in the following three chapters), there are statistically higher suicide rates and attempts within the LGBTQ community, with sexually active teens, and even within the BDSM community.[11] (If you don't know what that is, *don't* Google it.) *When people figuratively separate their body and their soul, they physically long for its completion.* When we separate physical pleasure from the *soul* purpose (pun intended) of sex, it makes people vulnerable to thoughts of suicide and death—at least, that's what the research seems to show.

Yes, sex is intended to be pleasurable. God created orgasms. But its pleasure was intended to reinforce a man's and woman's wedding vows in bodily form and prophetically point forward to the mystery of the church's eternal oneness with Christ. Even the chemicals involved (as we'll see in the next chapter) are intended to bind husband and wife together—spiritually, emotionally, and physically.

When we deviate from His plan, our bodies know it—even if our minds don't. If the Christian worldview is true—and especially what the Bible teaches about sex—then these suicide statistics make sense, sad as they are. We have separated our bodies from our souls and have an unfulfilled *telos*, which creates a longing that nothing in this world can satisfy.

Lie #3: All Judgments (Except This One) Are Wrong!

If you read our first book, you might remember the relativism chapter titled, "You're Wrong to Tell Me That I'm Wrong!" Moral relativism is the belief that objective truth (that is, truth that applies to everyone) doesn't exist. Only personal, subjective truth exists. You can believe whatever you want so long as your truth doesn't say my truth is wrong. Because it's wrong to tell anyone that they're wrong—right?

While sex-positivity claims that there are no objective standards (do whatever you want!), it *still* has an objective standard: judging another person's sexuality is objectively wrong. Sex-positivity is basically just relativism applied to your sex life.

This is especially difficult for our kids when they are taught that affirming a biblical sexual morality is not only wrong, but *oppressive*—which is essentially the message they are getting through their sex ed curriculum.[12] According to the new standards of worldly morality, they are required to not only affirm but *celebrate* the sexual choices of others.[13] Not doing so is a hateful form of disrespect. This is where our "I'm supposed to love like Jesus loved" kids are getting all turned around.

Lie #4: Sex-Positivity Leads to Freedom

The apostle Peter didn't know the phrase sex-positive, but he actually addresses this false teaching in his second epistle:

> They mouth empty, boastful words and, by appealing to the lustful desires of the flesh, they entice people who are just escaping from those who live in error. They promise them freedom, while they themselves are slaves of depravity (2 Peter 2:18-19).

What he means by "those who are just escaping error" are the people turning to Christianity from their sex-positive culture. They *just escaped the error*, and then, as we discussed in chapter 4, these false teachers hooked them right back in by teaching that Christianity and sexual immorality were compatible. Far from freedom, this kind of teaching leads people right back to the bondage they escaped from: bondage to their sexual desires.

The ideology also leads to some disturbing inferences about your worth as a person. But human beings have inherent value. This means your value isn't determined by anything outside of you. Not your job, your beauty, or your bank account. You are irreplaceable and immeasurably precious, with all the dignity and perks to life and liberty simply because you are a human being.

Remember the necessity of boundaries around something incredibly powerful and potentially destructive that we discussed in chapter 1? The same principle applies to things that have *value*. The more value something has, the more rules and boundaries we erect to protect it. This is why the Mona Lisa is behind glass—it is far too valuable to be exposed to a group of hacking, sneezing tourists all jockeying to snag a quick selfie for their Instagram.

It's only when something doesn't have any inherent value that you can do whatever you want with it, which turns out to be the skeleton lurking in the closet of sex-positivity. It encourages you to do whatever you want with whomever you want. The implicit message (that most people don't pick up on) is that you and your partner(s) have no inherent value worth protecting. Consent can't provide this value, and neither can pleasure. Sure, sex-positivity may sound like freedom, but in reality, it's saying that your body and what you do with it don't matter.

> Sex-positivity may sound like freedom,
> but in reality, it's saying that your body has
> no inherent value and is not worth protecting.

Lie #5: All Expressions of Sexuality Are Healthy

The new sex education standards place a huge emphasis on healthy sexuality. But as we saw in chapter 5, they define *healthy* as consensual and enjoyable. A big problem with this is that it outright denies that many of the sexual decisions that arise from sex-positivity (also called safer sex) are themselves dangerous.

Within the last 40 years, we've gone from two main STDs to 25.[14]

Every day there are 8,000 new cases—3 million a year—and that's just among teens.[15] And what is the medical community telling our girls about HPV? Do they tell them that, due to what is called the "transformational zone" on their cervixes, young women are at greater risk for contracting an infection?[16] Nope. Do they tell them that this zone gets smaller with age, so it's probably a good idea to wait for sexual activity? Oh, heck no. What about how birth control actually *enlarges* the transformational zone, increasing their risk? Of course not! That's sex-negative. So what are they told? Well, according to advice from Dr. Vanessa Cullins, the vice-president for medical affairs at Planned Parenthood, "*Expect* to have HPV once you become sexually intimate."[17] You know, no biggie.

How is this the advice from a medical professional? Myriam Grossman states, "Instead of aiming for disease *prevention,* as is done in the fight against heart disease or obesity, the goal [of this ideology] is risk *reduction*—aka 'safer sex'—followed, when it fails to be safe enough, by *damage control*."[18]

That's just the tip of the physical effects. What about the emotional toll? As Grossman says, there is no condom for the heart.[19] One study that sampled 6,500 students showed that teens who were sexually active were more likely to be depressed and attempt suicide.[20] Another study with 8,000 youth showed similar results among teens who were romantically involved.[21] And in both these studies, girls were impacted far more. Promiscuity, Grossman reminds us, is a heart risk.

This is common sense, people. Yet common sense has suddenly become politically incorrect rocket science for the sake of sparing people's feelings. What was once considered "risky behavior" is now promoted as healthy sexual exploration. As far as we can tell, about the only behavior designated as "risky," according to sex-positivity, is not having regular checkups to find out *which* disease you just picked up. Oh, and not using condoms. They're all about condoms.

Lie #6: You Can Be a Sex-positive Christian
Perhaps the most subtle lie that our kids have swallowed is that

Christianity and sex-positivity are compatible. To be both a Christian and sex-positive requires that you deny that God designed sex to be shared only between a man and woman in marriage. All those passages warning believers to flee from sexual immorality? Yeah, there's really no sin to repent of if you're sex-positive. In fact, there's even a Bible app your kids can use which will help them avoid such uncomfortable passages so that they can "ditch toxic theology."[22]

The whole "God loves you and He wants you to be happy" thing suddenly means that anything that gives you pleasure gets the heavenly green light of approval. With just a few quick "positive" concessions, the believer denies God's wisdom and design, ignores the existence of sexual sin, and rejects Jesus's atonement for those sins. That isn't Christianity, folks.

Lie #7: If You're Not for Us, You're Sex-Negative!

The final lie we'll mention here really stacks the deck against our Christian kids. Sex-positivity says unless you affirm that all consensual pleasures are good and healthy, you are sex negative! Booooo, you negative Nelly! This basically makes Christians sound like they hate sex, which is a flat-out lie and poor logic.

At the end of the day, the sex-positive movement is really just Romans 1:18-32 repackaged. Same outcome, different branding. If being the world's definition of "positive" means that we have to ignore God and His teachings, enthrone our sexual urges, and encourage everyone else to do the same, then you can keep it. We'd rather be countercultural anyway…#Romans 12:2.

ARGUE for a Healthier Approach

As we can see, the whole sex-positive approach is more mud than marble. Like the seductress in Proverbs 5, this worldview tells you everything you want to hear. But each lie leads to brokenness, hurt, and more than a few rounds of penicillin. If we want our kids to be wise to the schemes of the world, they have to be able to see beyond the pretty packaging. Here are a few reminders of truth.

Truth #1: God Created Sex

This concept is best summed up by the fictional demon Wormwood in C.S. Lewis's book *The Screwtape Letters*.

> Never forget that when we are dealing with any pleasure in its healthy and normal and satisfying form, we are, in a sense, on the Enemy's ground. I know we have won many a soul through pleasure. All the same, it is His invention, not ours. He made the pleasures: all our research so far has not enabled us to produce one. All we can do is to encourage the humans to take the pleasures which our Enemy has produced, at times, or in ways, or in degrees, which He has forbidden.[23]

God created sex and God created pleasure. We would do better to allow an all-good God to determine what's positive rather than sinful man.

Truth #2: Not All Judgments Are Bad

There's a difference between making a judgment and judging like God judges. Even the most tolerant person makes hundreds of judgments every day. We are judging when we decide which parts of town are unsafe to walk in alone at night. We are judging when we take a sniff of that chicken to see if it's gone bad. We are judging when we decide to marry our spouses instead of another person. Even our kids are judging when they decide to hold our hand while they cross the street. Making judgments involves using a set of standards to make decisions. It's a requirement for wise living, and there is nothing wrong with that.

God gave us His commandments in order that we might live in right relationship with Him. It's not judging (in the McJudgy-pants way) to abide by those standards while encouraging other *Christians* to do the same. Neither is it "being judgey" to point out the health risks and benefits of particular actions. That's just called knowledge, and we recommend er'body getting some, Christians and non-Christians alike!

Truth #3: Pleasure Is a Great Gift but a Terrible God

Sexual pleasure is a good thing. God designed us to experience it, and we are grateful for this aspect of our humanity. But all good gifts can be turned into idols, and pleasure makes a terrible one. Solomon experienced everything pleasure had to offer, and you know what he concluded? It was all meaningless apart from God. Men and women who seek the comfort of pleasure are overwhelmingly left depressed and saddened to find that it fails to give them hope and purpose.

A Final Word

To paraphrase General James Mattis, the most important battle-field is the six inches between your ears. Mamas, that's exactly where sex-positivity is waging war right now. And it's happening on every media platform. If we want our kiddos to stand firm against the cultural tide, then we have to help them understand God's design. They need to know which falsehoods are masquerading as truth and understand how God redeems the brokenness each lie brings. Once our kiddos can do that, they'll become beacons of hope to those around them. Let's do our part to help them shine!

REINFORCE Through Discussion, Discipleship, and Prayer

1. From infancy on up, we need to remind our kids where true plea-sure comes from. Whenever our kids enjoy something, remind them that God was the one who created that enjoyment. Horse-back riding? Sugar? Laughter? Puppy snuggles? Sex? All designed by God for our pleasure.

2. We don't need to go into sexual appetites with our little ones, so let's use another appetite to help them form the correct categories. In this instance, we'll use tongues and our bodies. Our tongues are part of our bodies, but they are only a *part*. There are things that our tongues enjoy, like ice cream. Ice cream is good! God created sugar so that we could enjoy ice cream! But ice cream doesn't have

a lot of potassium or magnesium or zinc or vitamins. There are other parts of our bodies that need these things in order to function well. How disrespectful would it be to our bodies to only eat what makes our tongues happy and not what makes the other parts of our body happy? As they get older, we can reinforce the same concept with sex. Instead of only making the tongue happy, it's... other body parts (wink!).

3. Pleasure can easily take over when we and our kids lack self-control. Discuss with your kids the importance of self-control. A few great passages you can use are Ecclesiastes 3:1-11, Proverbs 25:27-28, and Titus 2:11-12. Ask your kids (especially your teens) a few reflection questions: What does this passage say about the importance of self-control? Without self-control, how can pleasure turn out to be a bad thing? What are some practical benefits to controlling our desire for pleasure? What reasonable boundaries can we put in place to protect ourselves from walking into temptation? Which friends can I count on to help keep me accountable?

4. If you have older kids, read *The Screwtape Letters* together. Talk about different kinds of pleasures that can lead to disadvantageous outcomes because they are not being used the way God intended. How can food be misused? Alcohol? Nasal spray? I'm serious when I say that literally *anything* can be used to excess or in the wrong way and cause harm. As unfortunate frat boys have discovered, a person can even die from drinking too much water.

5. For high school or college kids, read Miriam Grossman's book *Unprotected* and Nancey Pearcey's *Love Thy Body* together. Then take an honest look at how media (movies, television shows, music) portray sex. Is it an accurate representation or not? What truths are missing? What messages have we believed that aren't actually true? Why do you think it's a struggle for young people to avoid believing the messages like the ones found in sex-positivity? When do I find

myself most tempted? What steps can I take to safeguard myself and a (current or future) boy or girlfriend from falling into sin?

PAWS for Prayer by Julie Loos

PRAISE God for Who He Is

Father God, I praise You for You reveal what is true, good, and positive. You are the protector of Your children. Your peace guards our hearts and minds through Christ Jesus (Philippians 4:7). You and You alone are the creator of life and therefore our sexuality. As its creator, You have authority over it.

ADMIT Where We Have Fallen Short of His Standard

Search me and show me, God, where I have fallen prey to the lies of the world about sexuality and not upheld Your view. Forgive me and forgive our nation for untethering sexuality from Your strong cord of goodness. Forgive us of promoting promiscuity, advancing abortion laws, and selling a sex ed curriculum that leads young people to "sell" their bodies to an unholy alliance with the world. For equating morality with consent, for making pleasure our god, for silencing Your Holy Spirit and common sense. We repent of celebrating sins clothed in deception.

WORSHIP WITH THANKSGIVING for the Things He Has Done

Thank You for the gift of sex and that in Your goodness You set up appropriate boundaries within which it should be opened. You have gifted us with worth and inherent value because we are made in Your image. Your words and Your ways are the true definition of sex-positivity.

SUBMIT Yourselves and Your Requests to God

Help us, we pray, that we may live and proclaim, positively, that the only healthy sexuality is holy sexuality. That we may value faith over feelings, logic over labeling. Give us the wisdom to recognize lies and point them out to our children. Help us be sensitive to Your Spirit and not desensitized by culture. Show us how to teach our children that Your boundaries for sex and marriage are not oppressive but freeing. That when they honor their bodies, they honor You. Help us raise up a generation as fierce as lions who will roar in the face of false narratives and positively proclaim that Your ways are higher and better.

Discussion Questions

1. **Icebreaker:** Was hookup culture a thing when you were in high school or college? Was dating still common? How have you noticed the dating scene change throughout the decades?

2. **Main theme:** *Sex-positivity teaches that sexual morality is summed up by pleasure and consent and nothing else.* Where have you seen the messages of sex-positivity in your parenting journey? Why are consent and pleasure a bad litmus test for health and morality?

3. **Self-evaluation:** Have you ever had any habits you enjoyed that really weren't good for you? Where have you believed the lie that one part of your body deserved pleasure to the detriment of your whole self?

4. **Brainstorm:** How have you seen the sex-positive movement displayed in recent movies? List as many reasons as you can think of for why our enemy is trying to sexualize our culture. In what ways does a lax view of sex prohibit the gospel? (Hint: think in terms of chapter 3 and Romans 1:18-23.)

5. **Release the bear:** Sometimes it's time for a media purge. Go through your movies and music with your kids. Really look at the messages there. Are there any DVDs or songs that are better left in the trash? Choose to not be a part of sex-positivity's messages, and make your home a safer place for *good* movies and music.

Part Three

Things That Are Tripping Everyone Up

PRAYER OF LAMENT

Ask Boldly

LAMENTATIONS 3:40-41;
EZEKIEL 11:19-20; 13:10-14; JUDE 12

Let us test and examine our ways, and let us return to the Lord. Let us lift up our hearts and our hands and then with them mount up in prayer to God in heaven. Give us ears that are sensitive and responsive to the touch of our God, that we may do what You say. The seducers of the age have built flimsy walls and covered them up with whitewash. But we say, by Your power, Lord, these whitewashed walls will fall—bring them down to the ground, Lord, so that the foundations will be exposed and all shall understand and realize that You are the Lord. Help us contend for the faith. Expose the hidden reefs, the elements of danger, in the midst of us.

———————

Father, we need Your help, and we need it now. Give us eyes to see evil and courage to call it for what it is. Give us ears to hear the voice of the enemy, no matter how beautifully disguised. Show us the boundary lines to set for our families, and incline our kids' hearts to not straddle them. Help us shine light in the darkness and bring hope to the hurting. Sanctify our children in the truth; Your Word is truth. You, O Lord, have delivered Your people before. You have brought justice and punished the wicked. You have preserved a remnant. What You have done before, You can do again. Do it!

Chapter 9

Pornography

It's Not Technically Sex if You're by Yourself, Right?

Hillary and Amy

Jesus often used stories to illustrate the upside-down nature of the kingdom of God. Higher truths were communicated through everyday, accessible characters and settings that made sense to the people at the time. But 2,000 years later, not all of us can relate to shepherds or oil-toting virgins. In our world, movies are the new parables, and one of the best examples I (Amy) have seen when discussing pornography can be found in an unlikely place: Disney's *Pinocchio*. Hold on to your crickets, folks, because you probably won't see this movie the same way again.

Pinocchio begins with a kindly woodcarver, Geppetto, whose visit from the Blue Fairy makes him the adoptive father of a wooden puppet. Talk about a modern family! Geppetto tries preparing the wooden boy for the real world, but temptation is right there with a slick hat and false promises. *Follow me*, says the creepy fox, *and I'll make you a real boy.*

The fox steers the young puppet to Pleasure Island. Here we watch Pinocchio happily riding on a wagon with rambunctious youngsters. On the ride, his buddy Lampwick tells Pinocchio how great it will be when they can do whatever they want. On Pleasure Island, no one will tell them what to do. It's a dream come true!

The boys clamber out of the wagon and disperse into the town, which

149

is positively overflowing with cigars, delectable food, and rocks just begging to the thrown through the windows. With all their newfound freedom, they don't notice the Wagonmaster's shadowy henchmen locking the gates of the island so no one can escape. Only after it's too late do the boys realize that they've fallen into a trap. They watch in horror as one-by-one they transform into donkeys and are crated up to be sold off. One boy who hasn't yet lost his voice cries out for his mother, begging the Wagonmaster to allow him to go home.

"You've had your fun!" the Wagonmaster growls, throwing the donkey-boy into a crate. "Now it's time to pay!" The boys thought they were just having innocent fun; they didn't know they were being forced into slavery.

If you were to rewind the movie back to the beginning of the scene, you would notice that it wasn't horses pulling the wagon, but donkeys. Boys who were already lost to the lies of Pleasure Island were now being used to drag the next batch to the same grisly fate.

Mama Bears, this exact same crisis is happening in our culture. But instead of pool tables and smashed windows, our children are being lured into bondage with pornography.

The Scope of the Problem

If you haven't personally struggled or known someone who has personally struggled with porn, the issue might feel a bit distant. Like, you *know* it's a problem, but you don't really understand how big of a problem it is. So just how widespread is porn now, anyway?

In 2019, the world's largest porn conglomerate reported *42 billion visits*. So basically the entire earth's population times six visited their site.[1] That's double what they had a mere two years prior. And the amount of *new* content added to the site? Enough to watch porn all day, every day… for 165 years. And remember that is just *one* porn site in *one* year. That doesn't even include the approximate 26 million other sites that exist, several of which *also* boast visits in the billions per year.[2] I don't think we are mentally capable of understanding the scope of this problem.

We would all like to think that porn is a "them" problem. Not *us*. Not *our* husbands. Not *our* kids. But we cannot afford to stick our heads in the sand on this one. According to Covenant Eyes, more than half of pastors have struggled with porn, and 57 percent of youth pastors "live in constant fear of being discovered" for their porn addiction.[3] When it comes to our kids' conception of porn, 90 percent of teens and 96 percent of young adults are *neutral, accepting, or encouraging* of porn consumption.[4] Yep, you read that right. Nearly every kid at school has no problem watching porn and will happily text their favorite videos to their friends so they can join in the fun.

Back in the day, the only way boys could get a peek at a pair of boobs was by swiping a dirty magazine from someone else's secret stash. Now our kids carry instant access around in their pockets. As for the grooming process? It starts with every screen in the house.

The Kaiser Foundation ran a study on the amount of sexualized content flashing across TV screens and found that 80 percent of TV programing and 60 percent of music videos had sexualized content and/or featured the objectification of women.[5] And that was 20 years ago!

Children's media now is especially concerning. In a survey of ten of the most popular children's shows, sexualization of female characters was present in *every episode evaluated.*[6] This was just in the most popular shows *for girls*. In content directed at boys, most commonly video games, 80 percent of female characters were sexualized, scantily clad, or looked like a supermodel; with a quarter of them being all three.[7]

With the rise of cell phones and social media platforms, the world has never had easier access to hyper-sexualized content. By the time our boys reach fifth grade, 90 percent of them will have been exposed to porn, with the lowball average age of first exposure being 8 years old.[8] As Vicki Courtney reminds parents in her book *5 Conversations You Must Have with Your Son*, the question isn't *if* your son will encounter sexualized material, it's *when*. Looking at the statistics above, the "when" can happen at almost every commercial break.

By the time our girls reach age 18 years old, 60 percent of them will have been exposed to porn themselves. And for the lucky 40 percent who haven't, more than likely they're dating guys who have or are regularly consuming it themselves.

Because the child brain is still forming, it can easily become wired in response to pornography exposure, resulting in lifelong consequences right as they are shifting into the, "How *you* doin'?" stage of sexual development. The younger a child is when they are exposed to suggestive images, the earlier their brains can be rewired to seek instant gratification and pleasure. They're also less likely to perceive the dangers and consequences of what they're viewing because the good judgment portion of the brain doesn't fully develop until adulthood. They just see a hot chick, so they'll buy the video game, or watch the movie with the shirtless hunk, and click on the website to see more because it feels good. The adult entertainment industry knows this and is happy to meet their demand. In short: they're using our kids' brains against them, grooming them to be *sensual* consumers instead of sensible ones. How do they get them to be sensual consumers? By hijacking the brain and using its chemicals against them.

> The adult entertainment industry is grooming our kids
> to be *sensual* consumers instead of sensible ones.

The Most Powerful Drug in the World

We talked in chapter 3 about how God made a pretty great design when followed, and especially what a powerful bonding agent sexual energy is when channeled toward one's spouse. But did you know there is research to back this up? While we appreciate the sentiment of Disney calling "true love's kiss" the most powerful thing in the world, neuroscience begs to differ. What is as powerful as crack cocaine? The almighty "O."[9] (Side note: this was the weirdest research I (Hillary) did for the book. *Did you know* that male macaque monkeys will forego the reward of a juice pouch in exchange for the dopamine rush of watching videos of a female macaque's bottom? Well now you do. And your life is richer for it. Moving on...)

There are several chemicals that are released during sexual arousal and orgasm. We'll talk about three specifically here—oxytocin and vasopressin, which lead to bonding, and dopamine, which leads to both pleasure and potentially addiction. To understand why pornography is such a huge problem in our culture, we need to look at what is happening on a physiological level. One key thing to keep in mind as we look at these three chemicals is that all three are "value neutral," meaning they can't discern right from wrong, beneficial from harmful. They just do what chemicals do. Brains reward all kinds of behavior without distinction.[10]

Oxytocin and vasopressin are the main chemicals that contribute to bonding, both between sexual partners and between parent and child. As a Mama Bear, you can probably appreciate the power of oxytocin in bonding with your child. Just think of the feelings you had when you first held your new baby. Now hold that thought…did you know that the same chemical is released during orgasm? It is. And our desires, motivations, and attractions become *directed to whoever or whatever is around us when that burst of oxytocin hits our brains.*

When we look at these chemicals from a Christian perspective, we can celebrate the way God made our bodies to reinforce our emotional attachments and emphasize that God created this chemical cascade. It's a great design—when it's used to enhance the bond between husband and wife. But what if these chemicals are released while watching porn? Yes, the human brain becomes wired to actually crave a two-dimensional image over the real thing—over a real person. We literally bond to a screen. This is actually one of the reasons porn usage *decreases* a person's likelihood to engage in real-life sex. And before your kid tries to rationalize that "porn helps them to save sex for marriage," just remind them: Sex with yourself is still sex. *Porn is not a more "moral" alternative to sleeping around.*

The fact that our bodies and minds are bonding to someone or something outside of marriage should be concerning, especially when we consider the devastating effects for future relationships. Neurologically, orgasm causes you to prefer the person (or thing) to whom your orgasm is attached. Ideally, it causes you to seek their attention and affection for future sexual experiences. So what happens when there isn't another person to seek or the image is constantly changing? Our brains get *used to the bond-breaking process*. We actually train the brain to think that breaking the bond is normal![11] This makes it ever more difficult to actually bond with a real person in the future. And even if we do bond, the bond is weaker because it's used to being broken.

So when we hear people complain about how sleeping with one person for the rest of their life sounds boring, what they're really lamenting is the damage they have created in their own brain that's preventing them from being comforted by the breast of the love of their youth (Proverbs 5:18-19). They're not celebrating their freedom. They are actually mourning the scope of their own brokenness, and they don't even realize it. It's immensely tragic, but through God's grace, fixable.

The Pleasure Chemical

The next chemical involved is dopamine. This little molecule is the reason why porn is so addictive. Dopamine is the reward chemical in the brain. We get little shots of it when we eat something tasty or see a piece of art that we like...or when someone "likes" our photo on social media. The problem with porn isn't that it releases dopamine; it's the *amount* it releases. Our body can only handle so much.

Dopamine would do nothing for our moods unless there were dopamine receptors in our brains for it to bind to. What happens when you flood your brain regularly with too much dopamine? Your body says, "Oh! I guess we don't need all these dopamine receptors. Let's get rid of a few." So your body actually *desensitizes itself* to pleasure. A person is less able to experience pleasure with normal things, like time with friends, a good meal, or a great concert. This also explains why there is such a link between porn usage and depression.[12] A person has altered their brain so that they are unable to feel joy. What that means is that to get the same feeling of "high" or happiness, a person now needs *more* dopamine because there are fewer receptors. And here's where porn use can turn into porn addiction. Not-so-fun fact, it's the exact same neurological pathway and mechanism as a crack cocaine addiction. And because of the added "learning" through oxytocin and vasopressin (which makes you crave that which follows the orgasm), it's even *more addictive*.

Porn and Violence

As mentioned above, regularly viewing porn decreases the dopamine receptors in a person's brain—which means, like in all addictions, that the person has to increase their consumption in order to get the same amount of euphoria. When it comes to pornography, it is not the amount of pornography, but the *type* that changes. The more habituated users are to watching the act of sex, the less sexually stimulated they become. This causes the user to crave ever more shocking and even violent forms of sex in order to become aroused.

This is where violent porn comes into play. I want to be gentle with my Mama Bears here, but at the same time, you need to know what is out there. Common in the *milder* forms of violent porn are men slapping, hitting, and choking women. The women are portrayed as *liking it*. And remember, *what a person orgasms to is what they will crave in a real-life partner.* As University of Michigan law professor Catharine MacKinnon states,

> The catharsis hypothesis—the notion that the more pornography men use, the less abusive sex they will seek out elsewhere—has been scientifically disproved. Closer to the reverse has been found: it primes the pump. As women have long known, use of pornography conditions consumers to objectified and aggressive sex, desensitizing them to domination and abuse requiring escalating levels of violence to achieve a sexual response. Use of pornography is also correlated with increased reports by perpetrators of aggressive sex and with increased inability to perceive that sex is coerced. Consumers thus become increasingly unable to distinguish rape from other sex.[13]

The link between real-life sexual violence and viewing of violent porn has been shown repeatedly in the scientific literature.[14] Not only is this trend hijacking our kids' sexualities, it is affecting how they interact with one another in real life and through social media.

Groomed to Consume and Groomed to Perform

Girls don't wake up one day and suddenly decide they're going to swing naked on a wrecking ball, but they certainly can be groomed to. Remember dopamine? Yeah, that's the same chemical that gets released when our girls see that someone has "liked" their social media post. The creators of platforms like Myspace and Facebook initially included this as a way to encourage positive interactions. Yet in the documentary *The Social Dilemma*, the creators admitted that they had no idea that it would morph into what it is now—fueling addiction and depression, especially among teen girls. Each platform has an addictive little feature called the "like" button that blasts the user with a hit of dopamine every time their phone dings. To keep the reward juices flowing, kids (and adults too, mind you) will often tailor their social media feeds to get the most attention—the most likes and the most dopamine. The more attention, the more likes, the more dopamine.

For most of their childhood, our girls will be in the "observer" role of the sexualization of women. They'll play with seductive-looking dolls and watch kid characters twerking like pop stars. Then they're given a cell phone, and all of a sudden, their role shifts from "observer" to "performer." And believe me, it is a performance. Most girls enter social media with no intention of degrading themselves for public approval. Yet when they notice that girls who act suggestively get more attention, some will start to compromise.

The boys are being conditioned to like what they see in porn, and the girls are being conditioned to perform to these boys' likings. And back and forth it goes.

The effects are not just limited to social media. One of the saddest pieces of research we came across involved interviews with a group of girls who were fed up with what porn had done to the guys at their school. One young woman in an article lamented that having sex was the only way to get her boyfriend to *watch a movie with her*.[15]

So, not only are these girls having sex at younger ages, but they aren't even doing it for their own sake. Due to the effects of porn, girls' primary worry is now *how they look* during sex. Girls are increasingly learning that their value changes according to their ability to turn a guy on and perform according to pornographic standards. Knowing that their boys consume so much porn, these girls have had to adapt their behaviors to give "the porn experience." Gynecological surgeons like Dr. Naomi Crouch report that girls as young as *nine* are contacting her for labiaplasties because they are "distressed by the appearance" of their vulvas.[16] (We didn't even know what a vulva *was* at nine, let alone that it could be unattractive.)

Kids spend an average of 6.5 hours a day plugged into social media.[17] While guys are more likely to record themselves playing sports or doing some moronic challenge, girls are more likely to fall victim to the comparisons game and feel pressured to use filters and produce sexualized content to "stay relevant." Filters and superficial highlights reels of another person's life have them focused on achieving beauty standards that don't exist while hating the reality that does. Instead of seeing themselves as wonderful creations of God, they base their value and self-worth on the number of followers they have and likes they receive. This can lead to increasingly risky online behavior in an effort to maintain a fickle definition of worldly value, resulting in what the American Psychological Association describes as "self-objectification."

So What Exactly Does It Mean to Objectify Someone?

When talking about pornography, the two most commonly used descriptors are objectification and dehumanizing.

Here's a thought experiment: Think about anything you use in your house—say, a pair of scissors, a computer, or a paperclip. Some objects have many functions (computer) and some have few (paperclip.) The only reason you interact with these objects is because you want them to perform a function to improve your life in some way—entertain you (like a TV) or make something easier (like a calculator). What happens when it can't perform its function anymore? You get rid of it and get a new one.

Objectifying something doesn't necessarily mean you don't love it. You can love something you objectify; it's just not the kind of love that we should have for our fellow human beings. I love my computer. I decorate it (fun case!). I protect it and take it to get fixed when it is wearing down. But ultimately, its value is not intrinsic. At the end of the day, if it doesn't do exactly what I want it to do when I want it to do it and at the speed I have grown accustomed to, then it's time to get rid of it. My attachment to it lasts only as long as it fulfills the needs for which I purchased it. That is how we treat objects.

Girls do not realize that this is what awaits them at the end of the objectification process. Many girls mistake *attention* for *attraction*, assuming their skimpy outfits and sexual wiles will attract a great guy. She may even find a guy who treats her well, buys her flowers, and takes her to dinner—for now. But at the end of the day, if she doesn't perform the duties he came to her for (a hot body and great sex), she is as useless as a broken stapler.

What About Dehumanizing?

Dehumanization is when you strip a person of their human rights or qualities. Men and women were created in the image of God, with free minds, free choices, and free emotions; they carry an inherent worth other creatures do not. When we dehumanize someone, we do not recognize their inherent dignity or even consider that they may have thoughts, desires, or emotions that are different from our own. Historically, most of the evils perpetrated against humans have been preceded by a dehumanization campaign. During the Holocaust, Jews were depicted as bugs or animals, an infestation which needed to be purged. Same thing for our Black brothers and sisters during chattel slavery. And now, in our supposedly progressive society, we do the same thing to babies-in-utero. People don't even like calling them babies. They are just "a fetus," and killing them is just "terminating a pregnancy." Very clinical. Very sterile. Pay no attention to the human being at the end of the suction stick.

Dehumanization, in general, is an exceptionally dangerous road to go down. The scariest part is that people usually don't even realize the shift in their thinking. The women in porn are always in the mood, just like my calculator is always in the mood to calculate for me. The men are abnormally well endowed, always perform on cue, and never interact with the woman beyond using her body. Pornography teaches boys that girls exist for the purpose of bringing them pleasure. And the girls learn to perform in whatever role will get the most attention from the boys. Nobody asks the porn star what her major is; she is there for one reason only. At the end of the day, we're all just animals doing what animals do. *De*-humanized.

ROAR Like a Mother!

RECOGNIZE the Message

As you can see, porn is absolutely destroying our kids' sense of what it means to be human and what healthy sexuality should be. If it sounds like we're losing the battle against pornography, it's because we are. We have underestimated the enemy and wandered onto the battlefield totally unarmed. But God has brought forth victory in worse circumstances. If we want to honor Him with what we view, we need to anticipate how the porn industry is reaching our kids, debunk its lies, and equip our boys and girls to stand firm against a porn-saturated culture. So what are the messages inherent in porn?

1. Women Are Always in the Mood for Sex

The television show *Friends* actually addresses this in the episode called "The One with Free Porn." After discovering that Monica and Rachel's apartment has accidentally been hooked up to the porn channel, Chandler and Joey refuse to let anyone turn off the television for fear that the channel won't come back. So enraptured are they by the free porn that they barely eat or sleep. By the end of the episode, we see them having a conversation about how "weird" their day was. Chandler went to the bank, and the super-hot teller didn't want to have sex with him in the bank vault.

Joey recounts, shocked, how the pizza delivery girl just took his money and left. After an awkward pause, they both decide that maybe it's time to turn off the porn.

2. Women Enjoy Being Degraded and Treated Like Sex Objects

The women in porn are almost always portrayed as *liking* everything a man is doing to them, no matter how violent or degrading. According to Robert Jensen, one of the main propagandas of porn is that "any woman who does not at first realize [that she likes] this, can be persuaded by force."[18] Imagine taking that belief into your dating life, or dating a guy who does. Or trying to convince yourself that *all the other girls like this stuff*. Our kids are in the monkey-see-monkey-do modeling stage up until their twenties. And when you have a powerful reinforcer (like an orgasm), this "observational learning" can become permanently seared in their psyche.

3. Porn Sex Is Normal Sex

According to a recent study in the UK, more than half the boys (53 percent) and a large number of the girls (39 percent) were under the impression that the acts depicted in porn *reflect how sex is in real life*. Even more disturbing was the number of children—more than a third of young teenagers—who responded that they'd like to "try out the behavior they had viewed." As the study's coauthor, Dr. Elena Martellozzo, put it,

> If boys believe that online pornography provides a realistic view of sexual relationships, then this may lead to inappropriate expectations of girls and women. Girls too may feel pressured to live up to these unrealistic, and perhaps nonconsensual, interpretations of sex. This is clearly not positive for developing future healthy relationships.[19]

Not to mention that consent, STDs, or condom use rarely occurs in these skin flicks. Obviously, we need our kids to come to us to learn about sex, not online videos featuring Fabian the well-endowed pool guy.

OFFER Discernment

While there is nothing (and we mean nothing) inherently good about pornography, we should still grapple with the reasons people watch it. Most people immediately point to the sin of lust, but that's a bit too simplistic. Yes, lust is occurring during the viewing, but it's what happens right before that is more telling.

Porn usage can often be due to a person trying to meet a legitimate need in an illegitimate way. In order to have victory, a person must identify the real issue. If we treat pornography as the main issue instead of as a symptom, we can miss the root cause.

In the book *Sex and the Supremacy of Christ,* contributor David Powlison recounts a story of a man named Tom who struggled with pornography and masturbation. Through just a little digging, he and his counselor discovered that his problem wasn't lust; it was anger at God for not giving him a spouse.

Desire for intimacy is often at the top of the list for girls and women who engage in pornographic material. Once the physical act of masturbation comes into play, however, they may experience the same level of addiction as the boys, but their desire was originally fueled by a need to connect. A desire to connect and be known is a God-given desire, one we shouldn't dismiss.

Likewise, there has been a noted link between pornography and feelings of loneliness, depression, and anxiety.[20] Now, which is the chicken and which is the egg has yet to be determined. (Do the negative emotions cause the porn usage or does porn usage cause the emotions? It's likely both.) And, furthermore, it doesn't take some fancy study to show that girls are often more comfortable talking about their feelings than boys. When our boys are experiencing extreme discomfort, they often can't even identify it, let alone admit to it. So they turn to something that makes them feel good without having to talk it out.

In conversations I've personally had with people who are honest about watching porn (and who are self-aware enough to describe what happens right before they stumble), frustration with some aspect of their life was at the top of the list. In other words, they weren't necessarily looking for sex. They were looking to…not feel so crappy. We are wired for intimacy and connection. And like any drug, a person's porn viewing habit can start out as a form of self-medication. That doesn't make it okay, but it should help us better understand how to help.

And yes, lust is going on as well. We are wired to respond to visual sexual stimuli. Song of Solomon wasn't shy about the beauty of the male and female body. Breasts like two fawns, drinking wine from her navel, blowing on her garden? Yup, that's all in Scripture. Our bodies are beautiful and desirable, and depictions of sexual expression are attractive to us because that's exactly how sex was designed! Being aroused by them is totally normal, and it's something to be fostered between a husband and wife.

Being attracted to visual displays of nudity isn't just a guy thing, either. Girls also like to see some skin, which is why Team Jacob never complained when their werewolf heartthrob from the hit teen series *Twilight* couldn't find himself a shirt. Finding an ancient vampire coven? Piece of cake. But a shirt? That was total mystery. So yes, we get it. We're all sexual creatures and porn recognizes (that is, exploits) that fact.

Furthermore, there really are health benefits to orgasms. Scientifically speaking, orgasms release chemicals that lower blood pressure, decrease anxiety, and promote better sleep. But we are not just bodies, and even if something has some benefits, it doesn't make it moral.

Porn is evil, period. We don't even care if someone thinks that their marriage is better because of it. I'm sorry, but having to get turned on by someone else so that you can have sex with your spouse is not a net gain.

So what lies are there in porn? Too many to list here. But here are a few of the biggies that our kids are being duped by.

Lie #1: Porn Isn't That Big of a Deal

We've said it before and we'll say it again: normal is not the same thing as moral. But unfortunately, that's what our kids think. It's part of the desensitization process. People experience shame over shameful things. You can tell when something has lost its shamefulness when kids openly talk about it. Both of us have heard young people (even Christian young-sters) loudly and openly discussing porn, which means they don't care who hears them. Why? *Because they aren't even embarrassed anymore.* They have forgotten how to blush (Jeremiah 6:15). Your kids may not talk to you about pornography usage because they expect that *you* think it is a big deal. But as we mentioned previously, upwards of 90 percent of youth today do not. And why should they? Their brains aren't fully formed to understand future consequences. As Abigail Shrier states, "Try convincing a teenager that something she wants to do carries risks…It's a little like informing her the sun will burn out five billion years in the future."[21]

Lie #2: Porn Is a More Moral Alternative to Sex

If your kids are brought up in church and youth group, they will likely hear the youth pastor entreating them to save themselves for their future spouses. Unfortunately, we may have mistakenly given them the impres-sion that if no other party is present, then it isn't really sex. If a girl watches porn, she assumes she has not given her heart away to someone other than her future husband. If a boy watches porn, he may justify it to him-self as technically "following the rules" because he hasn't deflowered any of the girls in the youth group. If it's just you and a screen, then nobody is getting hurt, right? They truly see porn as obeying the directive laid out by biblical teaching. But sexual faithfulness isn't just abstaining from sex with another person. As we've seen in the research above, a huge number of relationship issues are caused by porn usage—issues they *will take into their future relationships*.

Lie #3: Porn Is Harmless

This is a lie from the pit of hell. But often people aren't motivated to quit something until the harm hits them where it hurts. So let's explain this in terms that males will especially understand: *Porn is creating erectile dysfunction even for guys in their teens and twenties.*[22] In short, porn is rewir-ing brains and impeding people's ability to connect with other humans. So basically, if you want to be anxious, depressed, and ruin your future sex life, then by all means, watch porn. But I'm guessing you don't and neither do your kids. We don't always have to make everything uber spiritual. Sometimes good common sense will do the trick.

Lie #4: Porn Can Be Empowering

A common argument is that porn allows a woman to take control of her own body and use it as she wishes. But women in the sex industry disproportionately have histories of abuse and are so often victims of violence and poverty.[23] If you know a woman in the sex industry who is emotionally healthy and fulfilling her childhood dream of being paid for sex, please introduce me. I would like to hear her story.

Just because you choose to be exploited does not mean you are not being exploited. This is basically saying, "A guy can't take it from me if I give it up willingly." Ask the question: can someone be empowered and degraded at the same time? We say no. Wielding sexual power may *feel* empowering in the short run, but it's a sleight-of-hand trick of the enemy. These individuals may be completely unaware of how their sense of self-worth is slowly being siphoned away until there's nothing left. By the time they come to their senses, the industry is done with them, ready to move on and suck the soul out of the next wide-eyed ingenue. Thanks for playing; your services are no longer required.

Lie #5: Porn Can Promote Healthy Sexuality

This is a huge problem within secular psychology because many sex therapists recommend porn to their clients. But remember, much of their counseling training is based off teachers like Wilhelm Reich, Alfred Kinsey, Sigmund Freud, and others who held a materialistic worldview which states that we are only bodies. Their worldview isn't based on objective morality or a high view of the body, so their "treatment" is going to reflect the culture's view of sex, not God's.

Lie #6: Porn Can Be Ethical

"Ethically sourced" is a buzz phrase, especially for today's Gen Z'ers.

Just like diamonds and your favorite chocolate, some porn is now being touted as "ethically sourced." Ethical porn (sometimes called feminist or fair-trade porn) means all participants are willing and are fairly paid…and often paid *really* well. So, consent and fair wages equals ethical. Our kids assume that if someone is making a good living wage off their "work," then they aren't being exploited, so no harm, no foul. And even the word "work" is being twisted. Porn stars refer to having sex as their "job" or their "art," or their "business." Phrasing like this can be confusing to our kids when they hear us talking about the importance of getting a job. Why would they do one for $15 an hour when they could get a job paying $200 an hour? Work is work, right? #linguistictheft

ARGUE for a Healthier Approach

Porn is basically a cheap counterfeit for the beauty of God's design for sexuality. It uses our God-given sexuality, lures us away from the beauty and goodness of God's design for sex, and exchanges wholeness for brokenness. (What a deal!) One of the best ways to help combat pornography is to help our children distinguish between the real thing and a counterfeit. Though not guaranteed, there are generally lasting benefits that come from adhering to God's design and fallout from buying into the cultural lies.

As mentioned above, porn often hijacks real needs and seduces the individual with the promise of fulfilling them. Acknowledge those needs with your kids. Make a habit of helping them voice their needs. Kids are notorious for acting out when they don't understand a negative emotion. If your son or daughter is having a hard time voicing their emotion, maybe get them an emotion chart where they can point to how they are feeling. The more they learn to articulate a need, the less likely they'll need to express it in other ways.

Sex isn't just some act between bodies or screens, but a powerful testament to the goodness of God that bonds husbands and wives spiritually till death do they part. It nurtures the family unit as a whole. And you can bet your bottom dollar that this same power is equally destructive outside of God's intended use.

Every aspect that we have talked about shows how powerfully reinforcing the sexual act is, whether done in front of a screen or with a person to whom you have pledged your life. God created the act of sex for husbands and wives to recommit to each other bodily and to connect with another in a way that transcends logic or reason. It is an incredibly powerful chemical bond, and not one that you want to make with a person who has not pledged their lives to you in front of friends and family (or at least in front of a justice of the peace!).

As we'll see in our discussion on purity culture in chapter 12, we had a lot of well-meaning teachers trying to get this point across, but it's a tricky message to get across without inducing hopelessness in a person who has fallen shy of the ideal. As in most things in Christianity, we have to have a both/and approach. Who (or what) you share your orgasm with matters, *and* God has promised redemption to those who have fallen. There will likely be some emotional (and physiological) consequences, *and* God can make all things new.

The younger a child starts with porn, the harder the effects will be to reverse. It doesn't happen overnight, and there will likely still be lingering memories, but healing can happen. As Paul wrote in Philippians 3:13-14, "Forgetting what is behind and straining toward what is ahead, I press on toward the goal to win the prize for which God has called me heavenward in Christ Jesus." We don't want to forget the *lessons* we've learned in the past, but neither can we let our past failures dictate how much we strive for God's best in the future.

REINFORCE Through Discussion, Discipleship, and Prayer

As we've seen, the reasons for watching porn can be varied. But there are a few things that we can do as parents that can help mitigate the issues.

1. Get a filter on all your and your children's devices. Net Nanny, Safe Eyes, Covenant Eyes, Bark—take your pick. Parental settings on your streaming services are also a must. It's reckless not to have these.

2. No phones or computers in the bedroom or the bathroom. We

know you'll get pushback on this, but it would be like having a door connecting your house to a porn theater and refusing to lock it. Nearly all experts, regardless of faith, agree that it's a bad idea for kids to have smartphones or computers in the privacy of their own rooms. There's even a growing number who are against smartphones, *period*. We understand each family is unique, so we leave this up to the parents. But if you need a little encouragement to be countercultural, remember what your mom always told you: just because all your friends have one does not mean you have to. Part of being set apart as a Christian is making wise and healthy decisions. If our kids feel that giving up a smartphone is a cross too big to carry as a disciple of Jesus, you *might* have just uncovered a bigger spiritual issue that needs attention.

3. Prepare your kids for what to do if they accidentally see a pornographic image or if a friend tries to show them one. Talk to them about how it rewires the brain to crave things that aren't real.

   For girls, explain the prevalence of anxiety and depression associated with porn usage. Most girls want to avoid these emotions like the plague. They also need to know that a godly woman's identity is in Christ. She doesn't need to base her self-worth on a boy's reaction to a saucy social media post. She's too precious for that. Help her to be countercultural so that she can encourage her friends through her behavior to reject the lies that exploit them.

   Boys will need an escape plan as well as encouragement to know that they aren't weak or emasculated for choosing not to look at pornographic images when their friends are crowded around a screen. Part of being a godly man is protecting the men and women around them. Walking away from porn is one way to do that. Another is not asking for sexy pics from their girlfriends or sending and posting ones themselves.

4. Help your kids foster healthy *in-person* relationships. We are in a digital world, and while our kids are more connected than ever,

they are also lonelier than ever—an emotion that can lead to porn usage. Make your house the one that kids want to congregate at. Usually this is the house with the best snacks and where the parents are always up for a loud, rambunctious gaggle of teens to take over the living room TV till the wee hours. Yes, it's noisy and your food bill goes up, but it's a small price to pay for peace of mind and a connected kid.

PAWS for Prayer by Julie Loos

PRAISE God for Who He Is

Father God, You are the lover of our souls. You are faithful and jealous for our love. You designed us and made us wonderfully. You are wise in Your creation of man and woman, of the attraction and bond of husband and wife. Because You are an intimate and personal God, You made us for connection and intimacy as well. El Roi: the God Who Sees, knows everything; nothing is hidden from You. Yahweh Shammah: the Lord is there; there is nowhere we can go from Your presence.

ADMIT Where We Have Fallen Short of His Standard

Forgive me when my eyes have looked upon and my mind has entertained things not pleasing to You. Forgive our culture for allowing everything to be sexualized—for not making You the object of our worship but rather objectifying men and women who are made in Your image. We have not protected our young from the prowling lion who seeks to kill, steal, and destroy. We have idolized instant gratification and pleasure; even domination, abuse, and violence as poor substitutes for love. We have confused attention for attraction. Forgive us for losing the ability to blush.

WORSHIP WITH THANKSGIVING for the Things He Has Done

Thank You that our desire for intimacy is rooted in our desire to know You. You developed our minds and our bodies with intricate stages of development, with the ability to foster good judgment, with a need for bonding. Where we have allowed burning desires to be kindled by inappropriate means, You offer beauty for ashes. We are grateful that how we look in Your eyes is of much more worth than how we look in the eyes of others. There is no amount of shame that You cannot erase with Your grace.

SUBMIT Yourselves and Your Requests to God

Release us, we pray, from the bondage to pornography. Show us where and how to draw a line in the sand. Guide us as we teach our children to recognize dangers and realize consequences. Lead us to be sensible consumers and not sensual ones. May our desires and devotions be aligned under Your doctrine and not to our evil devices. To have eyes only for You and Your way. Expose the root causes leading loved ones, friends, and strangers to this quicksand of habits. Lord, we ask that You help us obey all Your commands so that we and our children may prosper forever as we do what is good and right in the sight of the Lord our God (Deuteronomy 12:28). May we set our sights on You.

Discussion Questions

1. **Icebreaker:** Did you remember the Pleasure Island scene from *Pinocchio*? What are some other movies you remember as a kid that were a lot darker when you watched them as an adult? (#FoxAndTheHound)

2. **Main theme:** *Pornography takes the beautiful design of sex to bond a husband and wife together and instead addictively bonds the porn user to a two-dimensional image on a screen.* What statistics about pornography in the chapter shocked you the most? Did you have any idea that porn was that big of a problem?

3. **Self-evaluation:** Have you ever struggled with watching things you shouldn't? What were your motivations for seeking them out?

4. **Brainstorm:** What are some ways you can prioritize in-person relationships for your children at your house? What might be some of the warning signs your child is experiencing loneliness?

5. **Release the bear:** Take this week to put all the advice into practice—put filters on everyone's devices. Move computers out of bedrooms, and make sure no screen in the house is difficult to see from other angles. Treat your home like you are battle-proofing for the war on porn!

Chapter 10

Same-Sex Attraction

Hurting People to Be Loved

HILLARY AND AMY

It should come as no surprise that having a family member or close friend who identifies as gay has been closely linked with Christians reevaluating the Bible's stance on homosexuality. And there is a lesson to be learned here: if we do not have any LGBTQ people in our family or circle of friends, we may have missed the legitimate pain that is taking place within this community. It is unwise to allow personal pain to reinterpret the truth of God's Word, but it should inform the way we treat this very delicate topic.

I (Hillary) have often said that the homosexual community has been treated as the scapegoat for all of the church's sexual sins. What do I mean by scapegoat? Originally, the concept of a "scapegoat" referred to a ritual element in the Jewish holiday Yom Kippur ("Day of Atonement"). Leviticus 16:20-22 gives a picture of what is going on:

> When Aaron has finished making atonement for the Most Holy Place, the tent of meeting and the altar, he shall bring forward the live goat. He is to lay both hands on the head of the live goat and confess over it all the wickedness and rebellion of the Israelites—all their sins—and put them on the goat's head. He shall send the goat away into the wilderness

in the care of someone appointed for the task. The goat will carry on itself all their sins to a remote place; and the man shall release it in the wilderness.

When applied to the gay community, no actual atonement is going on but rather a twisted and hypothetical transfer of guilt, as if our zeal for the *one* sin of homosexuality could replace our collective guilt for the rampant sexual immorality going on in our own fellowship. A colleague of ours recalled a time when, after speaking at a conference, a woman approached him asking what to do with her son who had just confessed same-sex attraction. She lamented to our friend, "Why can't he just be like his sister? She is engaged to a nice boy, and they are about to have their first child."

Hard stop. Did she just say that she wished her same-sex attraction son could be *more* like her daughter—the daughter who is living with a man she's not married to and is now pregnant by? *That situation is preferable?!?!*

Church, this is not okay. We can't treat one sexual sin as if it is worse than any another. Sexual immorality is sexual immorality.

A Long History of Hypocrisy

If we were to look back at church culture over the last 75 years, I'm pretty sure we'd recognize that the gay community is not the first group we've done this to. In our grandparents' generation, divorce was the scapegoat. You could be a gambling, alcoholic, abusive monster, but as long as you weren't divorced, you were still welcome in polite society. But when no-fault divorce became the law of the land, what was once the unforgivable sin became so prevalent in our churches that pastors just stopped preaching about divorce.

Then it was out-of-wedlock pregnancy. Girls and boys could do whatever they wanted in the back seat. As long as there was no concrete proof, we just looked the other way. Some churches still do this. Other churches came to the horrifying realization as to how the "evidence" was disappearing and instead started ministries to support unwed mothers so that they could be free to choose life for their babies without shame.

And now, it seems, we have set our sights on the *next* big sin—the battle we've lost in the culture, but not yet in the church: homosexuality.[1] You can have three kids from three dads or have as many baby-mamas as you like, but as long as you aren't gay, you are still welcomed in the fellowship of believers.

Church. We. Need. To. Stop. This.

If we consider homosexuality to be sin, then the church needs to be *the place* where people can be honest about their struggles. We cannot swing wide our doors to those struggling with pornography, addiction, and promiscuity but then get all shy and prudish with same-sex attraction. No wonder the LGBTQ community has run for the hills! And like the scapegoat, we have driven them there, purging our feelings of guilt over our own collective sexual sins.

I'm not saying that everyone in the church has individually done this, but I've talked with too many counselors who describe the pain that their homosexual clients have gone through—being disfellowshipped from their churches, rejected by their families, feeling that their attractions are the unredeemable or unpardonable sin. Isn't that exactly what the enemy would like us *all* to believe about ourselves? That there is something about us which disqualifies us from coming before the throne of God, cutting us off from the very One who desires to see us walk in freedom? So let's dispense with that nonsense now.

Same-sex attraction is not the unpardonable sin.

The gospel is not about making gay people straight.

The gospel is about transforming sinners into disciples of God.

How Should We Respond to Same-Sex Attraction?

A huge mistake we can make as Christians when it comes to homosexuality is confusing people for an agenda, mistaking captives for rebels. Are there some people who flaunt their homosexual practice and have no desire to change? Sure. Has there been a concerted effort in the west to normalize homosexuality through music, movies, advertising, and any other means possible? Also yes. You've seen it yourself; it's not a big secret.

As we've discussed, familiarity is not easily distinguished from truth. Our kids are constantly receiving the message that homosexuality is normal and healthy. So I'm going to make a contentious suggestion: maybe it's time that we start with the assumption that our kids will, at some point, question their gender and sexuality—especially if they struggle to fit in with their peers. Why? Because our society celebrates homosexual and transgender individuals who "bravely speak their truth." Kids model what they see heroized.

If your child comes to you saying they are gay or transgender, it is important to respond with gentleness and compassion. If they've watched the YouTube activists, they've been told to expect persecution and rejection from family. Don't go there. Listen. Ask questions. Remind them that you love them no matter what. And above all, remember that *when it comes to sexual desires, we are probably dealing with a symptom, not a root cause*. This is where listening to their stories is super important. The thing that we want to make absolutely clear is that *same-sex attraction is not the sum total of their identity*, nor does it separate them from the love of God. Desires are desires. It's what we do with them that matters.

Sexual identity and gender identity are, for many, an open and festering wound. We cannot go casually poking around an open wound and expect people to thank us. It is easy to forget that the words we say can cut someone to their core, to their very soul. We can't afford to do this kind of worldview surgery with a rough hand.

Author Bruce Marshall wrote, "The young man who rings the bell at the brothel is unconsciously looking for God."[2] As Peter Kreeft puts it, sex "gives us a foretaste of heaven, of the self-forgetful, self-transcending self-giving that is what our deepest hearts are designed for, long for and will not be satisfied until they have."[3]

At this point, many Christians find themselves at an impasse, caught between truth and compassion. On one side are people who say, "Marriage is between a man and a woman. The Bible said it, I believe it, that settles it." They stay true to Scripture but, like clanging cymbals, turn the Bible into a weapon, ignoring God's heart for people who are struggling in sin. On the other side is the (self-titled) "affirming churches." In their zeal to love their (gay) neighbor, they stand in solidarity with what the Bible says is not part of God's design. They twist Scripture, often leaving biblical inerrancy in the dustbin as they go.

We cannot fall prey to either of these two extremes, Mama Bears. We have to be the generation to disciple our children to truly love and understand their same-sex-attracted peers while maintaining a commitment to biblical truth about marriage. Because as we saw in chapter 3, if we mess with the picture God gave us through sex, marriage, and gender, we mess with people's ability to see God accurately. Who among us is willing to stand before God and say that they encouraged people to remain in bondage to a distorted view of Him when it was His desire for them to walk in freedom? We cannot afford to get this one wrong, Mama Bears.

The Scientific Complexities of Same-Sex Attraction

Sexuality is a difficult subject to study from a scientific perspective. Science usually waits until something breaks on a wide scale before people are willing to bankroll the study of said phenomena. Well, guess what? Sex done got broke. What was once a fringe topic discussed in the shadows is now catapulted to front and center, everywhere. And even when we try to talk about it, we talk past each other. But why?

We already discussed the first reason—the false dichotomy between truth and compassion. Some people are willing to pick one virtue over the other. The people who don't want to sacrifice either are left on the sidelines with everyone screaming "pick a side!" We refuse to choose between truth and love. We will always choose both.

The second difficulty is more scientific. There are some who feel either uncomfortable or ill-equipped to discuss same-sex attraction from a theological perspective, but they are more than ready to discuss the supposed science behind it. After all, *surely* science can provide a more clear-cut, less-polarizing answer. I posit that this is a dead end too, for a few different reasons.

Scientific Difficulty 1: No Clear Separation Between Demographics

There is a lot of research claiming to study the differences between heterosexuals, homosexuals, and bisexuals, as if these were nice, neat categories with no overlap. The problem is that upon further digging, discrepancies are found between people's self-identified "orientation" and their attractions and behaviors.[4]

Sociologist Lisa Diamond discusses the problematic nature of these "identities" in her presentation on Sexual Fluidity.[5] In comparing data from tens of thousands of randomly selected individuals, in studies spanning multiple countries and decades, she pointed out that many self-proclaimed heterosexuals report fantasies toward and sexual activity with people of the same sex. There are also self-proclaimed homosexuals who report fantasies toward or sexual activity with people of the *opposite* sex. At what point is a person officially classified as bisexual instead of gay or straight?

If you can't clearly identify and separate your subjects, you cannot study the differences between them. If you are waiting for "science" to settle this issue, you might be waiting a while. The studies we have are riddled with design flaws for the reasons explained above. For a scientific study to hold weight, researchers must be able to *clearly* differentiate between the groups. If there's not a clear differentiation, the results are invalid. (Side note: this says nothing about the people who do remain consistent in their sexual attractions. It just means that we have difficulty coming to any scientific conclusions about differences between sexual orientations at the population level.)

Scientific Difficulty 2: What Exactly Do We Mean by Sexual Orientation?

The most common argument is that our sexual desire is somehow intrinsic, like the title *sexual orientation* suggests—as if we were born with a sexual compass which points toward men or points toward women. We now realize that sexual attraction is much more fluid than that—at least on a population level. As we saw above from the Lisa Diamond meta-research, the majority of people who experience same-sex attraction are not *exclusively* same-sex attracted. And even if people were consistent, the question of orientation is not as simple as "which gender are you attracted to" because there is the *why* factor. *Why* do we experience the sexual desires that we do? And what constitutes a sexual desire?

There is a whole field of research devoted to *attachment theory*. Attachment theory teaches that humans have an internal drive to attach to both the same and opposite sexes for different reasons. Ricky Chelette, founder of Living Hope Ministries, has a fabulous talk on this. I recommend every parent get the DVD. As Ricky describes, failure to progress through certain attachment phases can leave a person craving the attachment that they missed, thereby *influencing* future sexual desires—whether directed toward same sex or opposite sex.[6]

We have amassed enough research (not to mention anecdotal evidence) which suggests that sexual trauma can *also* play a role.[7] As we discussed in chapter 9, pleasure and orgasm are powerful reinforcers that can direct our future sexual desires. What happens when a child's first exposure to sexual stimulation was with someone of the same sex? What happens when they have a traumatic experience with someone of the opposite sex? Both situations can affect which gender a person desires to be romantically involved with. The problem arises, though, that if part of their orientation is "nurture" instead of nature, then it cannot be considered an entirely inborn orientation.

Finally, the problem arises again as to how we differentiate between all these people for research purposes. How do we classify those who have had same-sex attraction from birth versus those who have had unhealthy or incomplete attachments in childhood versus those who have experienced trauma? It's almost impossible. When we look at the body of research as a whole, we can't say that *no homosexuals* are born that way, and we can't say *all homosexuals* are born that way.

As you can see, until we can clearly differentiate between groups, we cannot form concrete conclusions over what "the science" does or doesn't say. If you would like to see a summary of all the research, I recommend starting with the executive summary published in *The New Atlantis* by researchers Lawrence Mayer and Paul McHugh. You can find the link in note 7 to this chapter. If nothing else, it will give you something to keep your child busy when they come home claiming that science is "conclusive" about anything regarding homosexuality.

ROAR Like a Mother!

RECOGNIZE the Message

There are six main passages in Scripture that address homosexuality. These passages are often referred to as the "clobber verses" by progressives because they supposedly "clobber" everyone into a single interpretation of Scripture. These passages are found in...

1. Genesis 1–2 (original creation)

2. Genesis 19 (Sodom and Gomorrah)

3. Leviticus 18:22 and 20:13 (Jewish laws regarding homosexual behavior)

4. Romans 1:18-32 (basically the decline of a culture from all sorts of sexual sin)

5. 1 Corinthians 6:9-10 (the list of people who won't inherit the kingdom)

6. 1 Timothy 1:8-10 (the list of the unrighteous sinners)

There are two main camps when it comes to interpreting what the Bible teaches. These are commonly referred to as the traditional view and the revisionist view (also sometimes called the non-affirming and the affirming views). For the purposes of this chapter, we will use the words traditional and revisionist, because the main issue discussed here is textual interpretation, not the affirmation of same-sex-attracted individuals.

The revisionist view states that—for a number of reasons—the verses listed above cannot be used to prohibit loving, long-term, committed, monogamous, homosexual relationships for the following reasons:

1. These passages are only referring to abusive or reckless forms of homosexuality.

It is true that there was rampant sexual abuse occurring in pagan cultures of the Old Testament and throughout the Roman Empire. According to the revisionist readings, these abuses are what the Bible is prohibiting.

In the example of Sodom and Gomorrah, it is clear that the Sodomites weren't looking for romance. They were banging on Lot's door demanding to gang rape the visitors one by one. That's hardly a committed relationship. Most revisionists will cite Ezekiel 16:49, which reduces Sodom's list of sins to social justice—pride, excess food, prosperous ease, and a neglect of the poor and needy. Therefore, according to the revisionist, the Genesis 19 passage cannot be used to condemn loving, monogamous, same-sex relationships. The same is true, they argue, of the Corinthian and Timothy passages. These are all talking about things like pederasty (man-boy sex), temple prostitution, and slave-master sexual relations. Even the word "homosexuality" is, they argue, not in the original Greek.

2. The biblical writers had no concept of sexual orientation, so these verses can't apply to it.

Another one of the oft-cited arguments against the traditional reading of Scripture (i.e., that homosexuality is sin), is by appealing to the culture of the time. Revisionists will argue that there was no concept of a fixed, homosexual orientation. Therefore, the Bible is silent on the issue. Gay historians argue that sexual orientation was not recognized until the last 500 years, so the Bible cannot speak against it.

These arguments are especially prevalent now that embracing homosexuality is considered social progress. *USA Today* op-ed writer Hemal Jhaveri says that LGBTQ lifestyles are actually a sign of a "modern society."[8] These Bible passages are simply outdated, like parachute pants and shoulder pads.

3. The church is inconsistent in applying the Old Testament law.

When discussing homosexuality with a revisionist, you will inevitably have shellfish thrown in your face. "Why," the revisionists ask, "do we listen to the OT about homosexuality but not the other outdated laws?" It's a good question. How *can* we justify condemning homosexuality while happily eating shellfish on our anniversary (Leviticus 11:10), wearing an outfit with a patchwork of fabrics (Leviticus 19:19), or charging interest on a loan (Exodus 22:25)? When you look at *all* the laws, the ones against Adam and Steve seem to be unfairly applied while the laws that would prevent you from dining at Red Lobster are generally ignored.

4. Celibacy is only for those who choose it.

The revisionist also claims that when the church prohibits homosexuals from having same-sex life partners, they are commanding celibacy against the person's wishes. Jesus dignifies the celibate life in Matthew 19:12 when He says, "There are those who *choose* to live like eunuchs [celibate] for the sake of the kingdom of heaven. The one who can accept this should accept it." Since a same-sex-attracted individual doesn't want to *choose* celibacy, then this verse doesn't apply to them.

Their logic goes as follows: God said that being alone is bad (Genesis 2:18). Adam was able to have companionship when a *suitable* companion was found. Homosexuals do not find people of the opposite gender to be *suitable* sexual companions. To prohibit them from having a lifelong companion is to demand that they live in a state that God Himself declared "not good." Therefore, God's original statement regarding the goodness of companionship trumps any prohibitions of same-sex sexuality. Furthermore, the revisionist argues that it would be cruel for God to require all homosexuals to be celibate, and our God is a God of love, not cruelty.

5. God doesn't make mistakes.

With clobber passages safely reasoned away, the next step in gaining church acceptance for homosexuality is to argue that homosexual sex isn't actually wrong. Catholic ministry DignityUSA did just that when they reasoned that since people are created gay, and all that God creates is good, then they should have the freedom to live as they were created.[9] Anyone who disagrees is rejecting God's creation.

6. Prohibiting same-sex relationships produces "bad fruit."

Finally, this is a biblical argument that many in the revisionist camp cite. As Matthew Vines says in *God and the Gay Christian*, "Does that call to self-denial mean that gay Christians should view mandatory celibacy as part of what it means for them to follow Jesus? Or should we view that approach as causing unnecessary suffering—bad fruit, in other words."[10]

What exactly does he mean by "bad fruit"? Jen Hatmaker expands upon this concept in an interview with Pete Enns. "It was actually Jesus' teaching on fruit that locked us in hard…When you're not sure, when there's something…that feels ambiguous, or it feels contentious, or there's tension around its interpretation, look to the fruit…When I looked to the fruit of the [traditionalist reading] Christian tree, the fruit was so universally bad. It was suicide. It was broken families. It was folks kicked out of their churches. It was homeless teenagers. It was self-hatred and self-harm and depression, crushing loneliness, separation from God…If we are being honest, the fruit of the tree is rotten."[11]

OFFER Discernment

Having affirmed the legitimate grievances that the LGBTQ community has in the first pages of this chapter, we'll dive straight into answering the messages and asking ourselves if the theological claims are true.

1. Was the Sin of Sodom and Gomorrah Only Inhospitality?

The revisionist is only partially right. God does—according to the Ezekiel 16:49 passage—condemn Sodom and Gomorrah for more than just attempted homosexual gang rape. However, as Kevin DeYoung points out in his book *What Does the Bible Really Teach About Homosexuality?*, the Ezekiel passage mentions more than just inhospitality. Twice it mentions the word "abomination," (*to'ebah*).[12] In Leviticus 18:22, the law states that it is an abomination (*to'ebah*) for a man to lie with another man as with a woman. To be clear, it is not the person who is an abomination, but the act.

2. Is the Bible Really Silent About Long-Term, Committed, Monogamous Same-Sex Relationships?

Revisionists make a fair point that Scripture doesn't *specifically* talk about long-term, loving, same-sex couples. But where things get wonky is when they try to use this logic to argue that same-sex relationships then have God's approval. This is called an argument from silence. If we're going to take that route, then we can just as easily point out that there were plenty of opportunities for God to include loving, monogamous, committed, same-sex relationships in His plan for sex, but He didn't. The argument from silence goes both ways. It's a slippery slope to try and determine what God *might* have meant *had He said something*. All we have is what God said.

What we do know is that everywhere that homosexual sex is mentioned in Scripture, it is condemned. We cannot, in good conscience, assume that there must still exist another unscathed subset of homosexual practice, unmentioned in Scripture, that is morally sanctioned by God. The revisionist is reading into Scripture (eisegesis) rather than just reading Scripture. It has often been pointed out that there isn't a direct word that means "homosexuality" in the Greek. All the other examples of abusive homosexuality that the revisionists cite—the pederasty (sex with boys), the master-slave sex—all had terms that Paul could have used. From what we can tell, Paul created a new Greek word in 1 Corinthians 6:9 and 1 Timothy 1:9-10 (*arsenokoitai*) which translates as "man-bedder." It is a combination of the words used in Leviticus 18:22 and 20:13, both of which read "Do not sleep with a man (*arsenos*) as one beds (*koiten*) a woman."

3. Are Christians Inconsistent with Old Testament Laws?

We can definitely see why someone would make the argument that Christians cherry-pick Old Testament passages to follow. On the one hand, Paul says in Romans that Jesus is the *telos,* the *fulfillment,* the *completion,* the *end-goal* of the law (Romans 10:4). There are things from the Old Testament law that we as New Testament Christians are not required to follow. On the other hand, Jesus Himself also says that not one stroke of the law will disappear until everything is accomplished (Matthew 5:18). So which parts of the law were finished with Jesus and which parts weren't?

To answer this question, we need to search the New Testament for a few things:

1. Are there any parts of the law that are now *redundant* in light of Christ's final atoning sacrifice on the cross?

2. Are there any parts of the law that are specifically *retracted*?

3. Are there any parts of the law that are specifically *reiterated*?

The Jewish law is customarily divided into three types of law: moral, ceremonial, and judicial. The Hebrew has separate words for these, but the Greek is less clear. Since Jesus is the final atoning lamb of God, then all the actual sacrificial laws (along with the ceremonies attached to them) are considered null and void, having been accomplished by Jesus on the cross.

As to the second criteria, retracted laws, Peter's vision in Acts 10 nullifies the *dietary* laws of the Old Testament (so there goes the shellfish). In Acts 15:19-20, the Jerusalem council reduced their commands to Gentile believers to just a few requirements, including abstaining from sexual immorality. We also see Paul chastising the Galatians for thinking that anything exterior—like circumcision—would contribute to their salvation. One could reasonably assume that the other external signs, like fabrics, etc., would fall into this category, but we can't say that with absolute certainty. *What we do know is that at no point in the New Testament did any apostle reiterate the laws regarding clothing.*

Finally, as to which laws are reiterated, the New Testament broadly reinforces all ten commandments. Jesus reaffirms the Jewish Shema—loving God and loving neighbor—as the two greatest commandments. In many of the epistles, believers are commanded to abide by the fruits of the Spirit and to reject the deeds of the flesh—which are spelled out in

Galatians 5:19-23. Furthermore, what sin regularly tops the list whenever there is a long string of prohibitions? Sexual immorality.

4. Does the Call to Sexual Faithfulness Apply to Everyone?

This is a nonnegotiable for a follower of Christ. As we saw in chapter 1, it is how Christians have always been set apart from culture. And as much as we would love to be the ones to define what counts as moral and immoral, we do not have that authority. God alone, the creator of sex, is the One who defines how His good gift is to be used—between husband and wife in marriage.

5. Is a Person's Sexuality Their Whole Identity?

Our ethnicity, our denomination, our life experiences, and, yes, our sexuality are part of our identity. Christ says that He has reserved for Himself people from every tongue, tribe, and nation. But even with all these diverse parts of ourselves, we still have only one primary identity at the foot of the cross—*Christian* (Galatians 3:28). All our other identities fade into the background in the light of the one, unchanging truth that is Christ. Christ is the One who will never change, so our identity is grounded in Him alone.

6. Is Suffering the Same Thing as Bad Fruit?

This is where we need to be Nurturing Bears. As we mentioned before, the research isn't perfect in separating demographics. But studies show that psychological suffering pervades the LGBTQ community, and we can't ignore it. If there is one facet on which all the research is consistent, it is the prevalence of a whole bunch of other issues—depression, anxiety, suicide, body dysmorphia, substance abuse, and more—which plague the homosexual community.[13] And there's one more major issue which journalist Michael Hobbes chronicles in his article "Together Alone: The Epidemic of Gay Loneliness." The homosexual community is lonely, and nothing seems to alleviate the problem—being in the closet, being out of the closet, allowed to marry, wide public acceptance of homosexuality, nothing. The phenomenon persists. As one man in the article states, "For gay people, we've always told ourselves that when the AIDS epidemic was over we'd be fine. Then it was, when we can get married we'll be fine. Now it's, when the bullying stops we'll be fine. We keep waiting for the moment when we feel like we're not different from other people. But the fact is, we are different."[14]

So yes, we can heartily agree that the gay community is suffering. But might I posit that there is bad fruit on all sides when we deviate from Christ's love or Christ's truth?

Fruit, according to Luke 3:8, is repentance. When we see people continuing in a sexual relationship that is outside of God's design, that is bad fruit. When we see people trying to shame individuals into obedience, that too is bad fruit! There is not one side that produces bad fruit. Good fruit comes when we lean into God's love, submit our desires to Him in obedience, and allow Him to transform us. Whether or not the same-sex desires go away, we experience joy and peace and holiness. If you want an idea of what good fruit looks like, read Jackie Hill Perry's *Gay Girl, Good God*, Rosaria Butterfield's *The Secret Thoughts of an Unlikely Convert*, or Christopher Yuan's *Holy Sexuality and the Gospel*.

ARGUE for a Healthier Approach

There are so many ways in which the debate surrounding same-sex marriage and homosexuality has been derailed. There are so many lies flying around that people are slashing the swords of their tongues right and left until we are all left in tatters, unable to even look at one another without bitterness. We don't want the church to be divided over this issue anymore, but there is no unity apart from the unity of Scripture. We can't solve all the problems in the world, but maybe there are a few things we could all be reminded of.

Truth 1: We Submit All Parts of Ourselves to Christ... Including Our Sexuality

So many voices in culture tell people that submitting their sexuality to God's design is "being inauthentic" or "living a lie." Sorry to be the bearer of bad news, but it is much worse than that. Obeying Christ means that we die to ourselves and our desires (Galatians 2:20, Colossians 3:5, Luke 9:23). But in dying to ourselves, Christ brings life (John 12:24)! When a person sees the beauty and goodness of God, they can lay even their sexuality at the cross.

Truth #2: Having Proclivities Is Not the Same as Sinning

...and don't let anyone tell you otherwise. Temptation is not sin. Furthermore, sin did not enter the world when Adam and Eve were tempted; it entered when they disobeyed. That means that a person with same-sex attraction is allowed to have questions, confusion, and yes, even sexual temptation, and not be in sin. It is what he or she does with the questions, confusion and temptations that matters. Friends, we may not always have control over our feelings and sometimes not even our thoughts. But we have control over our choices.

Truth #3: Marriage Is So Much More than Just Sexual Attraction

The erotic part of marriage is wonderful, but it's not what keeps a marriage together. Being able to trust, and be vulnerable, and love, and forgive, and laugh, and fight, and repent—these are what happens in a happy marriage. There are millions of people in marriages who struggle with sexual dysfunction, and every one of them—when they are committed to their spouse—have had to learn other ways of being intimate. *Sex is not the only means of intimacy.* Furthermore, let me encourage you with the story of Ricky Chelette. Ricky was a lifelong homosexual. When he committed himself to the Lord, he committed himself to celibacy. But you know what? He too got married. Did God turn him into a heterosexual? *No.* Ricky openly admits that he is not attracted to women generally. But you know who he was attracted to? *His wife.* Just one woman. And they had a wonderful marriage until the day she died. His story is not the only one. We're not saying that this is God's path for every same-sex-attracted individual. But as followers of Christ *we need to at least leave that option open.*

Truth #4: Our Job as Christians Is to Make Disciples, Not Heterosexuals

Christopher Yuan notes that one of the biggest questions Christians have is what to do if a friend, child, or family member says that they are gay. Should they shun the sinner till they repent into heterosexuals? Institute a house-wide "Don't Ask–Don't Tell" policy? Fully embrace their alternative sexuality? The answer is: none of the above. None of those approaches are biblical. And they all lead to further brokenness.

Our relationship with our loved ones doesn't change per se, as Yuan points out; it's our ministry that shifts. We shift into being a faithful and loving witness of Christ to the other person. We don't have to bring up how homosexuality is wrong in every conversation. Trust us, people struggling with same-sex attraction usually know the Christian stance. What they need is to see Jesus in our actions, hear truth like the woman at the well, and find compassion for their struggles like the rich young ruler. It is the Holy Spirit who brings about change, not our hurling Bibles like dodgeballs at the wounded. We love like Jesus by eating with and ministering to others, not by shutting out or endorsing what they do.

REINFORCE with Discussion, Discipleship, and Prayer

1. If you're married, make "This is why I married you!" a regular household phrase between you and your spouse. Many of our kids are under the impression that sex and compatible personalities are the main reasons for marriage. Let them see your friendship, your banter, your laughter, your prayer, your service, your forgiveness. Whenever you are appreciating aspects of your spouse, remind them (in front of your children), "See? This is why I married you."

2. Remind your children that part of loving like Jesus is to find those who are on the outskirts and invite them into fellowship. Encourage them to look for kids in their classes who might not fit in or are lonely, and invite them over for playtime together. Emphasize how this is what it means to love others like Jesus did.

3. Talk to your children about identity. What makes them who they are? Which parts of them are unchanging? (Their ethnicity, their gender, their relation as your son or daughter, their status as children of God.) Which parts of them might change? (Their likes or dislikes, food, activities, clothing styles, and hobbies.) Remind them that a true identity is something that doesn't change, but it's okay to express their identities in many different ways. Teach them that there are many ways to express themselves while not confusing these expressions as part of their unchangeable identity.

PAWS for Prayer by Julie Loos

PRAISE God for Who He Is

O God! Jehovah Rapha, You are the Lord who heals. And we all need Your healing. We run to You, our refuge from hurt, our shield from deception, our fortress for protection, our dwelling place away from the sexual firestorm that bombards us. You heal the wounded and forgive the wounder.

ADMIT Where We Have Fallen Short of His Standard

First, Lord, we, Your church, ask forgiveness for the times we have inflicted pain on the LGBTQ community. Forgive us when we have rejected them, called them unredeemable, labeled them unpardonable, treated them as untouchable. We realize we have not always comprehended the depths of the hurt of sexual trauma which could push people away from Your design for their affections. At the same time, forgive us when we have reinterpreted Scripture through the lens of our own pain over the sexuality of a loved one. When our knees have buckled under the weight of "the right thing to do in hard situations," and we have not stood tall for Your truth, forgive us, Lord.

WORSHIP WITH THANKSGIVING for the Things He Has Done

Thank You that You hear our cries. When we abide in You, we can confidently draw near to Your throne of grace and receive mercy and find grace in time of need (Hebrews 4:16). When that need is for transformation—You give us power. For fleeing temptation—You give us self-control. For standing firm—You give us faithfulness. When we surrender to You, we become attached to the true vine. As Your branches, our identity is grafted in Christ alone.

SUBMIT Yourselves and Your Requests to God

Help us see this one, true fact. We are all born *this* way: sinners. And we are all offered the same rescue plan: by faith alone in Christ alone with our sin atoned. Give us eyes to see those who struggle. Help us clearly and lovingly show that one is so much more than one's sexual identity, and that to deny that is to sell oneself way short of God's glorious purpose for them. Let us teach our children to be faithful disciples submitting all their desires to You. In this world of so much confusion and so many evil darts targeting our children, we pray as You prayed for Peter: "I have prayed for you [child's name], that your faith may not fail. And when you have turned back, strengthen your brothers" (Luke 22:32).

Discussion Questions

1. **Icebreaker:** Do you have any friends or family who are gay? What was it like when they came out? How did other people react? How did you react?

2. **Main theme:** *Same-sex-attracted individuals are people to be loved, but that doesn't mean we affirm the lie that God approves of sexuality outside of a husband and wife relationship.* Read through Romans 1:18-32. Based on this passage, why do you think Scripture places such an emphasis on the sexuality of Christians?

3. **Self-evaluation:** Have you ever found yourself treating homosexuality like a worse sin than other sexual sins? Have you ever been tempted to compromise what God says about same-sex activity out of a desire to love someone? What is a proper balance?

4. **Brainstorm:** We are called to love like Christ loved without affirming lies. Brainstorm ways that you can include and love the same-sex-attracted people in your life without compromising on truth. If you don't have any in your life, get a plan in place so the news doesn't throw you for a loop. Distinguish between activities that affirm a lie versus ones that affirm a person. (Fun fact: my friend in California tried to "love" his gay friends by going to a gay bar with them. I loved his heart but counseled him that maybe that wasn't the best approach.)

5. **Release the bear:** Read the article "Overhauling Straight America," available online. Read it with your kids, as appropriate for their ages. The article should not change the way your children interact with their same-sex attracted peers, but it should open their eyes to what is going on in the media so that they don't blindly absorb its messages.

Chapter 11

Gender Identity

When Birds Identify as Bees

Hillary

The topic of gender identity may seem like an unnecessary tangent to some. You might be thinking, "If you have a penis you are a boy, vagina if you're a girl. Where's the confusion?" But I can assure you that there *is* confusion right now, and we can't afford to ignore it if we have kids. (If you'd like to see a more recent example, Google the story "Save James" about a boy in North Texas whose mother is fighting the courts to change his gender against his father's wishes. It's a tragic example of these ideologies at play.)

Do you remember when you were a kid and trying to figure out who you were? I do, and I remember observing the process in the high school girls under my leadership. I remember one girl in particular who reinvented herself every year. That's to be expected from teenagers. They keep trying on different identities and saying, "Does this feel like me? How about this one?"

Even I, in my twenties, found myself slightly different whenever I moved. As an extrovert, I have a tendency to take on others' expectations of me. It wasn't until my thirties that I had a really firm grasp on who I was apart from other people's perceptions. We cannot forget the tumultuous process that occurs as children grow into adults. Figuring out *who you are* is one of the most primary tasks of growing up, and it's not always an easy process.

In case you've forgotten, going through puberty is *hard*. If we look back at those days with rose-colored glasses, we forget the hormone-infused misery that defines adolescence. Brains are changing; bodies are changing.

The political push to separate biological sex from gender makes an already tumultuous time that much more chaotic. How in the world can we expect to help our kids to grow into men and women of God if they aren't even sure what it means to be a man or a woman? And what happened to make us question this aspect of our identity? It used to be a no-brainer. It was this *one beautiful thing* that we didn't have to "figure out." It never even occurred to most of us.

Let's Get Simple Before We Get Complicated

Before we dive in too deep, let's take this back to something that any kid can understand: let's start with the word "gender." The root word of gender is *gen*—which means "that which produces." (Think about it—genetics, genes, genealogy, genitals.[1]) Our gender is the means by which we, as humans, produce new life. We can contribute in two ways: a sperm or an egg. Them's the options. No spectrum. No rainbow. And our *gen*der is determined by our *gen*itals. No matter how someone feels, no matter their hobbies, if their theoretical contribution to a baby would be sperm, then their gender is male. If it's an egg, then female. No soul-searching required.

Now, are there some people who don't produce sperm or eggs? Yes. Which we'll talk about later. So that's the simple explanation first.

A Brief (and More Complicated) History of Gender Theory

A bunch of other differences have historically been associated with people who produce sperm (men) and people who produce eggs (women). What people have disagreed on is to the extent of the differences and how those differences came to be. Exactly *how* different are men and women? Did those differences always exist, or were they imposed over time?

Women are generally smaller, weaker, and more fragile than men. So they're basically children, right? Not funny—because that's how women used to be treated. In eighteenth-century Western society, men used innate gender differences as a justification to treat women as if they were second-class citizens. Women were regularly denied access to university education, were not allowed into mainstream professions, and lost all rights to their personal property upon marriage. When it came to men "disciplining" their wives, the law protected women from murder, but not much else.

Regarding the first "feminist" convention in 1848, Charles Murray states, "Women were rebelling not against mere inequality, but near total legal subservience to men."[2] Irish playwright George Bernard Shaw summarized the problem when it came to traditional gender roles within the home. "If we have come to think that the nursery and the kitchen are the natural sphere of a woman, we have done so exactly as English children come to think that a cage is the natural sphere of a parrot—because they have never seen one anywhere else."[3]

People naturally love to exaggerate differences, so *general* role differences (women being more nurturing, men being more pioneering) were treated like absolute role differences. By absolute differences, I mean that instead of saying that men and women tend to gravitate toward certain roles, people started acting like women were incapable of doing things that were traditionally masculine, and that men were exempt from doing things that were traditionally feminine. This dehumanized women and treated them as if they were merely breeding machines whose entire worth and utility was in the bearing and raising of children—as if they didn't have minds of their own. Yes, motherhood is a large part of what it means to be a woman, but it's not the whole part.

Second-wave feminism fought against this rigid stereotype, but in doing so, erred on the opposite extreme by denying *any* inborn differences between the sexes. Enter activists like anthropologist Gayle Rubin, who claimed that "gender is a socially imposed division of the sexes."[4] It's like women got so tired of all the baggage that came along with being called "woman" that they just threw it all down and demanded to start from scratch. Gender is just a construct! And if it can be constructed, then we can *deconstruct* it!

This way of thinking paved the way for intellectuals like Judith Butler, who taught that "gender ought not to be construed as a stable identity… rather, gender is an identity tenuously constituted in time, instituted in an exterior space through a *stylized repetition of acts*."[5] In other words, gender is about what you *do*, not who you *are*. Swirl in a little queer theory that we talked about in chapter 6, and here we are today, with everybody trying to figure out which pronouns to use.

We as a society loaded so many ad hoc expectations onto the words *man* and *woman* that people done lost their minds and buckled under the pressure. Universities had to advertise trigger warnings just to talk about it. And then they created an entirely new academic discipline to try to figure out what went wrong—Gender Studies. It's been spiraling out of control since.

And in case you think this is off in some ivory tower somewhere, it's not. In January 2021, Nancy Pelosi and House Rules Committee Chair James McGovern submitted the new rules for Congress that would promote "inclusion and diversity." One such rule called for Congress to "honor all gender identities by changing pronouns and familial relationships in the House rules to be gender neutral."[6] They literally banned any use of familial words that would identify the person's gender. No more husbands or wives or mothers or fathers. Triggered!! There are only spouses and parents now…and a list of about 30 other gender-neutral ways to reference family. I am not kidding when I say to get ready for phrases like "person who menstruates" instead of *woman*.

A Crash Course in Gender Terminology

Here's a little crash course on the some of the new terminology you've likely heard (or will soon), and a few words you *thought* you knew, but which have been redefined.

1. Gender

This word used to be synonymous with biological sex. That is not the case anymore. You'll remember back from the Genderbread Person chapter that gender is now this amorphous, undefinable, change-at-the-drop-of-a-hat term referring to how closely someone's self-perception and behavior aligns with gender stereotypes. (That's not complicated at all…) To keep it simple, we'll say that gender is the sex by which a person psychologically *self-identifies*.

2. Gender Dysphoria

This is a new phrase in the most recent Diagnostic and Statistical Manual of Mental Disorders (DSM-5). The condition was originally referred to as Gender Identity Disorder (GID) but was renamed in 2013 to decrease the stigma associated with having a disorder. Both phrases refer to a person who feels uncomfortable or mismatched with their biological sex. When the DSM treated it as an as a mental disorder (i.e., the person's mental state not lining up with biological reality), then therapy consisted of helping the individual to accept the reality of their biological body. And as we'll discuss later in the chapter, 60 to 90 percent of the time, the dysphoria disappeared after the child reached adulthood.[7]

This treatment had a mind-over-matter mentality. Treatment of gender dysphoria today is often the opposite and consists of affirming the person's self-perceived gender while prescribing social, hormonal, and surgical interventions to change the body rather than counseling, which focuses on the mind.

3. Cis and Transgender

Coming from a background in chemistry, these terms make more sense to me. They are used to describe whether or not an organic molecule (molecule with carbon) has chemical attachments which are on the *same side* (cis) or on the *opposite side* (trans) from each other. Knowing this basic definition will help you understand the terminology:

- Cisgender male/female—To be cisgender means that you are a biological male or female whose gender identity matches (i.e., is on the same side) as your biological sex. Most people are cisgender. Some people remember this by turning *cis* into an acronym—comfortable in skin.

- Transgender female—A transgender female is a *biological male* who self-identifies as a female. This person is also denoted by the abbreviation MtF, which stands for "male to female" transition.

- Transgender male—A transgender male is a *biological female* who self-identifies as a male. Their acronym is FtM which stands for "female to male" transition.

4. Binary

A binary is anything that has only two options. Binary computer language is a series of 0's and 1's. There is no ½ in binary code. Similarly, biological sex is a binary. We have male and female gametes (sperm and eggs). Queer theory rejects that gender is binary and insists that it exists on a spectrum, and thus language should reflect that spectrum.

5. Intersex

Intersex is when a person is born with a genetic, hormonal, and sometimes genital variation from the traditional understanding of chromosomal sex (XX = girl, XY = boy). Intersex is *not the same thing as transgender*, and people who are intersex generally affirm binary gender rather than attempting to forge a non-binary norm.

These are the main terms you'll hear, along with the panoply of "genders" like "non-binary" (meaning not identifying as male or female), "gender fluid" (sometimes identifying as male and sometimes female), "agender" (basically not identifying with either), and dozens of others. (A link to a complete list is in this chapter's notes.[8]) And just a heads-up, all this terminology gets even more complicated when combined with a person's sexual orientation, since sexual orientation depends on which gender you are sexually attracted to. If you can't define the genders, how do we then define an individual's sexual orientation *toward* one gender or another? We can't.

What Does the Science Show?

This could be a really short section or a really long section. We'll keep it short. When it comes to fetal development, the genitals usually form during the first trimester, while the brain continues to develop throughout the whole pregnancy. Since the genitals and brain develop at different times and the mother's hormones can change during pregnancy, some have theorized that a person could have a "male" body with a "female" brain (or vice versa). So what does the science show?

In short, it's inconclusive.[9] By inconclusive, I mean a gazillion studies were published, and some of them showed brain similarities between transgender people and the sex of their gender identity, but sometimes they still best matched their birth gender. If your kids come home saying that "science affirms transgender brains," show them the bibliographies of the two sources mentioned in note 9. I've gone through many of them myself, and the science is indeed inconclusive.

Genes and Hormones

We're going to keep this simple as well. We do not have room for all the details, but these are the most pertinent things you need to know when it comes to biological sex: the SRY gene and the role of testosterone.

SRY Gene

The SRY gene is basically what gives a boy his boy-parts. The "undifferentiated gonadal tissue" in a developing embryo that will become *one* of two types of tissue—tissue that produces sperm or tissue that produces eggs. If the SRY gene is present, the embryo produces a protein (testes-determining factor) which turns the tissue into testes. If there's no SRY gene, that tissue will turn into ovaries. The testes and ovaries later determine which sex-specific hormones will be produced by the baby (testosterone or estrogen) for further sexual development, both in utero and in adolescence.

The SRY gene is usually located on the Y chromosome. This is why, for most people, XY = male and XX = female. But as we discussed in chapter 2, when sin came into the world, things got messed up. So, sometimes people are born intersex, which means that their genitals aren't always as clearly defined. Sometimes, it's because the SRY gene jumped ship and attached itself to another chromosome. In this case, a person could have XX chromosomes but physically develop into a boy—because the SRY gene is still present and producing the testes-determining factor (this is called XX male syndrome). In other cases, the SRY gene is damaged or the baby's androgen sensors are blocked (meaning that even though their SRY gene produces testes-determining factor, their body can't respond to it). The body acts like there's no SRY gene and develops as a girl, even though she's got XY chromosomes and an SRY gene.[10] There are dozens of such conditions, accounting for 1.7 percent of the population—which may not sound like a lot, but that's at least statistically one or two intersex people in any church congregation with more than a hundred members.[11]

It is important to distinguish between intersex and transgenderism. Intersexuality is all about sex organs and chromosomes. It is an objective trait about which a person has zero control. Transgenderism is all about how a person *perceives* him or herself. If there was anyone on this earth who had the right to say that there might be more than just two genders, it's people who are born intersex but—if you might remember from the Genderbread Person chapter—the Intersex Society of North America does not think this is helpful.

Testosterone

The second thing you need to know is the role of testosterone. Testosterone plays a large continuing role in forming the rest of the boy-parts. Prenatally, the amount of testosterone a boy experiences can affect the amount of testosterone his body produces during puberty and beyond.[12]

But testosterone doesn't just affect the giblets. I cannot point to any studies involving humans as such studies are unethical. But in studies involving rats, monkeys, and other mammals, changing prenatal levels of testosterone affected "gendered behavior"—meaning animal behavior that is typically associated with one of the two genders. High levels of testosterone have been shown to increase aggressive play (considered masculine behavior) and lack of testosterone has been linked to feminized behaviors among rats.[13] *This was true whether or not the unborn rat was male or female.* What does that mean? Based on prenatal testosterone levels, you could have feisty female rats or calm and gentle male rats. Nothing wrong with either of them; they both sound like fun.

The same has been observed in humans, with levels of prenatal testosterone playing a role in play type and toy selection.[14] If you're like me and loved roughhousing as a kid and didn't care much for dolls, maybe good ol' mom had some heightened testosterone while you were a bun in her oven. And you know what? *There is nothing wrong with that, and it doesn't make you less of a girl.* Conversely, if you were a boy and your uterine environment had low levels of testosterone, you might enjoy playing quietly and *not* imagining yourself as a Tyrannosaurus rex, attacking every person in sight. And you know what? *There is nothing wrong with that either, and it doesn't make you any less of a boy.*

When it comes to gender, we want our kids to know that, while there are *general* sex differences, they can bring their own version of masculinity and femininity into *whatever interests them.* And if they encounter kids in their classes who are confused about their gender, *don't ridicule them,* and stand up to anyone who does.

What Does the Bible Say About Transgenderism?

This one is quick to answer: the only real, hard-and-fast rule I can find when it comes to gender identity is in regards to people who are trying to look like the other gender. Deuteronomy 22:5 says, "A woman must not wear men's clothes, nor a man wear woman's clothing." The Bible says nothing about particular interests or having to act any way, except in holiness. There is, frankly, a *lot* of biblical freedom when it comes to gender expression—as long as the person isn't trying to make people believe something that isn't true—namely that they're a boy when they're not, or a girl when they're not. So basically, just respect what the Designer gave you, and then be who He created you to be!

ROAR Like a Mother!

RECOGNIZE the Message

Now that we have a general understanding of gender, let's ROAR through the messages present in gender theory and transgenderism.

1. Biological Sex and Gender Describe Two Different Things

According to current mainstream scientific literature, "sex refers to the biological and physiological properties of a person, whereas the term gender refers to one's psychological identification as male or female."[15] Your kids (from pre-K on up) will be learning these new definitions.

2. Biological Sex Is Only Relevant to Your Identity if You Want It to Be

Nobody quibbles about whether or not biological sex exists. The going narrative is rather that biological sex *doesn't matter* (or doesn't have to) in telling a person anything meaningful about their identity. It's just a label someone slapped on them at birth.

3. Sex Is Assigned

Rather than sex being discovered by looking at the child, activists are now pushing for the language "sex *assigned* at birth." (If you see AMAB or AFAB, those stand for "assigned male at birth" and "assigned female at birth.) This is nonsense according to the average person. You assign a parking space. You don't assign a gender. My husband wasn't assigned sperm, and I wasn't assigned eggs. The very use of this word "assigned" is intended to convey that biological sex and gender are subjective perceptions rather than objective facts. After all, if you can assign something, you can *reassign* it—change it at will. Which is, consequently, the exact message being taught to our kids.

4. Why Are You So Obsessed with What's Between My Legs?

I've heard several variations on this statement by people in documentaries who are clearly proud of their androgynous appearance. In their mind, if anyone attempts to determine their sex or gender, it's because that person is obsessed with genitals, as if all the relevant and meaningful information that go along with gender is illusory. This statement is a strawman fallacy, intending to make anyone who questions the gender theory dogma sound like a total pervert.

5. I Want to Be My Authentic Self

You'll hear the words "authentic self" a lot within the transgender movement. The idea behind this is that it is constraining and oppressive to equate gender with biological sex. Doing so "forces" people into an unnatural box and prevents them from just being who they are. I personally think that they have this logic exactly backwards, and I'll explain why in the OFFER Discernment section.

6. The Male-Female Binary Is Oppressive

Since male and female have now been redefined in psychological terms, people can argue that gender is on a spectrum. Forcing a person to choose between the two identities is, to gender theorists, a false dichotomy that does not take into account the full range of gender experiences. As discussed in chapter 6, this kind of binary language "marginalizes" those who don't fit the gender stereotypes. (And marginalizing someone is the same as oppression, and oppression is injustice.)

OFFER Discernment

As with all discussions, we must look at what real points the gender theorists and transgender community offer and stand with them in truth. First off, I think that we as a church must acknowledge the way we have treated the transgender community. If you've never met a single trans person in your church body, ask yourself why. Well, part of the reason is that they are such a small group, statistically speaking, accounting for between 0.005 and 0.014 percent of boys and 0.002 and 0.003 percent for girls.[16] (So, a few out of every 100,000 people.) But we should still ask ourselves whether there are any other reasons a transgender person might not feel comfortable darkening the door of our church. Have we loved like Christ loved? In many cases, I would say no. It is easy to demonize that which we don't understand, and most of us don't understand how someone could think that they could change genders.

In regards to suicide, the numbers don't lie.[17] There *is* a much greater statistical probability for suicide attempts within the transgender population, even after transitioning.[18] However, the prevalence of co-occurring anxiety and depression is *also* very high.[19] As we discussed in chapter 8, this might have more to do with a rejection of the body rather than the feelings of rejection by society. What we do know is that this population is hurting a lot more than the average population. As Christians, this should concern us.

Like the Viet Cong analogy we discussed in chapter 4, dangerous ideologies have attached themselves to the most vulnerable among us. While we can't affirm the ideology, we can't reject the person either. It is difficult to address a person's ideology while they feel unsafe and unloved. Our love, however, *must be grounded in truth and guided by the Holy Spirit.*

Some studies do show trans individuals doing better (psychologically) after transition—but in most of these studies, subjects were only followed for one to five years post-operation.[20] In a long-term study in Sweden, transitioners were followed for up to 30 years, and right around the 10-year mark, all hell breaks loose in terms of increased deaths—often death by suicide (27 times higher than the control group!). If nothing else, this should at least give us pause to consider that *just maybe* sex reassignment surgery has a honeymoon phase and is a temporary fix for a more persistent underlying issue.

Finally, another legitimate point offered by gender theorists is their rejection of artificial and confining gender stereotypes. I am so glad I wasn't born in the Victorian era. I am way too opinionated, way too talkative, and cooking is my own personal phobia. (I'm working on it, Mom!)

I'm also grateful to live in a time and place where I, as a woman, was allowed to get my master's in biology, and my worth in society isn't contingent on being able to bear or raise children. As discussed in chapter 7, I never really fit into the girly-girl category. Once I realized that I didn't *have* to fit into a preconceived mold, it was like the whole world opened up. I even began to revel in my femininity; I just had to come to terms that I didn't express it the same as other girls, and that's okay.

So, while we can stand arm in arm with the truths the transgender community has brought to our attention, we must still recognize that there are lies that have snuck into the message.

Lie #1: Gender Is on a Spectrum

While gender *expression* may exist on a spectrum, gender itself does not. A person may have more traditionally masculine or feminine interests or mannerisms, but that doesn't change the fact that the men produce sperm and women produce eggs. You can be a burly, biker sperm producer and still cry over a good rom-com. You can be a sexy, feminine egg producer who loves working on old cars. There are men who excel at hairdressing and makeup artistry, and women who enjoy construction, mixed martial arts, and spitting contests. Our ability to *fit in* with others of our gender does not determine our gender!

Lie #2: It Is Possible to Change One's Sex

It *is* possible to change your genitals. (Sorta?) But this does not and never will change your sex because you can't change your DNA. There are not enough surgeries or hormone shots in the world that will erase biological sex. In fact, emergency doctor Dr. Alyson McGregor has an entire lecture on the differences between males and females when administering medical aid.[21] Why? *Because men and women are biologically different on a cellular level.* Biological sex is not just about what's going on down under;

it is stamped into every cell in our bodies. Furthermore, if gender is *not* rooted in biology (as activists claim), then there's no need to *change one's biology* in the first place.

> If gender is not rooted in biology, then there's no need to change one's biology in the first place.

Lie #3: Sex Reassignment Surgery Is Freeing

Ironically, the group that rages the most against gender stereotypes is also the group that rigidly reinforces the same gender stereotypes they claim to abhor. As soon as you see a person transition, they start adopting all the same clothes and mannerisms of the opposite gender—*they are reinforcing the binary*!

And here is where I promised to argue against the idea that transitioning allows someone to more fully be their "authentic self." Since transitioning often means that the person adopts the opposite stereotype from how they were born, then they are forced to now play by those rules. Maintaining their new gender identity pressures them away from expressing any of their inborn traits—even if some of those traits are trying to peek out. Isn't that *more* constraining?

I know there will be plenty of people who disagree with these statements or accuse me of not understanding. But from what I understand of freedom, true freedom seems like living in the body that you were born with, free to pursue the interests that you have, free from surgeries, free from lifelong hormonal treatments, and free from having to live in a societally determined stereotype. That freedom is already granted to us from birth, *prior to transition*. Why would I advocate for someone I love to give up those freedoms? I can't.

Lie #4: If You Feel Uncomfortable in Your Body, You Are Probably Transgender

While gender dysphoria has traditionally plagued boys (and usually the signs are present in early childhood), researcher Abigail Shrier has written extensively about a new phenomenon called "rapid onset gender dysphoria" where girls suddenly (and without warning) declare that they have always felt like a boy—despite the lack of any evidence from childhood. This is *drastically* different from the kids—usually boys—who start out at age three with clear and observable and persistent gender dysphoria. According to Shrier, these girls "flee womanhood like a house on fire, their minds fixed on escape, not on any particular destination."[22]

Transgender advocates are openly saying that if you don't fit in, if you feel like a misfit, if you don't love makeup as a girl or football as a boy, then you are transgender. And if you're wondering *if* you're transgender, then you probably *are* transgender.[23] And our kids are swallowing these lies in droves!

I mean, kudos to you if you *always* felt comfortable in your developing adolescent body or *always* felt like you fit in in high school. The glorious and horrifying reality of adolescence is that most everyone felt awkward or like they didn't belong in some way. Even the people who were the "popular kids" have told me stories of how they felt like nobody really knew the "real" them. If not fitting in means you're probably trans, then we're all trans—which means these feelings are not a reliable indicator of gender or reality. Our kids need to hear this from us! They need to hear about our horror stories, not just the glory days.

ARGUE for a Healthier Approach

There is so much confusion in our world regarding what it means to be a man or a woman. How does the Bible address these concerns best?

1. Your Interests Don't Affect Your Gender

Most of the lies within gender and transgender theory are predicated on fixed masculine and feminine roles. *These are not how God describes men and women.* As we saw in chapter 7, biblical stories represent a whole range of masculinity and femininity. Furthermore, when it comes to the distribution of spiritual gifts, nowhere does Scripture say that there are male gifts and female gifts. The Spirit gives generously to *all* (1 Corinthians 2:7-11; Romans 12:6-8). As we saw in chapter 7, we need to especially be affirming this for our boys because we live in a society that seems to allow a lot more freedom of expression for girls than for boys.

2. God Planned Variety in the Way We Think

As we saw in the science section, the genitals form separately from the brain over different times in the pregnancy. Some might say, "See! Proof! A child can develop the wrong sexed brain!" But that is a secular perspective. Let's look at this from a Christian perspective, assuming that God planned every step of the gestation process. God knew that the brain and genitals would develop during different time periods. This tells me that God didn't want to have a one-to-one link between genitals and brains. Thank God for the variety! We'd all be so boring and predictable otherwise.

3. Puberty Is Hard for Everybody

Puberty has always been rough. But today, "rapid onset gender dysphoria" has been tacked on to the concept of adolescnece. Again, I don't say this to nullify the individuals who experience real, true, gender dysphoria—these are two different beasts. Neither do we want to dismiss the *real pain* that these teenagers are facing. They probably aren't lying about feeling miserable. We just have to be smart about not coming to bad conclusions in culture's misguided attempt to alleviate their pain. Our Christian mental health practitioners have never been so needed.

4. It's Not Harmless to Indulge a Kid Who Says They Are the Wrong Gender

Sexologist Deborah Soh points out in her book *The End of Gender* that of the 11 known longitudinal studies of children who experienced gender dysphoria, 60 to 90 percent of the kids desisted in adulthood (meaning that they came to terms with their biological gender). You hear that? That is 60 to 90 percent.[24] Expect to be hearing a different statistic on this in the future, because there are a few things media won't tell you. The first is that *once gender identity is affirmed*, the child will tend to persist into adolescence. And once they persist into adolescence, they will more than likely persist into adulthood—when 60 to 90 percent of it could have been avoided. There is a chain reaction happening here, and it starts with affirming a child's transgender identity prematurely. All our currently known persistence statistics will soon change because we have changed our approach to how we treat children with gender dysphoria. We will turn it into a self-fulfilling prophecy if we're not careful.

Just My Two Cents...

I really believe that God gave us unique personalities because He plans on using us in unique ways. That being said, I will give this one piece of advice: If you have a child who has gender atypical interests, *find out why*. What is it that attracts them to whatever it is? Do you have a boy who feels jealous of his older sister and wants the same treatment? Maybe he's closer to his sister, so that's who he's modeling. Maybe you have a girl who feels horribly excluded by other the girls because, frankly, girls can be mean.

Sometimes, kids don't have the words to express what they are actually feeling, and it comes out as them saying that they are the opposite gender. We can't assume that just because a five-year-old says, "I think I'm a girl," he understands what that means.

In summary, there is a difference between a child being *drawn to* gender atypical activities and one who is *backing away* from gender typical activities. Both root causes can show up as gender atypical behavior but have very different reasons behind them.

Either way, let's remind our kids that it's okay to be interested in the things that interest them. Let's show our boys and girls how they can bring their maleness and femaleness *into* their interests, whatever those interests may be. If they express distress at their gender, remember that they might lack the verbal skills to explain themselves. Yes, it may sometimes be legitimate gender dysphoria, but let's not *assume* that to be the case 100 percent of the time. Don't feel pressured to be "woke" when it comes to your kids.

REINFORCE Through Discussion, Discipleship, and Prayer

Check out the article "Raising Gender Healthy Kids" by Sue Bohlin.[25] She has a lot of great ideas for things to do with your kids that will encourage your boys to be happy they are boys and likewise for the girls. Constantly reinforce that their gender doesn't change with their interests.

1. If your child knows another kid at school who appears to not fit in well with other kids of the same gender, encourage them to befriend them—especially if they are the same gender. Remind them that *this is what it means to be Jesus*. Jesus purposefully befriended the outcasts, not the class favorites.

2. Prepare your kids to accept rejection when necessary. At the end of the day, if a person has decided that your love is only real if you affirm their chosen identity, that's on them. We can't force our love on them. Our kids need to know that we do not change our stance on truth even if a person says it hurts their feelings.

3. Know your child's tendencies and adjust instruction accordingly. If they have grown up in a bubble and are horrified by transgenderism, maybe discuss the pain that comes with gender dysphoria. Pain is pain, no matter the cause. On the flip side, if your child is overly empathetic and their first instinct is to alleviate any distress in another person, then you might need to have a conversation about why it's important to affirm truth even if it causes someone distress. Our goal is to have children who can love the person without sacrificing truth. More than likely they'll instinctively lean toward one extreme. As they get older and are able to understand gray areas, teach them how to embrace both virtues without letting go of the other.

PAWS for Prayer by Julie Loos

PRAISE God for Who He Is

You are Elohim, Mighty Creator. You alone are our source of identity. You assign us purpose. Your creation is good and beautiful. You are not the God of confusion or chaos but of order and design. You are immutable, unchanging, and Your design stands firm. You are the God who counsels and who delivers. We praise You!

ADMIT Where We Have Fallen Short of His Standard

We have exchanged the glory of the immortal God for images resembling mortal man (Romans 1:23) and exchanged the truth of God for a lie (Romans 1:25). We have built "social constructs" and torn down biblical foundations when it comes to identity, denied DNA, raised up the knowledge of intellectuals over the wisdom of God, and believed fabrications and false research. By valuing the subjective over objective truth, we have become the subject of our own worship and participated in the idolatry of gender identity. We have affirmed lies in the name of compassion and bowed to the god of emotional manipulation. Father, forgive us.

WORSHIP WITH THANKSGIVING for the Things He Has Done

We thank You that from the beginning You knit our biology and gender into our genes. We are fearfully and wonderfully made in Your image. Thank You that theology outweighs theories. You, Your Word, and Your purpose are fixed, not fluid. We are grateful that our biology is biblical and binary. As far as it goes, we are thankful for science. For the wonders and ways of masculinity and femininity, we rejoice. We declare, with thanks, that no one can erase what You have written into our genes.

SUBMIT Yourselves and Your Requests to God

Lord, help us navigate this identity crisis. May we be beacons of clarity in the confusion. For those struggling with gender identity, bring their minds and bodies into alignment with the truth of Your Word. Show them the deception of needles and knives, injections and resections. Reorient attractions to holiness and wholeness. Help us see that self-perception is deceiving because the heart is deceptive above all things, and desperately wicked (Jeremiah 17:9). Give us courage to show others that the greatest self-harm is self-deception, and that the most loving thing we can do is expose that deception. Help us teach our kids what is true, pure, lovely, and of moral excellence (Philippians 4:8). To know that they are created in Your own image; they are created male or female (Genesis 1:26-28). And then confirm their God-given identity as truth.

Discussion Questions

1. **Icebreaker:** How well do you fit into your gender stereotype? Are there parts of you that are more like the opposite gender? Did you fit in with the other kids of your gender back when you were in school? How comfortable did you feel as a teenager?

2. **Main theme:** Gender is biologically defined as whether a person's body was designed to produce male gametes (sperm) or female gametes (eggs). It is an objective fact; it is not on a spectrum; and it is not determined by someone's interests or self-identification.

3. **Self-evaluation:** When discussing transgenderism, have you ever been tempted to ridicule? How do you think Jesus would have us treat people who are confused about their gender?

4. **Brainstorm:** List men and women in the Bible whose traits match a gender stereotype. Make a separate list of characters who break stereotypes. How is gender stereotyping not a useful way of determining gender?

5. **Release the bear:** Enjoy your kids this week with whatever it is they like to do. Have them pick any activity they like and do it together. Whatever it is, tell them how much you enjoy seeing them exercise their gifts as a boy or a girl. Talk together about what they picture themselves being like one day as a man or a woman.

Chapter 12

Purity Culture

When Our Best Efforts Went Kablooey

AMY

Not too long ago, my Twitter feed blew up with news articles covering a book launch for Pastor Nadia Bolz-Weber. Normally this sort of thing wouldn't have made the nightly news, but Weber wanted to celebrate her tell-all exposé of the failings of purity culture by commissioning a very unique statue...of a golden vagina.[1] The statue was crafted out of purity rings donated by former adherents to the True Love Waits movement. Bolz-Weber believes the statue was metaphorically crafted by the evangelical church when purity culture launched in the spring of 1993, and thousands of hearts were sacrificed to the golden calf of virginity.

The purity movement had not been an unmitigated success, too often inadvertently sending the message that sexual sin was the one sin God couldn't forgive. As shame-filled testimonies came to light, Christian parents were called to stop the cycle of hurt by abandoning the toxic message of chastity. Instead, Christian sexologists like Dr. Tina Schermer Sellers said that what we should be teaching our children is that, as long as you are committed to your partner, you are modeling God's intent for love regardless of who they are or when you sleep with them—something Sellers calls the "New Covenant Sexual Ethic."[2]

Did you feel your discernment alarm going off just now? Yeah, me too.

That's because Sellers and other liberal Christians are using the abuse of the chastity message to advocate a humanistic view of sexuality. This message has just enough Jesus to make premarital sex sound biblically supported and morally right.

Our kids deserve the truth—that God's plan for sex starts with marriage—but when the truth has been abused and twisted by the people we trust most, it no longer looks attractive…and can seem downright terrifying. We don't abandon truth because of its abuses. We correct the abuses and stand firm in the truth. So let's start by tackling what went wrong in the purity culture a lot of us grew up in. To get off on the right foot, we have to first look at what was being taught and preached to teens.

The Original Message

In 1992, Dr. Richard Ross and Jimmy Hester first sketched out the ministry that would eventually become True Love Waits (TLW).[3] Their goal was to speak over the voice of the sexual revolution and advocate the superiority of the biblical sexual ethic to teens and singles. To be effective, though, this message required more than just a fatherly, "Don't do it." They believed Christians needed to present truth while making the message appealing, practical, and rooted in the redemptive power of Christ. And they couldn't do it alone; they needed parents.

You read that right. No more passing off "the talk" to the middle school health teacher. (Seriously, they suffer enough.) Instead, parents were called to take the lead role as primary sexual educators to their children and were invited to attend training classes. These trainings explained the TLW curriculum and offered written materials to help them have meaningful discussions about sexuality at home. Youth leaders would then reaffirm these "home chats" by teaching that God designed sex to be shared exclusively between a husband and wife.[4]

Now, it didn't take long for teens to get all philosophical about what *actually* counted as sex. So to avoid any confusion, TLW leaders advocated purity instead of just abstinence. This broader emphasis better communicated the biblical standard for holy living while rejecting potential gray areas like pornography, impure touching, lustful thoughts, and inappropriate banter. Teenagers were told that they were not slaves to their raging hormones. They could avoid STDs and unplanned pregnancies and remain "pure" until marriage by relying on Christ, maintaining an active support base, and setting healthy boundaries between themselves and the opposite sex.

These boundaries were most recognizably outlined in Joshua Harris's book *I Kissed Dating Goodbye.*[5] In it, Harris told teens they could avoid the heartache of superficial relationships—those made without any intention of commitment—and the temptation to compromise their moral convictions by giving up the "selfish" pursuit of a boyfriend or girlfriend. This didn't mean that they couldn't hang out with friends in groups—only that intimate dating should be avoided until a couple was ready to head to the altar. In the meantime, teens were encouraged to protect one another's purity as well. Guys were told not to mislead girls into thinking the relationship was more than it was in the hopes of luring her into the bedroom. Girls were encouraged to dress modestly, as a guy's mind easily wandered when revealing clothing left little to the imagination. Both were advised to seek friendship rather than romance first, as it is a person's character, not an emotional state, that withstands the stresses of marriage. If the good-looking hunk of creation they admired didn't want anything serious, teens were encouraged to move on. It wasn't worth the risk of giving a piece of themselves to someone who never intended to stay in the first place.

But what if this message came too late? What about the teens who had already gone too far? Were they beyond redemption? Not at all. Christ's death and resurrection meant that we were no longer slaves to sin. They could find forgiveness and love in Him. But the Jesus who said, "Neither do I condemn you," also said, "Go now and leave your life of sin" (John 8:11). This meant that some teens needed to avoid one-on-one situations, install Internet and TV restrictions, and refrain from certain conversational topics. For others, it meant that their relationship had to end so they wouldn't fall back into impure habits. No book, ministry, or speaker said it would be easy, but all the teachers, pastors, writers, and speakers agreed that pursuing God's design is always the best choice.

Many churches held a form of commitment ceremony to help families and teens unite around God's design. For some this was a simple affair of signing a pledge form at the back of a workbook or buying a purity ring. Other churches pulled out all the stops and had formal pledge ceremonies and purity balls for girls. Pledge ceremonies were typically held before the church and involved the whole family (or at least the parents and the child) committing to protect the purity of the child as they entered the dating sphere. Purity balls, on the other hand, were like a Southern debutante ball, complete with gowns, fancy dinners, the works! (And yes, in some places they still go on today.) Instead of being presented to society as a woman of marrying age, however, girls pledged to be chaste until marriage, and their fathers vowed to cover and pray for them. As one attendee reflected, "Purity balls are a symbol telling people that this is what I'm doing...Making a promise to myself and to God that I will stay pure until I get married."[6]

Balls were often a special time for parents and children to come together in mutual commitment before God, encouraging each other to stand against cultural pressure to have premarital sex. They were fun events that many girls looked forward to. (Who doesn't like an excuse to dress up?)

What Went Wrong

If what you just read sounded totally different from your purity culture experience, you aren't alone. In the original curriculum, truth and grace were fairly balanced. By the time this message reached youth groups, however, things often went sideways.

For starters, the movement itself wasn't perfect. Stories, skits, and metaphors in the leader guides devalued the human body while seemingly idolizing virginity. Students who weren't virgins were compared to chewed-up gum, half-eaten lollipops, juice that someone had already spit in, flowers without petals, and used pieces of tape. There were even group activities to emphasize these points. For instance, a student was handed a rose and encouraged to touch it, smell it, crush it, and pass it along to the next person. After the whole youth group had manhandled the rose, only a few bruised petals were left clinging to the stem. And then the leader would ask, "Who wants the rose now?" (And leaders never gave the right answer...*Jesus.* Jesus wants that rose.)

Kids, too, often felt pressured by pushy parents or friends to make a pledge they weren't ready for or didn't fully understand. They knew they didn't want to let their youth pastor or mom down, so they played the part...until the boyfriend or girlfriend came along, that is.

These activities were supposed to be analogies for what happened during premarital sex, but overly zealous church leaders made virginity their primary focus, neglecting the redemptive work of Christ. Some even ignored the original design of the curriculum by excluding parents, refusing to be transparent about what was being taught, or by integrating their own perverted twists to the lessons.[7]

Then you had the more legalistic parents. These folks were so committed to keeping their kids on the straight and narrow that they barely told them what sex was. After all, you can't desire what you don't know exists, so sex ed was avoided like the plague. (I mean, seriously...what could *possibly* go wrong?) By the time these students reached adulthood, they'd received so many legalistic or false teachings that they found themselves struggling with intimacy in their marriages. They were ashamed of their bodies, or thought that their sexual development and attraction toward others was a threat to their salvation. Talk about unintended consequences!

As a result, women harbored such resentment toward the traditional teaching of chastity that here we are now—with "Christian" teachers now encouraging parents to avoid these "shame-filled messages." And to be fair, some of the messages really were poorly thought through. Let's look together at the most damaging ones that came out of 1990s purity culture and see if we can't clear the air, dispel the myths, and offer a more biblical approach.

ROAR Like a Mother!

RECOGNIZE the Message

As we saw above, the original purity message was biblically accurate, but there was also a lot of damage done under the banner of biblical sexuality. We here at Mama Bear Apologetics have no problem admitting when the church made some missteps, and we're going to look at three big ones that have caused many people to walk away from the church and God's teaching about biblical sexuality for good. Spoiler alert: they're all fixable!

1. Purity Is the New Holiness

When a former classmate shared his experience with purity culture, one of his greatest frustrations was the legalistic teaching that purity was synonymous with holiness. As author Jessica Valenti scathingly remarked, "You can be vapid, stupid, and unethical, but so long as you've never had sex, you're a 'good' girl (i.e., 'moral') and therefore worthy of praise."[8]

Your worth as a person depended on who you *didn't* sleep with. The fragility of this worth was communicated through some powerfully black-and-white examples. One teacher had her class take turns spitting on an Oreo to illustrate a girl's undesirable state after she lost her virginity. Boys stuck tape to different pieces of construction paper to show how useless you become if you get too handsy with too many girlfriends—as useless as unsticky tape. At a TLW rally, a teen leader remarked that Christians who lost their virginity were like rumpled magazines that no one wanted to buy. Countless books referred to those who had slipped as "impure" or "damaged goods."

Once damaged, any spiritual blessings that come with marriage were out of reach. If you went too far, you could kiss your chance at a happy marriage goodbye! Who would want an apple other people had bitten into? And all the married sex that was supposed to be *a-maz-ing* once you walked down the aisle on your wedding day? Nope, that's only for the chaste couples. The best you could hope for was for some other non-faithful person to settle for you—two perfectly matched pieces of chewed up, spit on, crumbled up garbage living in mutual compromise. How romantic.

2. You Give a Piece of Yourself Away to Each Person You Date

In case you haven't read *I Kissed Dating Goodbye*, Harris retells a friend's dream in which she and her husband were joined at the altar by every woman he had ever dated. Even though he had broken up with these women years ago, they remained permanently connected because each possessed a piece of his heart. (Harris was not clear about what causes this piece to be joined to another. It could have meant that he was sexually intimate with these women, or that he fell in love with them emotionally. In his book he implies both.)

Fifteen-year-old Elise made a similar reflection for Oprah's magazine series "The Innocence Project." She said, "I think your life is kind of like a flower, and every time you have a relationship or a boyfriend or something, you're taking a petal of your flower and giving it to that person. So you're giving all these petals away. Pretty soon you're not left with anything to give your husband."[9]

For Harris and Elise, whenever you enter into a romantic relationship outside of marriage, your very self becomes fragmented and a piece is transferred to your partner. If you aren't careful, by the time you find Mr. or Miss Right, you'll have run out of pieces to give.

But since virginity can only be lost once, it doesn't make sense to refer to someone as progressively giving "pieces" away to different people. It's this ambiguity that allows for a variety of interpretations, and Harris later implies that even falling in love with another person has the same effect. This line of thinking raises a host of questions regarding the nature of self. For example: if we gave every bit of ourselves away while simultaneously gathering bits from other people, who or what do we become? How can one's self endure while becoming fragmented? Must it remain whole to exist?

This flawed philosophy sent many people, the majority of them women, into a panic whenever they began dating someone new. *How far is too far? What if I get too close, and he doesn't turn out to be the one? How many pieces do I have left?* No one knew. What they did know was that they couldn't get those pieces back—and worse, a piece of each partner stayed with them too, so any future relationships only added to an ever-compounding orgy.

Is it any wonder that people felt like they were in a legalistic trap? Like I said, it's a mess. Look, dating does not turn people into metaphysical vending machines because—surprise!—God made you in His image, not in the image of a Pez dispenser.

After hearing endless stories of his writings being used as a hammer, Harris denounced his book and stopped further publication. Unfortunately, in 2019, he renounced his faith entirely.

3. Your Body Is His Problem

This lie was exclusively directed toward the girls of the group, and good grief was it a doozie. It wasn't just your actions that could be sinful, it was your *body itself*. In elementary school you were basically a ticking time bomb of temptation. Once puberty entered the scene, you exploded from a Shirley Temple into a Delilah looking for a Samson. A girl's figure suddenly became a threat to the souls of the boys in the youth group as well as to the faith of the girl herself.

This meant that girls were totally on the hook if their brothers in Christ couldn't keep their eyes to themselves. And that womanly figure you had been waiting for your whole preteen life? You had better cover that up, because now that puberty has kicked your development into high gear, the body you were told was fearfully and wonderfully made is starting to make you look like a harlot. As author Linda Kay Klein put it, female bodies were "nothing more than things over which men and boys could trip," shameful stumbling blocks waiting to drag you and the boys who liked you away from God.[10]

Tucked within this body-shaming nightmare was the belief that guys just couldn't help themselves. They're wired to respond visually to girls, after all. If their imaginations started running wild, it wasn't their fault.

That's just how they're made. And there were plenty of matronly women hovering around the church who would happily clutch their pearls while pointing out all the different ways girls were going astray. So you best watch how you dress, or else!

OFFER Discernment

It's no surprise that the purity fallout looks like it was inspired by the book *The Handmaid's Tale*, but that doesn't mean that everything that was taught was unbiblical. There's a good amount of truth that we can point to even in the mess, and no, we're not donning a proverbial white cap and a red dress by doing so.[11] This is just good, old-fashioned discernment in action.

For starters, abstaining from sexual activity before marriage is God's design for biblical sexuality. (See Hebrews 13:4, 1 Corinthians 7:2, and all of the bride's warnings not to awaken love before it pleases in Song of Solomon.) It falls under the spiritual fruits of self-control and faithfulness (Galatians 5:19-24), and thus is a demonstration of holiness. Holiness calls for Christians to be set apart. Chastity—avoiding sexual activity before marriage—is an *aspect* of holiness, but it's not the whole measure of it, as many students were led to believe.

This important distinction was missing from much of the purity movement. TLW material was very clear that we are made clean through Christ. The problem was that kids who had already fallen were less likely to believe that message because of how virginity was often idolized. As one holier-than-thou teen put it, "I can be a non-virgin whenever I want, but they can never be like me."[12] Prideful much?

Since you can only be a physical virgin once, this meant there was no unringing that bell once it had been rung. Many students mistakenly thought that their physical virginity was essential for salvation, making throngs of kids think there was no hope once they had gone too far.

Secondly, actively sinning *does* hinder your walk with God (Proverbs 15:8, 28:9; 1 John 3:9-10). And it's also true that having multiple sexual partners before marriage *can* cause emotional, physical, and spiritual harm.

Studies have shown that marital happiness is higher between couples who have no previous sexual partners as opposed to those who do.[13] Promiscuity also brings an increased risk of STDs, which can result in infertility and transmission to the future spouse. Some couples struggle with guilt from having past partners. Others felt *compared* to their spouse's past lovers—whether they were or not. All of this could have been avoided if each partner had chosen chastity.

Lastly, as much as our world loves to deny it, what we wear does convey a message. This is true of every culture and time. It's why you don't wear sweatpants to a job interview or on a first date. It's why so many professions have uniforms. *What we wear communicates something about us.*

There's a reason Paul encourages women to dress themselves in good deeds rather than pearls and braids. To say that our clothes don't communicate a message just doesn't make sense. For now, though, let's check out the most common lies within purity culture.

Lie #1: No One Will Want You if You Aren't a Virgin

Remember all those awful examples we read about? These illustrations tried to show the seriousness of losing one's virginity outside of marriage, but they ended up reducing the value of the individual to the state of their purity, leaving many feeling hopeless, dirty, and irredeemable.

This also caused immense confusion about sex. Some had the idea that sex was so wrong and dirty that marital intimacy was difficult or unappealing. Many women saw sex as more of a duty than a God-given pleasure, which caused tension within their marriages.

These illustrations were particularly damaging to children and teens who were survivors of sexual assault. Much of the TLW campaign completely failed to account for the spiritual and emotional needs of these young people. Even if their loss of innocence was through no fault of their own, they were still left with the impression that they had lost their purity, were offensive to God, and had no chance at a fulfilling marriage and sex life.

Metaphors and similes are an invaluable tool when you're telling a story, but they are painfully inadequate when you compare the complex human person to a single-purpose inanimate object. What kids need to hear is that they are not an object. Their value isn't found in their virginity, but grounded in a Savior who can make all things new.

Lie #2: Following This Formula Will Guarantee a Great Marriage and Sex Life

Oh yes, this was totally a selling point within purity culture. If you saved yourself for marriage, the sex was going to be better than anything you can imagine! Your marriage was going to be great! You and your spouse were going to be happier than those smiling families in the car commercials! Purity was *the* formula for marital and bedroom success.

Those teens grew up and got married. And far from mind blowing, their wedding nights were awkward and painful. For some, intimacy felt anything but intimate with ten years of "sex is evil" messages ingrained in their heads. Some grew up in fundamentalist households and turned to pornography because they didn't even know what they were supposed to do! When purity failed to deliver on the promise of easy intimacy and perfect spouses, many couples felt lied to and ended up walking away from the church forever.

Using future sex to bribe teens not to have sex should never have happened. Great intimacy has to be nurtured, sometimes through Christian counseling, and it sure as heck has some awkward, fumbling, "I got a leg cramp" moments that never made their way into the highlights reel of the purity scene. God never promised mind-blowing bedroom skills for the chaste. He does promise that sex is good, pleasurable, and able to satisfy and sustain a husband and wife. It's not a person's virginity that nurtures a successful marriage, but the mutual and continued practice of the biblical fruits of love that enable a relationship to weather the storms of life.

Lie #3: The First Time Is the Only Time That Matters

This was the huge lie that green-lighted promiscuity among teens. Once they had crossed that bridge, there was no going back. Might as well enjoy some debauchery with the rest of the sinners! What was often missing was a proper understanding of chastity.

When we look at the beatitudes, we see Jesus blowing the false binary of sexual purity out of the water. Matthew 5:27-28 shows that chastity isn't only a body issue, but a heart issue. Virginity wasn't just lost by those who got too carried away on prom night; it's any sexual act outside of marriage. This meant that the virgin college student watching porn is just as guilty as the sophomore who slept with her boyfriend. The unmarried couple living together is just as broken as the guy waking up from a one-night stand.

When you really study it, chastity becomes like the law: revealing our brokenness and pointing us toward our need for a Savior. It completely leveled the sexual playing field, but no one knew it because all anyone seemed to care about was the wedding night, not the heart.

ARGUE for a Healthier Approach

If we want to raise our kids to have a healthy sexuality, we don't do it by ditching God's design—as many progressive teachers encourage. We do it by aligning what we teach with His Word. This starts by affirming the beauty and purpose of sexuality. Sex is good! It feels good! And it's a blessing to be completely vulnerable, intimate, and loved by one person for the rest of your life in the covenant of marriage. The most romantic moment isn't the first kiss; it's the one-millionth kiss from the wrinkled-faced sweetheart of your youth.

Redemption is possible for everyone. No amount of sexual brokenness can keep you from the healing power of God. Yes, physical virginity is a one-time deal, STDs have to be treated, and babies have to be cared for. But as a classmate once said, "If Paul, who persecuted believers and had them put to death, can be redeemed, so too can our broken past."

Next, our kiddos need to understand that chastity is faithfulness in body, mind, and heart; and Satan is going to attack all three. To be effective in the battle requires total dependence on Christ, honesty with parents, and a great support group of like-minded friends. Make no mistake, we cannot act like the world and expect to end up with all the benefits of godly obedience. Instead, we have to live counterculturally. We have to understand that dating isn't a hobby; it's the act of searching for a spouse, and it places you in a whole lot of tempting situations. Christian dating will mean setting healthy boundaries and honoring the other person like Christ.

This countercultural defense also involves how we dress and act. Now for guys, clothes aren't as much of an issue. Just the other day some radio jockeys were debating whether guys could have sexy outfits, and the best they could think of was unbuttoning an extra button on their shirts. The awful truth is that women are objectified through clothing more so than men. Just compare men's and women's Halloween costumes if you have any doubts.

For ladies, there is a lot more baggage here. Let's start off by saying no outfit justifies or will prevent abusive behavior. If a guy is going to be a creep, he's going to be that way whether you're dressed like a nun or wearing a miniskirt. And no, you weren't asking for it. Who would?

However, this doesn't mean that how we dress doesn't communicate a message. It does. We need to exercise discernment in our style choices because we can't look like the world and expect to convey an other-than-worldly message. It's not a black-and-white matter of the right clothes or wrong clothes. But there is something to be said about dressing in a way that honors God and ourselves. Luckily there are a few really practical tips on how to be attractive and modest for any body type.

An outfit is probably too short, tight, or low cut if....

- You have to take off your underwear to look good in an outfit.

- You lean forward and expose what only a doctor or a nursing infant should see.

- You can't walk or pick something up off the ground without exposing yourself to the people behind you.

- Anything that would normally be covered by underwear is hanging out the bottom or sides.

- You still look naked even with it on *cough scrunch butt leggings*

For those clothes that might be a bit on the showy side, camisoles, a pair of bike shorts, or a longer-waisted shirt are easy additions to up the modesty without compromising style. Our goal is to encourage our kiddos to dress in a way that gives honor to God while teaching them to be respectful of each other no matter what the other person is wearing.

REINFORCE with Discussion, Discipleship, and Prayer

1. The word *purity* has been put through the ringer, and sometimes we have to concede when it might be too far gone to be saved. Instead, let me offer "sexual integrity" as an alternative. Integrity better encompasses the mind, body, spirit unity that is comprised within discipling your child's sexuality—all these pieces are *integrated* in the Christian worldview. It also dispels the legalistic pure/impure dichotomy so often found within the early purity teachings—one can display sexual integrity before and after marriage. Chastity or sexual faithfulness are also great choices.

2. Discuss with your child how you can honor God and foster sexual faithfulness within your home. For teens this may include things like avoiding shows that display people having sex, dates where teens spend extended alone time together, and unsupervised media access. Parents can likewise model sexual faithfulness by also avoiding sultry shows and avoiding alone time with members of the opposite sex—especially if you are a single mom or dad with a significant other. Make sure everyone is aware of the agreed upon expectations—and that everyone follows them. Make sure they're reasonable, achievable, applicable, and fair. Discuss which boundaries will be in place and how you and your child be accountable to them. Teens will also need to know what steps are to be expected if these boundaries are violated.

3. Make sure you and your child have a support network that is outside of your family. Your child should seek friends and mentors that share their convictions and will ask the tough questions. Who are

these people? Do they regularly meet? If you do not have an outside support network, we encourage you to become involved in your local church and start making connections.

4. Encourage your child to pursue purposeful dating. This is counter to the world's approach to dating for entertainment and reinforces that the purpose of dating is to find one's spouse. The goal should be to get to know the person and see whether they would be a good ministry partner—since life is ministry! Activities could include volunteering together at the church, group trips, cooking together at home, and service projects. Pick activities that help you learn each other's character, family background, and beliefs. Set boundaries for your kids that will help them avoid situations that would lead to unnecessary temptation, like being alone together. Remind them that if they are deliberately acting in a way to encourage sexual affection (stroking, making out, looking for a dark, quiet place to be alone), they should find a way to restore boundaries (meet up with friends, change the activity) and, if need be, call it a night. Again, discuss these with your child so you can come to a sensible agreement.

5. Teach your boys how to ask a girl out, how to talk to her parents, how to behave on a date, and how to respect the girl's parents' wishes. Have mother-son dates where he can practice his gentlemanly and chivalry skills. Have father-daughter dates where your husband demonstrates to your daughter how a gentleman is to behave.

Talk to your kids about the specifics of what is okay and what is not in a dating relationship. A guy or girl wanting your teen to break his or her convictions or send sexy photos is not okay. Make sure your daughter knows that she doesn't owe a guy *anything*, no matter how fancy the steakhouse.

If you don't feel your teen is mature enough to date, encourage him or her to demonstrate maturity by being respectful of your wishes. Offer to revisit the conversation at a later time, reminding your teen that sneaking behind your back won't prove maturity.

And teach your teen how to end a relationship in a way that preserves the dignity of the other person. No social media bullying, shaming, or text breakups. Look the person in the eye and explain your reasons. Delete pictures, return sweatshirts, and be above reproach.

PAWS for Prayer by Julie Loos

PRAISE God for Who He Is

We praise You, Yahweh Nissi—The Lord Our Banner. We lift Your name high because You have the power to overcome any enemy that comes against us. Not only are You holy and pure, but You are our Redeemer when we fall. No matter what we have done or failed to do, You are Jehovah M'Kaddesh—the Lord who sanctifies and sets us apart for holy use—our bodies included.

ADMIT Where We Have Fallen Short of His Standard

Forgive us for abandoning Your biblical standard for holy living. There are times when we have parented out of fear, peer pressure, and trying to make up for our own past mistakes. Intending good, Your church has made missteps in our teaching about sexuality. At times we have promoted legalism over love and have equivocated purity with holiness. Out of fear of communication, we may have actually turned our kids toward brokenness.

WORSHIP WITH THANKSGIVING for the Things He Has Done

We are so thankful, Lord, that You redeem the broken, turning ashes to beauty. No one is out of Your reach or Your loving repair. You have the balm that heals our loved ones' emotional, physical, and spiritual wounds. Gratefully, we come acknowledging that You foreordained male and female, marriage, family, and boundaries for our sexuality and for our good. Any discipline that You bring on us is for our good and our sanctification.

SUBMIT Yourselves and Your Requests to God

Lord, as we try to guide our children in purity, help us balance truth and grace on the beam of Your Word. Help us model self-control and faithfulness for them. When they are tempted to compare themselves to others, help us guide them to use Your Word as their mirror. Protect them from the schemes of the evil one and his masquerading minions. May our children want to honor one another by setting boundaries and living above reproach. Help us train them in sexual integrity of mind, body, and spirit. If they give in to temptation, let them run to us and to You for help rather than hiding in shame or fear. May they purify their souls in obeying Your truth through the Spirit in sincere love of the brethren, loving one another fervently with a pure heart (1 Peter 1:22).

Discussion Questions

1. **Icebreaker:** Did you go through a True Love Waits ceremony in high school? Do you know anyone who did? What was your impression of TLW? What did your youth group teach about sex? If you weren't in church as a teenager, what were your impressions about what Christians thought about sex?

2. **Main theme:** *The church tried to encourage chastity but used bad analogies that scarred some people for life.* How are some ways that the church's attempts to teach sexual faithfulness backfired?

3. **Self-evaluation:** What are your thoughts about sexual activity for single parents? Do you think it's the same for them as for teenagers? Why or why not?

4. **Brainstorm:** This is actually a fun thought experiment. Brainstorm together to make a list of every single social problem that would go away if people had sex only with their spouse. (Seriously...it's mind boggling.)

5. **Release the bear:** This week, make a point of discussing integrity with your kids. If you need to correct behavior, ask them how they would have handled the situation if their thoughts, heart, and words were fully aligned with God's Word.

Chapter 13

Taking Up Your Sexual Cross

Because We're All Born That Way

Hillary

I was meeting with two high school students, Jared and Gina, at a conference a few years back. I had just given a talk, and they both had further questions. Gina was a devoted Christian and intended to go into ministry. She just had one hang-up: what about abortion? She knew abortion was wrong, but she had a hard time condemning it in cases of rape. "What would happen," she asked, "if I were to be raped and get pregnant? I would have to give up college, delay my entire life. I didn't ask to get pregnant. There was no sin I committed. What then?"

I could tell she was waiting for me to go into a pro-life apologetic monologue, but I considered my audience. This wasn't a girl who needed to be convinced abortion was wrong. This was a girl who was scared of being put in a difficult situation. And her fear was legitimate! She needed encouragement—and I mean *encouragement* the way the Bible means it.

A lot of people are confused about what it means to truly encourage someone. We use it to remind people that they're good enough, smart enough, and stable enough to conquer anything that comes their way. Or we (mis)use parts of Scripture written for someone else and assure our friends that God won't ever let anything bad happen to them. They will soar on wings like eagles in all situations (Isaiah 40:31)! The Lord has promised them freedom from pestilence and disease (Psalm 91)!

This stuff sounds *great,* but the problem is, it might not be true. *God does not promise us safety here in this life* (just ask the first-century martyrs). Nor does God promise us health, wealth, or long lives (just ask the present-day martyrs). Statements in the Bible that were made to individuals or to Israel are not necessarily promises which we can claim for ourselves and demand that God fulfill.

While ooey-gooey statements about conquering all our enemies and success in all circumstances might feel good, they are not necessarily encouraging—in the biblical sense. Encouragement literally means *to infuse courage.* We don't infuse courage by telling people there is nothing to fear when there is. We infuse courage by reminding them that whatever comes, they can face it head-on with God's help. We infuse courage by reminding each other of God's presence in the midst of our fear, pain, grief, and discouragement.

After a few moments of thought, I looked at Gina and said, "It comes down to this. We are all called to carry the cross of Christ. The unfortunate reality is that you and I, as women, may be called to carry a different cross from the one Jared is given. Yes, either one of us could become pregnant through no decision of our own. And you know what our cross is at that moment? To care for and protect the baby growing inside us. Jared will *never* have to carry this cross, and it's horribly unfair, but we don't decide the right thing based on what's fair."

Gina was quiet for a minute, and then, with a look of fierce resolve in her eyes, she said, "Okay."

Gina loved the Lord and desired to serve Him. Thinking that she might be put in an unfair situation scared her. But submitting to Christ? Remaining faithful no matter the situation? She had already made that decision a long time ago. So she looked that fear square in the eye and decided, "Nothing will change my resolve to follow the Lord—not even the fear of rape and pregnancy." Once she realized that the issue was ultimately about submission to God, it became a nonissue, and I could see a weight lifted from her shoulders. I felt privileged to stand there in that moment, witnessing a warrior for Christ preparing for the battle. *That, my friends, is what infusing biblical courage looks like.*

Christian encouragement means that we see this world for the broken mess that it is and remind each other that we were created for another world (John 15:18-19). Christian encouragement means that we acknowledge the pain, the strife, the difficulties of being a disciple of Jesus, but then remind each other *why* we are running the race (Hebrews 12). We remind each other that the glories that await us will far outweigh these momentary trials (2 Corinthians 4:17) and that we are storing up for ourselves treasures in heaven that moth and rust cannot destroy (Matthew 6:19-20). That is biblical encouragement.

Gina needed encouragement that God had already given her the strength and the ability to be faithful. Mama Bears, we all need someone who infuses courage in us from time to time. And part of our jobs as mamas is to infuse that courage into our kids.

The call to discipleship with Jesus is a heavy one, and we shouldn't pretend otherwise with our kids. In Luke 9:23-24, Jesus says to His disciples, "Whoever wants to be my disciple must deny themselves and take up their cross daily and follow me. For whoever wants to save their life will lose it, but whoever loses their life for me will save it." Here, Jesus is saying bluntly that the Christian walk will not be an easy one; we'll all have burdens to bear. Is this scary? Yup. Do we know what crosses we'll be called to carry in our own individual lives? Nope. Do we know what crosses our *children* will be called to carry? Also, no. So what can we know?

First, we can know God's will for our lives.

> It is God's will that you should be sanctified: that you should avoid sexual immorality; that each of you should learn to control your own body in a way that is holy and honorable, not in passionate lust like the pagans, who do not know God…For God did not call us to be impure, but to live a holy life. Therefore, anyone who rejects this instruction does

not reject a human being but God, the very God who gives you his Holy Spirit (1 Thessalonians 4:3-5, 7-8).

Yes, friends, sexual holiness is itself a cross we will have to carry—each one of us. As Christopher Yuan puts it, "Holy sexuality—chastity in singleness and faithfulness in marriage—is God's good standard for *everyone*."[1] Our kids need us to infuse them with the courage it will take to follow this command.

Carrying Our Sexual Crosses

A popular argument surrounding LGBTQ issues is that same-sex attraction and transgenderism are burdens too heavy to carry. After all, none of us privileged cisgendered heterosexuals have to carry this cross. God made us for relationship. Who are we to tell people that they're doomed to a life without love?

It is good to acknowledge others' burdens, and it is also good to help each other carry our burdens (Galatians 6:2). But this assumption that homosexuals and transsexuals are the only ones with a sexual cross to bear is just not true. Everyone has a cross they are called to carry. If we want to live with our brothers and sisters in kindness and in compassion, it helps to see what crosses they may be carrying that we might not.

Cross 1: Being Young and Celibate

We older Mama Bears (and Papa Bears, and Grandma and Grandpa Bears) may have forgotten what it is like to be young and struggling with a strong sex drive. Biologically speaking, humans are created with a certain window of time during which our bodies are practically *begging* us to go out and make a baby. And our society is *not* structured according to our biology. A hundred years ago, it was fairly normal to get married right out of high school. Even further back, societies were structured so that when young people hit puberty and sexual maturity, they didn't have to wait long before fulfilling their biological destiny.

Nowadays, that is not the case. And we who are older must recognize what a massive cross this is for our young people to carry. They are having to wait for sexual relationships ten, sometimes twenty years beyond the time when their bodies become ready. For those of you who are young and still maintaining sexual chastity, I commend you. You are loved by God and He sees your suffering. *How can we as the church help you carry this cross?*

Cross 2: Being Male and Celibate

Male and female sex drives are different. This has been common knowledge for eons, but it's now suddenly politically incorrect to say so. Are there some women who have higher than usual sex drives? Sure. But they aren't the norm. And God bless the men who find them! For the most part, girls, we will *never* understand what our guys go through to remain sexually chaste. Yes, we want to be loved. Yes, we long for touch. Yes, it can feel like we have to chew on a piece of leather to prevent ourselves from going full sex-kitten on the guy we're dating. But no matter how hard it is for us to maintain self-control, *we will never fully understand what is going on in our guys' bodies* and the struggle they face to obey God in this area.

So ladies, we need to be kind to our guys, especially the ones who are trying to maintain a faithful witness as disciples of Jesus. And for our guys out there who are trying to not only keep it in their pants but also fend off all the predatory girls who read *Teen Vogue*, I salute you. Your plight is not easy, especially not in a society where sex is so visible, so prevalent, so easily accessible, and where you are encouraged to "be a man" by disobeying God. You have a cross to carry that most of your sisters in Christ will never understand. You are loved by God and He sees your suffering. *How can we as the church help you carry this cross?*

Cross 3: Being Single and Celibate When Your Friends Are Married

Married people, remember the plight of your single friends. Human bodies were created for touch. Scientific studies have shown the importance of touch for normal childhood development[2]—and I suspect we will start seeing studies on the elderly population being deprived of touch during the pandemic lockdowns. Skin hunger is especially painful for people whose love language is touch.

Married people receive regular touch that their single friends do not—a quick kiss as you're running out the door, your husband's hand lingering on your back—and it isn't easy for single people to watch, knowing that their sexual faithfulness means waiting for a spouse who may never appear. For those of you who are single while all your friends are married, taking up your sexual cross means that you suffer from not having touch. Sexual faithfulness means waiting for a guy or girl who may never appear. My eyes fill with tears as I remember the longing I had during my time as an older single. Friends, you are loved by God and He sees your suffering. *How can we as the church help you carry this cross?*

Cross 4: Living in a Loveless Marriage

Maybe your marriage hasn't gone the way you hoped. Perhaps you can't even remember why you got married. You know what the only thing lonelier than being single is? Feeling alone in a marriage. Not only are you isolated, but you're stuck in a lifelong commitment, and you can't imagine feeling in love again. At least a single person has the possibility of meeting Mr. or Miss Right! For those of you carrying this cross, I commend you, friends. Taking up your cross means being sexually faithful to a person whom you may not even like. You are loved by God and He sees your suffering. *How can we as the church help you carry this cross?*

Cross 5: Inability to Have Sex in Marriage

This is one of those topics that few people ever discuss. Maybe you had a traumatic birth and carry scar tissue that makes sex almost impossible now. Maybe there's been illness, accident, or paralysis, and sex is no longer an option. Or maybe you have no clue what is going on with your body. All you know is that sex hurts…a lot. What do you do then? Who has it worse—the spouse in pain, or the other spouse who would cause pain by trying to be sexually intimate?

There are no winners in this situation. But there are disciples of Jesus, who, despite the hardships they have been handed, continue to be sexually faithful in whatever situation they have been placed. For those of you who have been given this hand, we mourn with you. You are loved by God and He sees your suffering. *How can we as the church help you carry this cross?*

Cross 6: Infertility

We have an epidemic of infertility in our world. Men and women who desire so badly to start a family suffer miscarriage after miscarriage. They grieve the death of child after child, hope after hope. Looking around, it seems everyone else has children. *The 16-year-old down the street just got pregnant. What's wrong with me? This is supposed to be a natural process!* For those of you in this situation, we grieve with you. Being a disciple of Jesus may mean not having children, or it may mean loving children you did not carry in your body. The Lord can make beauty from ashes. You are loved by God and He sees your suffering. *How can we as the church help you carry this cross?*

Cross 7: Unwanted Pregnancy

Women were given the unique ability to grow the next generation in their bodies. However you ended up in this situation, whether by your own sin or the sin of another, you have unexpectedly found yourself with child. We stand with you as you choose life. Being a disciple of Jesus doesn't mean having to choose motherhood now; it just means providing this new life a place of safety until it can join the rest of us out in this world. Even if you can't raise this child to adulthood, another family will. Sacrificing the next nine months might be a greater sacrifice than anyone even knows. Or maybe it will be the most life-changing blessing you never saw coming. Either way, we acknowledge your fear. We grieve that this blessing did not happen at a time that you preferred. But you are loved by God and He sees your suffering. *How can we as the church help you carry this cross?*

Cross 8: Same-Sex Attraction

You grew up feeling different from the other kids of your gender. You watched them all get crushes, and then boyfriends and girlfriends. Maybe someone suspected your secret and ridiculed you. They made you feel like a freak, like you didn't belong, like you were broken. Maybe people told you that you were an abomination, hated by God. Carrying your cross could mean never kissing your lover goodnight. Never having a family. Never having that wedding, growing old with someone you love. Your parents might grieve the loss of potential grandchildren, and you could feel like you aren't just breaking your own heart, but theirs as well. Being a disciple of Jesus means willingly laying down a part of yourself and denying its power. It's lonelier than anyone ever knows. You are loved by God and He sees your suffering. *How can we as the church help you carry this cross?*

Cross 9: Not Fitting in with Other People of Your Gender

You're a girl and you feel like there is some mysterious girl-codebook that all the other girls got...and somehow you missed out. All the adults say to "be yourself," but when you are "yourself," the other girls withdraw. They don't want to play with you. Every time you've tried to be vulnerable, you got crushed. The Lord sees you.

Maybe you are a boy, and the other boys called you a sissy. You were picked on, harassed, bullied, and made to feel like you'd never be man enough, so why even try? All the things your mom praised you for, the other boys used to ridicule you for.

I know it feels easier to go where you fit in, to change yourself to match other people's expectations. For you, taking up your cross means that you might walk a lonely road and have a harder time making friends. *You will find them.* God created you as a man or woman with the exact qualities He wanted you to have as a man or a woman. You don't have to act like all the other men or women. For our guys, I celebrate the unique way God has created you as a man. For our girls, I celebrate the unique way God has created you as a woman. You can be your authentic self while still remaining in your God-given body. Taking up your cross means that you accept the body He gave you while pursuing the gifts He also put inside of you—even if other people make fun of you for it. Do it anyway! You are a perfect fit in God's family. He loves you and He sees your suffering. *How can we as the church help you carry this cross?*

Cross 10: Sexual Abuse

Someone ripped a part of you away that you can never get back. You can't look at people the way you used to. You can't trust the way you used to. Maybe some people said it was your fault. You might have nightmares; you may have anger. You have an entire burden placed on you which clawed its way from your body to your brain, tainting the way you see everything and everyone around you.

Being a disciple of Jesus means that you place your anger in His hands so that it doesn't come out on other people, people who have nothing to do with what happened to you. It might mean that you protect future survivors by coming out and carrying your cross publicly. Or maybe that is just too much to bear, so you carry it silently.

The abuse was not your fault, and you are not forgotten. You are loved by God and He sees your suffering. *How can we as the church help you carry this cross?*

Submit...Even When It's Unfair

You see, Church, we all have a cross to carry. If we could stop looking at our own, we might just see that we are truly all in this together. We all suffer. Maybe it shows up in our sexuality; maybe it shows up in other ways. There are those who struggle with finances, those who struggle with mental illness, those who struggle with relationships, learning disabilities, chaotic families of origin, betrayal, lust, addiction...should I go on? There are innumerable ways that sin can break this world. And yet, it is in this world that we are called to follow Christ.

Believers can submit to God no matter how unfair the circumstances. There are a lot of crosses to bear—a lot of sexual burdens we might be asked to carry. No matter how unfair they are, no matter how inborn the desire is, they do not negate Jesus's command to carry the cross of Christ. When we submit to Christ as Lord, we submit to Him in every area of our lives. Some areas are more difficult to surrender than others, but our submission isn't predicated on the ease of the task.

And here's the secret about sin: *we were all born that way*. We are all on equal footing—equally flawed, equally guilty, and equally burdened with hardships. And we are all equally covered by the grace of Jesus Christ. When we realize how much we've been forgiven, we can turn and extend that same grace and compassion to others.

Sometimes the grief and trials feel too great to bear. But we can rejoice that "we do not have a high priest who is unable to empathize with our weaknesses" (Hebrews 4:15). Jesus doesn't look down from heaven thinking, "Gee, that looks hard." No, He suffered all that we suffer so He could look back at us and say, "Here's how you suffer. I'll do it first so you won't be afraid."

He is the imminent, the ever-present, the good God whom we serve. And He is infinitely worthy of us taking up our crosses—no matter what they may be—and following Him unto death. Nothing we lose here can compare to the life that we have gained. May the Lord grant us love and compassion and understanding as we all carry our crosses, together.

Discussion Questions

1. **Icebreaker:** Give an example of encouragement that didn't fill you with courage. Share the situation with the group and have them reimagine the response as biblical encouragement. What words would have helped you to face the situation with strength?

2. **Main theme:** *We are all called to submit to God's will, no matter how unfair His will seems.* Describe a time you felt God's commands were too burdensome to take up. What was the cross God asked you to carry?

3. **Self-evaluation:** Have you shown judgment and lacked compassion toward those carrying sexual crosses? Bring this confession to God and receive His forgiveness.

4. **Brainstorm:** Discuss ways you can support those in your community who carry sexual crosses. Are there any tangible ways you can care for those who are struggling with the burdens of same-sex attraction, singleness, or past abuse?

5. **Release the bear:** Talk with your kids this week about the crosses they carry as disciples of Christ.

PRAYER OF LAMENT

Choose to Trust

LAMENTATIONS 3:21-22,55-57; JUDE 20,21,24

This we recall and therefore have hope and expectation: Your mercy and kindness allow us not to be consumed by all this. Your tender compassion fails not. We called upon Your name, O Lord, out of the depths of the mire of the (filth). You heard our voices: O hide not Your ear at our prayer for relief. You drew near on the day we called to You; You said, "Fear not." You are the One who can help us build up our children on our faith, rising higher and higher, praying in the Spirit. Guard and keep us in the love of God. You are able to keep us from stumbling or slipping or failing to present ourselves and our children blameless and faultless before the presence of Your glory.

———————

You are worthy to be trusted, Lord, even when things don't look so good. You are the lamp to our feet and the light to our path. The Good Shepherd who can keep the enemy from slipping in the side door. You have already overcome the evil one. We can trust You to help us implement what we know for now. Just as we want our children to accept our discipline, we want to accept Yours as well. You are the Way when we lose ours, the Truth when we are surrounded by lies, and the Life when our world is trying to be the death of us, our sanity, and our kids' sexuality. Let us boldly live and proclaim the truth that despite what the world looks like: You have overcome the world. By Your power, You will bring us through it! Amen. So be it.

Things to Repeat to Your Kids Until They Want to Gag

The Lasting Effects of a Good Maxim

HILLARY

See if you can complete the following sentences:

If you don't have something nice to say…

Do unto others as you would have them…

Well, life isn't always…

Growing up in the South, we heard these statements constantly. If we didn't have anything nice to say, we didn't say anything at all. We did unto others what we would have them do unto us, and we learned not to complain about fairness because any adult within hearing distance would remind us that life wasn't fair. My favorite maxim came from my grandmother as I was learning to drive. She would scream in terror whenever I pulled away from a four-way stop sign in the presence of another car. I'd lovingly reassure her, "It's okay, Grandmommy. I have the right of way." And each time she'd snap back, "Well, there's a graveyard *full* of people who had the right of way."

Maxims are easy-to-remember, bite-sized pieces of a worldview that were repeated to us so many times we could recite them in our sleep. They tell us *general* truths about the world and how we should behave as humans. These little sayings not only teach us how to act, but also reinforce what is *true* about our world, our identity, and our life's purpose. Through the sayings above, I learned my words shouldn't be used to tear people down, that life wasn't always fair, and that I could follow the rules and *still* get hurt because there was no guarantee that other people were following the rules.

Today, maxims about self-control and common courtesy are less common, and in their place are battle cries to "speak your truth," "follow your heart," or "you deserve the best." Those are the nuggets of wisdom that culture is passing on to your child, and they ain't *gold* nuggets, if you know what I mean.

As we said in chapter 6, human beings have a difficult time distinguishing that which is true from that which is familiar. The purpose of a maxim is to reinforce a particular worldview. And reinforcing biblical concepts for your kids through maxims might seem cheesy, but it's only weird if it doesn't work. (And yes, that's my life motto.)

Let's face it. An oft-touted maxim can be harder to shake than mono. My cousin's parting words to her daughter whenever she leaves the house are, "Have fun! Keep your clothes on!" I can all but guarantee that if her daughter even *thinks* about stripping down with a boy, she will immediately hear her mother's voice in her head—the last person you want in your thoughts when you are trying to get jiggy with Mr. Right Now.

Here, then, are some maxims you can try repeating to your kids. When they've heard it enough for it to really sink in, you'll know. Their eyes will roll back in their heads and there will be audible gagging sounds. At which point, you have permission to pat yourself on the back for a job well done.

1. What You Do with Your Body Matters

This one deals not just with sexuality, but with basically *every* aspect of human life, and there is no age too young to reinforce this truth. So, Mama Bears, when you ask your kids to take a bath or brush their teeth and they ask why, remind them that it's because *what they do with their body matters*.

The more you say it, the more this truth will be reinforced across different areas of life. But for the young kids, this statement will usually be followed by an even longer "But *whyyyyy*? Why does it matter what I do with my body?" Instead of saying "Because I said so," follow this maxim up with the next one.

2. God Gave You Your Body to Take Care of It

This one *also* applies to most anything you can think of. When they ask why they have to eat broccoli instead of candy, you can remind them that God gave them their body to take care of it, and too much candy can make their body sick.

Now, some parents try to get this point across by telling their child that their body is a gift from God, but I would discourage this language. First, gifts imply ownership, and that's not what our bodies are. First Corinthians 6:19-20 says, "Do you not know that your bodies are temples of the Holy Spirit, who is in you, whom you have received from God? You are not your own; you were bought at a price. Therefore honor God with your bodies."

A more practical second reason I don't recommend using the "gift" language is because your child has probably seen you throw away or regift a gift. And if you think they don't pick up on that kind of minutiae, to our chagrin, they do. So when they ask *why* we are to take care of our bodies, the statement above presents the concept of stewardship, a theme which is heavy throughout Scripture.

Adam and Eve were stewards of God's creation. We as humankind continue that stewardship. Not only does this reinforce how to be a good steward, but also how to be a good *authority*. Part of authority is taking care of that which you rule. We are to rule over our bodies (and our urges) in a way that reflects *self-control*. This is an example of being a good steward *and* a good authority.

3. Sex Is the Bodily Renewal of Marital Vows

This would have changed my whole outlook on sex as a teen. When sex is properly defined, "sex outside of marriage" becomes nonsensical. How can you repeat vows you haven't taken?

4. Authority Means Leading by Serving

When the concept of authority is seen as inherently bad, our kids will not know what to do with the authority of the Bible or any other authority in their lives. We can also ask them, "How are you exercising your authority?"

Our kids need to recognize that a hierarchical structure itself is not bad. It's what you do with it. With the proper definition of authority, our kids can learn to recognize a person who is a good authority and one who is a bad authority. Some authorities you can get out from under and others you can't. It is important that we recognize and place ourselves under good authority—if we have the option.

5. God Created Everything with a Purpose, but There Are Few Limits to What Sin Can Break

This is one of those both/and statements which we cannot separate. The first part reinforces the truth of God's sovereignty. God indeed designed everything for a purpose. At the same time, much of our physical world is ruled by the prince of this world (Ephesians 2:2). That means that God's original purpose is not always apparent.

Some people fall into the trap of thinking that since God created everything with a purpose, then everything we experience reflects that purpose. That's a *dangerous* road to go down. This discounts natural evil and suffering in the world and also teaches us that any sinful desire that comes to us "naturally" is part of God's plan for our lives. (Yikes!) Nope. Not everything that comes naturally is good. Yes, God created everything with a purpose…but there's almost no limit to what sin can break.

6. You Can Say the Right Thing in the Wrong Way

We want our kids to speak truth, but we don't want them to become little crusaders for God by dropping a bunch of truth-grenades and letting the pieces fall where they may. As women have complained for millennia, "It's not *what* you said, it's the *way you said it*." They aren't wrong, y'all. Our delivery matters.

7. Just Because You Feel It Doesn't Make It True

This bit of wisdom goes against ev-ah-ree-thing the world is telling our kids. It cuts to the heart of emotional reasoning and helps remind our kids that we don't determine truth by our feelings. We can't prevent culture from following after the god of emotions; all we have control over is ourselves. Our kids need to remember that they will experience all sorts of feelings that are not grounded in truth. We don't ignore feelings. We dignify them for what they are. We also care about other people's feelings, but we don't judge *reality* based on feelings. You can press this maxim a little further from time to time by asking them, "Are your feelings lying to you right now?" This allows them to express the emotion while still understanding that it may not be pointing toward truth. (Fun fact: my husband frequently asks me this.)

8. Not All Change Is Progress

As humans we have a tendency to think that any change is for the better. But anyone who saw my first-grade haircut knows that ain't the case. Some change is progress, some is regressive. Some is neutral. It's best that we don't take a naive approach by assuming that anything different is automatically *better*.

9. What Do You Mean by That? How Did You Come to That Conclusion? What Actually Happened?

Remember from chapter 6 that there is a difference between categorical words and actual information. Linguistic theft is alive and well. When someone uses a categorical term (healthy, good, wrong, right, oppressive, injustice, harmful), we should never assume we're all on the same page unless they have defined the word and we know the circumstances surrounding the label.

When someone is trying to get your kids to agree with them without giving them details, teach them to ask, "What do you mean by that word?" and, "How did you come to that conclusion?" or even, "So what *actually* happened?" This reminds our kids that they are *not* to turn their brains off. We should all ask clarifying questions before committing ourselves to a position. Remember: if they can't accurately reenact the situation, then they don't really know what happened. They are believing the category without knowing the facts.

10. It's Okay to Be Normal and It's Okay to Be Different

When I was a kid, all I wanted in life was to be like everyone else. All the other kids seemed to have a handle on their personality. They were shy, or boisterous, or funny. I was just *intense.* My brain was constantly seeking to understand every facet of the world I lived in, to find patterns, explain behaviors. I wanted everyone to be as keenly interested in life as I was. It's a great trait to have as a 40-year-old writer. It does *not* make you popular on the playground as a 10-year-old, though. I would always think, "Why can't I just be like everyone else?" I would have loved to know that it was okay to be different and that God had a plan for my special kind of weird.

Fast-forward to now, and suddenly the world belongs to the geeks, the nerds, and the weirdos (just like *Breakfast Club* prophesied!). Now the struggle kids face is "how can I be different?" Suddenly being average, ordinary, dare I say *the norm* is what terrifies them. Being a minority used to mean sitting on the fringes. Now, it confers status to the point that all the kids in the majority-type are squeezing and reshaping their identities so that they, too, can be different and special, just like everybody else.

But let's look at this objectively: *trying* to fit in or *trying* to be different both carry baggage because neither reflects being at peace with how God made you. We'll all have areas where we blend in and areas where we stand out. Do you have a little boy who doesn't fit the rough-and-tumble mold? What about a little girl who's more mud than Malibu Stacie? There are some molds that are just fine to break, so honey, go right ahead.

11. It's Okay to Be on the Wrong Side of History if You're on the Right Side of Eternity

The phrase "being on the wrong side of history" pops up a lot, especially with the politicization of sex. And there's a legitimate point there. Humans do have a history of misquoting Scripture to justify the mistreatment of other people. Heroes like Abigail Adams and Rosa Parks improved our world by pushing back against the status quo—*when the status quo was wrong.* Kids today are being taught that every act of rebellion is just as noble. Uhhhh…no. Some rebellion is just good, old-fashioned rebellion and not to be admired. So if they are told that following Jesus means "being on the wrong side of history," then get used to being hated—because it's a *lot worse* to be on the wrong side of eternity.

12. Just Because It Feels Good Doesn't Make It Good for You

Now, there are some things that feel good that are actually good for you! Like a massage! But that's not the way it is for everything. This applies to food. It applies to pleasure. It applies to sex. It applies to most everything. Pleasure is not the same thing as moral or good, and just because it tastes good, looks good, or feels good doesn't mean it's good for you.

13. You Can't Keep a Bird from Flying over Your Head, but You Can Keep It from Making a Nest in Your Hair

Far too many people focus their energy on things they can't control, which makes them ignore the things they can. Our kids need to know what's under their control and what to release to God. Emotions? We can't always control those. Thoughts? They're like the birds flying over your head. We can shoo them away, though sometimes they don't shoo very easily. But we do have some control, and if we're not careful, those thoughts can set up camp in a really unhealthy way. Behaviors? We've got even more control. Take responsibility for what you can control. And the stuff you can't, give it to God.

14. Feelings Are Terrible Leaders but Great Followers

When it comes to obedience, discipline, and forming good habits, you can't wait till you *feel* like it or it'll never happen. So lead your feelings in the right direction till they catch up. Obedience becomes a lot simpler when we accept the fact that we can do the right thing even when we don't feel like doing it. The beautiful thing about how the mind works, though, is that when a person chooses to do stuff they don't want to do, it eventually helps them *want* to do those things. So give your feelings to God, and do the right thing anyway. With practice, it gets easier over time.

15. Neurons That Fire Together Wire Together, or You Train Your Brain What to Crave

We like to think that habits are things we can make or break at will. The reality is that every decision you make, every action you take, every thought on which you choose to dwell is laying down neural pathways in your brain, rewiring it to focus on that which you are choosing to focus. It doesn't distinguish between good and bad; *it just responds to repetition.* (This is especially true when it comes to pornography.) These neural connections *can* be undone with time, but it is difficult. You are training your brain what to crave.

16. We Are Only Responsible for What We Have Been Given

Kids (okay, let's be honest…all of us) tend to play the game of comparisons. It's easy to judge ourselves by looking at the gifts and resources God has given someone else. But remember: you are not responsible for what the Lord has given me, and I am not responsible for what the Lord has given you. Each of us is only responsible for that which He has put on our plate. If your child has been blessed with intelligence, athletic ability, or popularity, remind them that to whom much is given much is expected (see Luke 12:48). For the child who feels like they aren't as smart or talented as other people, remind them that they are responsible only for cultivating what God has given them. None of us will be judged in comparison to others. We stand alone before the throne of God, giving account for what we did with what we had. And remember, this also means that we can't judge others, because we don't know the load God has given them.

17. Everyone Is Suffering, Just in Different Ways

It's easy to imagine that everyone else's life is easier than our own. But everyone suffers in a unique and different way. Instead of letting our own pain steal all our attention, letting it isolate and divide us, we can remember how pain and suffering are global realities. These are ties that bind us together, in shared humanity. We can find company in our struggles, vulnerable connections through our pains, and shared community in overcoming adversity. Tracing each trail of tears, we can find lines of empathy and understanding. We are all human, and we are all in this thing together. Let's start living like it.

A Final Word

We are so grateful to have been able to journey alongside you as we tackled some of the biggest ideological challenges facing you and your children. Each one of these chapters could have been a book in itself, and naturally some points didn't get their due turn under the microscope. But here's the great news: there are a wealth of books, articles, and studies to explore next.

We challenge you not to let your studies stop with this book. The cultural conversation is always shifting. New arguments will be neatly packaged and offered as Turkish Delight to your little ones. Let's do our best to arm our little Lucys and Susans and Peters while taking hope in the God who rescues every Edmund who calls out to Him!

You also have a whole community of Mama Bears standing beside you, ready to equip and encourage you on your journey as you disciple your children in their sexuality. We take great joy in pouring into one another, so if you have a question or concern, please reach out to us through our website.

Finally, know that we are praying for you. The conversations we need to have as parents can be awkward at times, but God's design is worth it. Take up your cross, Mama Bears, and put on the armor of God, so that "you may be able to stand your ground, and after you have done everything, to stand" (Ephesians 6:13).

Notes

Introduction. My Kid's Cartoon Showed *What*?

1. Juli Slattery, *Rethinking Sexuality: God's Design and Why It Matters* (New York: Multnomah, 2018), 31.
2. Jeff Diamant, "Half of U.S. Christians Say Casual Sex Between Consenting Adults Is Sometimes or Always Acceptable," Pew Research Center, August 31, 2020, www.pewresearch.org/fact-tank/2020/08/31/half-of-u-s-christians-say-casual-sex-between-consenting-adults-is-sometimes-or-always-acceptable/.
3. Erik Kain, "Study Finds Majority of Young Evangelicals Have Premarital Sex," *Forbes*, October 1, 2011, www.forbes.com/sites/erikkain/2011/10/01/study-finds-majority-of-young-evangelicals-have-premarital-sex/.
4. Slattery, *Rethinking Sexuality*, 24.
5. "Survey Says: Parent Power," Power to Decide, October 2016, https://powertodecide.org/what-we-do/information/resource-library/parent-power-october-2016-survey-says.
6. *Pliny's Letters*, trans. Alfred Church and W.J. Brodribb (Edinburgh and London: William Blackwood and Sons, 1872), 153-54. Emphasis mine.

Part One. Things I Probably Already Knew...But Kinda Forgot

1. Prayers of Lament based on the work of Mark Vroegop, *Dark Clouds, Deep Mercy: Discovering the Grace of Lament* (Wheaton, IL: Crossway, 2019).

Chapter 1. Sexually Set Apart

1. Clay Jones, *Why Does God Allow Evil?* (Eugene, OR: Harvest House Publishers, 2017), 29.
2. Clay Jones, "Killing the Canaanites: A Response to the New Atheism's 'Divine Genocide' Claims," Christian Research Institute, January 13, 2011, www.equip.org/article/killing-the-canaanites.
3. Clay Jones, "We Don't Hate Sin So We Don't Understand What Happened to the Canaanites," *Philosophia Christi* 11, no. 1 (2009), https://www.clayjones.net/wp-content/uploads/2011/06/We-Dont-Hate-Sin-PC-article.pdf.
4. Ezekiel 16:36; Leviticus 18:21, 20:2-5; 2 Kings 23:10; Jeremiah 32:35.
5. Tim Keller, "The Gospel and Sex," The Gospel and Life Conferences, 2004 and 2005, https://gospelinlife.com/downloads/the-gospel-and-sex.
6. Peter Kreeft, *How to Win the Culture War: A Christian Battle Plan for a Society in Crisis* (Downers Grove, IL: InterVarsity Press, 2002), 95.
7. Christopher West, *Our Bodies Tell God's Story: Discovering the Divine Plan for Love, Sex, and Gender* (Grand Rapids, MI: Baker, 2020), 47.

Chapter 2. Sex Is Spelled W-O-R-L-D-V-I-E-W

1. John Piper, *Sex and the Supremacy of Christ* (Wheaton, IL: Crossway, 2005), 26.

2. C.S. Lewis, *The Weight of Glory* (New York: HarperCollins, 1980), 140.

3. In the appendix of *The Abolition of Man*, C.S. Lewis compares the laws and codes of multiple societies throughout time. The similarities among them demonstrate how the moral law is written on the hearts of humans.

Chapter 3. A Pretty Great Design, When Followed

1. For excellent examples of this type of biography, see Jackie Hill Perry, *Gay Girl, Good God: The Story of Who I Was, and Who God Has Always Been* (Nashville, TN: B&H Publishing Group, 2018) and Rachel Gilson, *Born Again This Way: Coming Out, Coming to Faith, and What Comes Next* (Epsom, UK: The Good Book Company, 2020).

2. Rachel Gilson, *Born Again This Way: Coming Out, Coming to Faith, and What Comes Next* (Epsom, UK: The Good Book Company, 2020), 39-40.

3. West, *Our Bodies Tell God's Story*, 82.

Chapter 4. Demolishing Arguments, Not People

1. The Shema is considered the most important Jewish prayer—the first to be memorized by children—and is often spoken or sung at important moments, like Shabbat.

2. Jen Hatmaker, *Fierce, Free, and Full of Fire: The Guide to Being Glorious You* (Nashville, TN: Thomas Nelson, 2020), 91.

Chapter 5. Are You Sex Smarter than a Fifth Grader?

1. *National Sex Education Standards: Core Content and Skills, K-12, Second Edition,* 2020, https://advocatesforyouth.org/wp-content/uploads/2020/03/NSES-2020-web.pdf.

2. Miriam Grossman, "A Brief History of Sex Ed: How We Reached Today's Madness," *Public Discourse: The Journal of the Witherspoon Institute*, July 16, 2013, https://www.thepublicdiscourse.com/2013/07/10408.

3. *National Sex Education Standards*, 7.

4. John S. Santelli, et al., "Abstinence-Only-Until-Marriage: An Updated Review of U.S. Policies and Programs and Their Impact." *Journal of Adolescent Health* 61, no. 3 (2017): 273–80, doi: 10.1016/j.jadohealth.2017.05.031.

5. Planned Parenthood, "How Do You Know If Someone Wants to Have Sex with You?" YouTube video, September 21, 2015, www.youtube.com/watch?v=qNN3nAevQKY.

6. Nadia Bolz-Weber, *Shameless: A Case for Not Feeling Bad About Feeling Good (About Sex)* (New York: Random House, 2020), 17.

7. William H. Jeynes, "A Meta-Analysis on the Factors That Best Reduce the Achievement Gap," *Education and Urban Society* 47, no. 5 (2015): doi: 10.1177/0013124514529155.

8. William H. Jeynes, "The Effects of Black and Hispanic 12th Graders Living in Intact Families and Being Religious on Their Academic Achievement," *Urban Education* 38, no. 1 (2003): doi: 10.1177/0042085902238685.

   Conclusions: "The results indicate that Black and Hispanic children who lived in an intact family and showed a high level of religiosity scored as well as White students on most measures of academic achievement, even when controlling for socioeconomic status and gender. These same Black and Hispanic students also performed better than their Black and Hispanic counterparts who were not from intact families and/or were not high in religiosity. These results suggest that parental family structure and religiosity may play a larger role in explaining the academic gap between Black and Hispanic students, on one hand, and Whites, on the other hand, than was previously believed."

9. Right now, a woman can choose to have the child without the father's permission and demand child support for 18 years. Under this definition of "equity," men could theoretically demand that they, too, be allowed to terminate the pregnancy without the mother's consent. All in all, "equity" when it comes to reproduction is not necessarily the goal we should strive for.

10. *National Sex Education Standards,* 11.

11. Russell Goldman, "Here's a List of 58 Gender Options for Facebook Users," ABC News, February 13, 2014, https://abcnews.go.com/blogs/headlines/2014/02/heres-a-list-of-58-gender-options -for-facebook-users.

12. Michel Foucault, *The History of Sexuality* (New York: Random House, 1990), 25.

13. Erin R. Markman, "Gender Identity Disorder, the Gender Binary, and Transgender Oppression: Implications for Ethical Social Work, Smith College Studies in Social Work," *Smith College Studies in Social Work* 81, no. 4 (2011): 314-27, doi: 10.1080/00377317.2011.616839.

14. Judith Butler argues against the reductive categories of normal in her book *Gender Trouble: Feminism and the Subversion of Identity* (New York: Routledge, 1990).

15. *Encyclopedia Britannica,* s.v. "Command Economy," February 10, 2017, https://www.britannica .com/topic/command-economy.

16. C.S. Lewis, *God in the Dock: Essays on Theology and Ethics*, ed. Walter Hooper (Grand Rapids, MI: Eerdmans, 1970), 292.

17. Maurianne Adams, Lee Anne Bell, and Pat Griffin, eds, *Teaching for Diversity and Social Justice*, 2nd ed. (New York: Routledge, 2007), appendix C.

18. Jeffrey M. Jones, "LGBT Identification Rise to 5.6% in Latest U.S. Estimate," Gallup, February 4, 2021, https://news.gallup.com/poll/329708/lgbt-identification-rises-latest-estimate.aspx.

19. Abigail Shrier, *Irreversible Damage: The Transgender Craze Seducing Our Daughters* (Washington, DC: Regnery Publishing, 2020), 38.

20. Gordon Rayner, "Minister Orders Inquiry into 4,000 Per Cent Rise in Children Wanting to Change Sex," The Telegraph, September 16, 2018, www.telegraph.co.uk/politics/2018/09/16/ minister-orders-inquiry-4000-per-cent-rise-children-wanting/.

21. Shrier, *Irreversible Damage*, xxi.

Chapter 6. The Enemy's New Playbook

1. For a broader discussion of these tactics, see Gabriele Kuby, *The Global Sexual Revolution: Destruction of Freedom in the Name of Freedom* (Kettering, OH: LifeSite, 2015).

2. Saul D. Alinsky, *Rules for Radicals: A Practical Primer for Realistic Radicals* (New York: Random House, 1971), 36, 44.

3. Daniel Kahneman, *Thinking, Fast and Slow* (New York: Farrar, Straus and Giroux, 2011), 62.

4. These are two main themes in Greg Koukl's book *Tactics: A Game Plan for Discussing Your Christian Convictions* (Grand Rapids, MI: Zondervan, 2019).

5. Bolz-Weber, *Shameless*, 82. Emphasis mine.

6. The Council on Biblical Manhood and Womanhood, *Nashville Statement* (August 2017), https:// cbmw.org/nashville-statement.

Chapter 7. The Genderbread Person

1. "Genderbread Person & LGBT+ Umbrella," The Safe Zone Project, http://thesafezoneproject .com/wp-content/uploads/2015/08/GenderbreadPersonLGBT+Umbrella.pdf.

2. *Merriam-Webster Dictionary,* s.v. "identity," accessed December 8, 2020, www.merriam-webster .com/dictionary/identity.

3. "Genderbread Person & LGBT+ Umbrella."

4. Ibid.

5. Ibid.

6. Sue Bohlin, "Raising Gender Healthy Kids," Probe for Answers, July 30, 2015, https://probe.org/ raising-gender-healthy-kids.

7. Lianne Laurence, "Court Orders Christian to Pay $55,000 to Trans Politician for Calling Him 'Biological Male,'" LifeSite, March 28, 2019, www.lifesitenews.com/news/court-orders-christian-to-pay-55000-to-trans-politician-for-calling-him-biological-male.

8. "Genderbread Person & LGBT+ Umbrella."

9. Jeannie Visootsak and John M. Graham, "Klinefelter Syndrome and Other Sex Chromosomal Aneuploidies," *Orphanet Journal of Rare Diseases* 1, no. 42 (October 24, 2006): doi: 10.1186/1750-1172-1-42.

10. "Genderbread Person & LGBT+ Umbrella."

11. "Does ISNA Think Children with Intersex Should Be Raised Without a Gender, Or in a Third Gender?" Intersex Society of North America, accessed December 8, 2020, https://isna.org/faq/ third-gender.

12. Paula Johnson, "His and Hers…Health Care," TED: Ideas Worth Spreading, December 2013, https://www.ted.com/talks/paula_johnson_his_and_hers_health_care.

13. "Genderbread Person & LGBT+ Umbrella."

14. Cara Lee Arndorfer and Elizabeth A. Stormshak, "Same-Sex Versus Other-Sex Best Friendship in Early Adolescence: Longitudinal Predictors of Antisocial Behavior Throughout Adolescence," *Journal of Youth and Adolescence* 37, no. 9 (October 2008): 1059–70, doi: 10.1007/ s10964-008-9311-x.

15. "Genderbread Person & LGBT+ Umbrella."

16. Ibid.

17. Evan L. Ardiel and Catharine H. Rankin, "The Importance of Touch in Development," *Paediatrics & Child Health* 15, no. 3 (March 1, 2010): 153–56, doi: 10.1093/pch/15.3.153.

Chapter 8. Sex-Positivity

1. Reich is not the only one who encouraged this movement. Alfred Kinsey, Margaret Sanger, Robert Rimmer, and others led the charge for sexual liberation. Nancy Pearcey gives an excellent account of each of these people in her book *Love Thy Body: Answering Hard Questions About Life and Sexuality,* which we encourage you to read ASAP!

2. Pearcey, *Love Thy Body*, (Grand Rapids, MI: Baker Books, 2018) 133.

3. Quoted in Gail Mitchell, "The Real Story Behind 'WAP': Cardi B's Business Partner Brooklyn Johnny Tells All," *Billboard*, August 28, 2020, www.billboard.com/articles/business/9441667/ wap-cardi-b-business-partner-brooklyn-johnny-story.

4. Pearcey, *Love Thy Body*, 135.

5. Chantelle Ivanski and Taylor Kohut, "Exploring Definitions of Sex Positivity Through Thematic Analysis," *The Canadian Journal of Human Sexuality* 26, no. 3 (2017): 216-25, doi: 10.3138/cjhs.2017-0017.

6. Jess O'Reilly, "What Sex Positivity Means to Me," Sex with Dr. Jess, March 6, 2019, www.sexwithdrjess.com/2019/03/what-sex-positivity-means-to-me.

7. Erica Smith, quoted in "What Does It Actually Mean to Be 'Sex Positive'?" by Gabrielle Kassel, *Healthline,* September 3, 2020, www.healthline.com/health/healthy-sex/sex-positive-meaning.

8. The K-2 standard requires children to define the different kinds of "family" including same-sex parents and non-married cohabitating parents (Standard CHR.2.CC.4). Grades 3-5 begin defining sexual orientation (Standard SO.5.CC.CC.2). 6th-8th graders have to explain the difference between people who are heterosexual, bisexual, lesbian, gay, queer, two-spirit, asexual, and pansexual (Standard SO.8.CC.2). See *National Sex Education Standards: Core Content and Skills, K-12, Second Edition,* 2020, https://advocatesforyouth.org/wp-content/uploads/2020/03/NSES-2020-web.pdf.

9. NSES Standard SH.8.CC.1

10. West, *Our Bodies Tell God's Story,* 8.

11. Sarah L. Brown, et al., "Suicide Risk Among BDSM Practitioners: The Role of Acquired Capability for Suicide," *Journal of Clinical Psychology* 73, no. 12 (December 2017): 1642-54, doi: 10.1002/jclp.22461.

12. CHR.12.INF.2 – "Analyze cultural and social factors (e.g., sexism, homophobia, transphobia, racism, ableism, classism) that can influence decisions regarding sexual behaviors." See *National Sex Education Standards: Core Content and Skills, K-12, Second Edition,* 2020, https://advocatesforyouth.org/wp-content/uploads/2020/03/NSES-2020-web.pdf.

13. By the end of eighth grade, your child should "Develop a plan for the school to promote dignity and respect for all people of all sexual orientations in the school community." While we are all in favor of promoting dignity for all people *period*, the only reason to specify sexual orientation is to get kids to be promoting the orientation under the guise of promoting the person. Just another example of sneaking in the ideological bomb attached to a hurting person in need of love.

14. Myriam Grossman, *Unprotected: A Campus Psychiatrist Reveals How Political Correctness in Her Profession Endangers Every Student* (New York: Penguin Group, 2007), 23.

15. Meg Meeker, *Epidemic: How Teen Sex Is Killing Our Kids* (Washington, D.C.: Regnery Publishing Company, 2002), 12.

16. Grossman, *Unprotected,* 27.

17. Planned Parenthood, "Let's Talk About Sex—Sexual Health Advice from Dr. Vanessa Cullins," YouTube video, October 20, 2009, www.youtube.com/watch?v=wvlCx3w_tss.

18. Grossman, *Unprotected,* 16.

19. A phrase Grossman borrows from the literature from the Medical Institute for Sexual Health.

20. Kirk Johnson, "Sexually Active Teenagers Are More Likely to Be Depressed and to Attempt Suicide," The Heritage Foundation, June 3, 2003, www.heritage.org/education/report/sexually-active-teenagers-are-more-likely-be-depressed-and-attempt-suicide.

21. Kara Joyner and J. Richard Udry, "You Don't Bring Me Anything but Down: Adolescent Romance and Depression," *Journal of Health and Social Behavior* 41, no. 4 (December 2000): 369, doi: 10.2307/2676292.

22. See the app "Our Bible App" at www.ourbibleapp.com.

23. C.S. Lewis, *The Screwtape Letters* (New York: Touchstone, 1961), 44.

Chapter 9. Pornography

1. Pornhub Team, "The 2019 Year in Review," Pornhub, December 11, 2019, www.pornhub.com/insights/2019-year-in-review#2019.

2. Josh McDowell, "The Porn Epidemic: Facts Stats & Solutions," accessed March 25, 2021, www.josh.org/wp-content/uploads/Porn-Epidemic-Executive-Synopsis-9.25.2018.pdf.

3. Ron DeHaas "What Are the Most Up-to-Date Stats on Porn?" Covenant Eyes, January 19, 2016, www.covenanteyes.com/2016/01/19/what-are-the-most-up-to-date-stats-on-pornography.

4. "Pornography Statistics," Covenant Eyes, accessed March 25, 2021, www.covenanteyes.com/pornstats.

5. Dale Kunkel, et al., "Sex on TV: A Biennial Report for the Kaiser Family Foundation," accessed March 25, 2021, www.kff.org/wp-content/uploads/2013/01/sex-on-tv-a-biennial-report-to-the-kaiser-family-foundation-1999-executive-summary.pdf. Unfortunately, an equally exhaustive survey of the presence of sexualized content has yet to be repeated on today's content. Something tells me the numbers would not be pretty, especially in music videos.

6. Elizabeth McDade-Montez, "New Media, Old Themes: Sexualization in Children's TV Shows," ETR.org, March 28, 2017, www.etr.org/blog/research-childrens-media. Sexualization and objectification ranged from seductive clothing to unwanted touching and suggestive behavior.

7. Karen E. Dill and Kathryn P. Thill, "Video Game Characters and the Socialization of Gender Roles: Young People's Perceptions Mirror Sexist Media Depictions," *Sex Roles* 57, 851–64 (2007), doi: 10.1007/s11199-007-9278-1.

8. "Consider This," The Novus Project, accessed March 25, 2021, http://thenovusproject.org/resource-hub/parents. We can't even go to the store anymore without having a game plan in place to distract their attention from the eye-level backside hanging out of the bottom of a pair of "fashionable" cutoffs waiting to check out in front of them.

9. Ryan Singel, "Internet Porn: Worse than Crack?" *Wired*, November 19, 2004, www.wired.com/2004/11/internet-porn-worse-than-crack.

10. Joe S. McIlhaney, Jr., and Freda McKissic Bush, *Hooked: The Brain Science on How Casual Sex Affects Human Development* (Chicago: Northfield Publishing, 2019), 32.

11. Frances E. Jensen, *The Teenage Brain: A Neuroscientist's Survival Guide to Raising Adolescents and Young Adults* (New York: Harper Collins, 2015), 107.

12. Brian J. Willoughby, Dean M. Busby, and Bonnie Young-Petersen, "Understanding Associations Between Personal Definitions of Pornography, Using Pornography, and Depression," *Sexuality Research and Social Policy* 16 (2019): 342–56, doi: 10.1007/s13178-018-0345-x.

13. Catharine A. MacKinnon, "X-Underrated: Living in a World the Pornographers Have Made," in *Big Porn, Inc.: Exposing the Harms of the Global Pornography Industry,* Melinda Tankard Reist and Abigail Bray, eds. (North Melbourne, Victoria: Spinifex Press, 2012), 12.

14. Gert Martin Hald, Neil M. Malamuth, and Carlin Yuen, "Pornography and Attitudes Supporting Violence against Women: Revisiting the Relationship in Nonexperimental Studies," *Aggressive Behavior* 36, no. 1 (2010): 14–20, doi: 10.1002/ab.20328.

15. Melinda Tankard Reist, "Growing Up in Pornland: Australian Girls Have Had It with Porn-Conditioned Boys," Feminist Current, March 13, 2016, www.feministcurrent.com/2016/03/13/growing-up-pornland-australian-girls.

16. Jean Mackenzie, "Vagina Surgery 'Sought by Girls as Young as Nine,'" BBC, July 3, 2017, www.bbc.com/news/health-40410459.

17. "Landmark Report: U.S. Teens Use an Average of Nine Hours of Media Per Day, Tweens Use Six Hours," Common Sense Media, November 3, 2015, www.commonsensemedia.org/about-us/news/press-releases/landmark-report-us-teens-use-an-average-of-nine-hours-of-media-per-day.

18. Robert Jensen, "Stories of a Rape Culture: Pornography as Propaganda," in *Big Porn, Inc.: Exposing the Harms of the Global Pornography Industry*, Melinda Tankard Reist and Abigail Bray, eds. (North Melbourne, Victoria: Spinifex Press, 2012), 30.

19. Sandra Laville, "Most Boys Think Online Pornography Is Realistic, Finds Study," *The Guardian*, June 14, 2016, www.theguardian.com/culture/2016/jun/15/majority-boys-online-pornography-realistic-middlesex-university-study.

20. Colin Hesse and Kory Floyd, "Affection Substitution: The Effect of Pornography Consumption on Close Relationships," *Journal of Social and Personal Relationships* 36, no. 11-12 (2019): 3887–3907, doi: 10.1177/0265407519841719.

21. Shrier, *Irreversible Damage*, 47.

22. See Gary Wilson, *Your Brain on Porn: Internet Pornography and the Emerging Science of Addiction* (Kent, UK: Commonwealth Publishing, 2018). You can view the associated website at www.yourbrainonporn.com. It has both anecdotal evidence and a lot of scientific studies.

23. Linda Cusick, "Youth Prostitution: A Literature Review," *Child Abuse Review* 11, no. 4 (July August 2002), 230-251, doi: 10.1002/car.743.

Chapter 10. Same-Sex Attraction

1. There are still churches fighting to remain orthodox regarding this issue, but the culture is not on their side. And another side note, for those feisty enough to look at the endnotes, the next big ones are polyamory and then pedophilia. Gird your loins, Mama Bears. It's a coming.

2. Bruce Marshall, *The World, The Flesh, and Father Smith* (Boston, MA: Houghton Mifflin, 1945), 108.

3. Peter Kreeft, *How to Win the Culture War: A Christian Battle Plan for a Society in Crisis* (Downers Grove, IL: InterVarsity Press, 2002), 95.

4. Lisa Diamond, "Sexual Fluidity in Males and Females," *Current Sexual Health Reports* 8 (December 2016): 249-56, doi: 10.1007/s11930-016-0092-z.

5. Lisa Diamond, "Lisa Diamond on Sexual Fluidity of Men and Women," YouTube video, December 6, 2013, www.youtube.com/watch?feature=player_embedded&v=m2rTHDOuUBw.

6. The best talk I've ever seen on this is by Ricky Chelette, executive director of *Living Hope Ministries* in Arlington, Texas. I recommend that any parents of boys watch his video on the development of homosexuality in males available at www.livehope.org/product/why-understanding-male-gender-development-on-demand.

7. Lawrence S. Mayer and Paul R. McHugh, "Sexuality and Gender: Findings from the Biological, Psychological, and Social Sciences," *The New Atlantis*, Fall 2016, www.thenewatlantis.com/publications/executive-summary-sexuality-and-gender.

8. Hemal Jhaveri, "Oral Roberts University isn't the feel good March Madness story we need," *USA Today*, March 23, 2021, https://ftw.usatoday.com/2021/03/oral-roberts-ncaa-anti-lgbtq-code-of-conduct.

9. "Sexual Ethics: Experience, Growth, and Challenge. A Pastoral Reflection for Lesbian and Gay Catholics," Dignity USA, accessed April 5, 2021, www.dignityusa.org/sites/default/files/digusa-sexual_ethics.pdf.

10. Matthew Vines, *God and the Gay Christian: The Biblical Case in Support of Same-Sex Relationships* (New York: Convergent Books, 2014), 17.

11. Jen Hatmaker, "Episode 34: Jen Hatmaker—Changing Your Mind About the Bible: A Survivor's Guide," *The Bible for Normal People* podcast, January 29, 2018, http://thebiblefornormalpeople. podbean.com/e/episode-34-jen-hatmaker.

12. Kevin DeYoung, *What Does the Bible Really Teach About Homosexuality?* (Wheaton, IL: Crossway, 2015), 36.

13. Ibid.

14. Michael Hobbes, "Together Alone: The Epidemic of Gay Loneliness," *The Huffington Post*, March 1, 2017, https://highline.huffingtonpost.com/articles/en/gay-loneliness.

Chapter 11. Gender Identity

1. West, *Our Bodies Tell God's Story*, 28.

2. Charles Murray, *Human Diversity: The Biology of Gender, Race, and Class* (New York: Hachette Book Group, 2020), 12.

3. George Bernard Shaw, *The Quintessence of Ibsenism* (Boston, MA: Benj. R. Tucker, 1891), 43.

4. Gayle Rubin, "The Traffic in Women: Notes on the 'Political Economy' of Sex," in *Toward an Anthropology of Women,* ed. Rayna R. Reiter (New York and London: Monthly Review Press, 1975), 179.

5. Judith Butler, *Gender Trouble: Feminism and the Subversion of Identity* (New York: Routledge, 2007), 191.

6. "Pelosi and McGovern Unveil Details of Rules Package for the 117th Congress," House Committee on Rules, January 1, 2021, https://rules.house.gov/press-releases/pelosi-and-mcgovern-unveil -details-rules-package-117th-congress.

7. Deborah Soh, *The End of Gender: Debunking the Myths About Sex and Identity in Our Society* (New York: Simon & Schuster, 2020), 141.

8. Mere Abrams, "64 Terms That Describe Gender Identity and Expression," Healthline, December 20, 2019, www.healthline.com/health/different-genders#why-it-matters.

9. See Jonathan Wells's Transgenderism Series on *Evolution News and Views* at https://evolutionnews .org/tag/transgenderism-series. You can also see the executive summary of all the literature summarized by Lawrence S. Mayer and Paul R. McHugh at www.thenewatlantis.com/publications/ executive-summary-sexuality-and-gender.

10. There are about 15 known intersex conditions. For more information, see The Intersex Society of North America at www.isna.org.

11. Leonard Sax, "How Common Is Intersex? A Response to Anne Fausto-Sterling," *Journal of Sex Research* 39, no. 3 (2002), 174-178, doi: 10.1080/00224490209552139.

12. T. Beking, et al., "Prenatal and Pubertal Testosterone Affect Brain Lateralization," *Psychoneuroendocrinology* 88 (February 2018): 78-91, doi: 10.1016/j.psyneuen.2017.10.027.

13. Arthur P. Arnold and S. Marc Breedlove, "Organizational and Activational Effects of Sex Steroids on Brain and Behavior: A Reanalysis," *Hormones and Behavior* 19, no. 4 (December 1985): 469-98, doi: 10.1016/0018-506X(85)90042-X.

14. Melissa Hines, "Prenatal Testosterone and Gender-Related Behaviour," *European Journal of Endocrinology* 155, supplement no. 1 (November 2006): S115-S121, doi: 10.1530/eje.1.02236.

15. Elke Stefanie Smith, et al., "The Transsexual Brain: A Review of Findings on the Neural Basis of Transsexualism," *Neuroscience and Biobehavioral Reviews* 59 (December 2015): 251-66, doi: 10.1016/j.neubiorev.2015.09.008.

16. *Diagnostic and Statistical Manual of Mental Disorders,* 5th ed. (Washington, D.C.: American Psychiatric Association, 2013).

17. Noah Adams, Maaya Hitomi, and Cheri Moody, "Varied Reports of Adult Transgender Suicidality: Synthesizing and Describing the Peer-Reviewed and Gray Literature," *Transgender Health* 2, no. 1 (April 2017): 60-75, doi: 10.1089/trgh.2016.0036.

18. Cecilia Dhejne, et al., "Long-Term Follow-Up of Transsexual Persons Undergoing Sex Reassignment Surgery: Cohort Study in Sweden," *PLoS ONE* 6, no. 2 (2011), doi: 10.1371/journal.pone.0016885.

19. Richard Bränström and John E. Pachankis, "Reduction in Mental Health Treatment Utilization Among Transgender Individuals After Gender-Affirming Surgeries: A Total Population Study," *American Journal of Psychiatry* 177, no. 8 (August 2020): doi: 10.1176/appi.ajp.2019.19010080.

20. For instance, see Yolanda Smith, et al., "Sex Reassignment: Outcomes and Predictors of Treatment for Adolescent and Adult Transsexuals," *Psychological Medicine* 35, no. 1 (2005): 89–99, doi: 10.1017/s0033291704002776.

21. Alyson J. McGregor, "Impact of Sex and Gender on the 'Medicine' of Emergency Medicine," YouTube video, May 18, 2017, www.youtube.com/watch?v=0mhyPoU-tk8.

22. Shrier, *Irreversible Damage,* 7.

23. Ty Turner, "How to Tell If You Are Transgender," YouTube video, February 20, 2015, https://www.youtube.com/watch?v=f1rT7xOumO4.

24. Deborah Soh, *The End of Gender: Debunking the Myths About Sex and Identity in Our Society* (New York: Simon & Schuster, 2020), 141. This section references and cites all 11 studies.

25. Sue Bohlin, "Raising Gender Healthy Kids," *Probe for Answers,* July 30, 2015, https://probe.org/raising-gender-healthy-kids/.

Chapter 12. Purity Culture

1. Leah MarieAnn Klett, "Liberal Lutheran Pastor Melts Purity Rings into Vagina Sculpture, Presents It to Gloria Steinem," *Christian Post*, February 15, 2019, www.christianpost.com/news/liberal-lutheran-pastor-melts-purity-rings-into-vagina-sculpture-presents-it-to-gloria-steinem.html.

2. Tina Schermer Sellers, "How the Purity Movement Causes Symptoms of Sexual Abuse," TinaSchermerSellers.com, September 12, 2019, www.tinaschermersellers.com/post/how-the-purity-movement-causes-symptoms-of-sexual-abuse.

3. You can see a complete timeline of the True Love Waits movement at www.lifeway.com/en/product-family/true-love-waits/history.

4. *True Love Waits: Crossing Bridges with Purity* (Nashville: Lifeway Press, 1998), 10-12.

5. Joshua Harris, *I Kissed Dating Goodbye: A New Attitude Toward Romance and Relationships* (Colorado Springs, CO: Multnomah, 1997).

6. Hannah Lee Powers, quoted in "My Life Inside the Purity Movement," YouTube video, October 10, 2018, www.youtube.com/watch?v=c0vTn177UVg.

7. Linda Kay Klein, *Pure: Inside the Evangelical Movement that Shamed a Generation of Young Women*

and How I Broke Free (New York: Touchstone, 2018). This happened in Klein's small-town church, and she implied that all evangelical churches were the same.

8. Jessica Valenti, *The Purity Myth: How America's Obsession with Virginity Is Hurting Young Women* (Berkeley, CA: Seal Press, 2010), 24.

9. Elise Forte, quoted in Amanda Robb's "The Innocence Project," *O: The Oprah Magazine* (March 2007), www.oprah.com/relationships/father-daughter-purity-balls-to-promote-abstinence-chastity -pledges/6.

10. Klein, *Pure,* 3.

11. In case you haven't read Margaret Atwood's book *The Handmaid's Tale* or seen the show or the feminist protesters, this was the dress code of the enslaved fertile women forced to bear children for the wealthy couples of the Republic of Gilead.

12. As quoted in the documentary *Give Me Sex, Jesus* at www.youtube.com/watch?v=wp5HkXw9Rag.

13. Nicholas H. Wolfinger, "Does Sexual History Affect Marital Happiness?" Institute for Family Studies, October 22, 2018, https://ifstudies.org/blog/does-sexual-history-affect-marital-happiness.

Chapter 13. Taking Up Your Spiritual Cross

1. Christopher Yuan, *Holy Sexuality and the Gospel: Sex, Desire, and Relationships Shaped by God's Grand Story* (New York: Multnomah, 2018), 52.

2. Evan L. Ardiel and Catharine H. Rankin, "The Importance of Touch in Development," *Paediatrics & Child Health* 15, no. 3 (March 2010): 153-56, doi: 10.1093/pch/15.3.153.

Acknowledgments

Hillary

This book is the epitome of what it means for me to conquer fear. Thank you, Harvest House, for pushing me to write it even when I kept saying no.

Thank you, Amy and Lindsey, my partners in ministry, who were willing to listen to every insecurity and fear, and especially for Amy for agreeing to conquer this cultural behemoth with me.

Thank you to my husband, who loves me like Christ loved the church.

For my editor, Kathleen, who endured about five FaceTimes per day to discuss anything and everything. You are officially part of my "writing process."

For Lindsey and Robin, who kept our ministry running while Amy and I worked on this book.

Thank you to those who read early versions and lent support—Teasi Cannon, Hillary Short, Bethany Woodward, Beth Barber, Chris and Alice Morgan (the best publicists and parents anyone could ask for), Katie Hoksbergen (you and Leah and Jenna were my happy place through this book), Ricky Chelette, Julie Loos (and her amazing prayers), and countless others who were willing to lend feedback.

As with everything that is Mama Bear Apologetics, this is a group project. Mama Bear is all of us. We truly are all in this together. And as in all things, to my God and Savior who is the Artist of artists. May we all have eyes to see and ears to hear how He reveals Himself through our bodies, our sexuality, our gender, our marriages, and our families.

Amy

This book would never have been possible without the support of so many. Thank you to R.K.L., T.D., P.G., and R.I., who first sparked the love of apologetics in me and gave me my first chance to speak.

To Kyle, Travis, and countless ladies who shared their stories, advice, and wisdom.

To my folks, who knew I always wanted to be a writer but probably didn't think it would be on this topic!

To my kiddos, who ate cereal for dinner more than once and never complained. Who always cheered me on and brought me fresh coffee. I know you were sneaking snacks while I worked, but you were quiet so we'll call it even. I'm so proud of the godly men you're growing up to be.

To my gorgeous, the love of my life. You were my first editor, sounding board, and vent for my crazy. Thank you for all of the sacrifices you made, dinners you cooked, and for telling me I was pretty even when I wore the same sweatpants for days on end. You are my greatest blessing.

But mostly to God, whose beauty and wisdom guided this whole process. May the many mamas and papas who read this feel Your love, grace, and truth.

About the Authors

Hillary Morgan Ferrer, founder of Mama Bear Apologetics®, has a burden for providing accessible apologetics resources for busy moms. She has a master's in biology, and her specialties are scientific apologetics, dealing with doubt, and identifying causes and solutions for youth leaving the church.

Amy Davison is a former Air Force veteran-turned-writer and podcast cohost for Mama Bear Apologetics. She received her BS of Religion from Liberty University and MA in Christian Apologetics from Southwestern Baptist Theological Seminary. She speaks at conferences, and her work has been published by the Evangelical Philosophical Society and The Stream.

Julie Loos, the contributor of the "Prayers of Lament" and the P.A.W.S. for Prayer sections, marries her passion for prayer and apologetics in her ministry roles as the College Groups Liaison for Moms in Prayer International and as a contributing writer for Mama Bear Apologetics. She equips moms to pray strategically for the college campus and writes about stemming the tide of youth exodus from the faith.

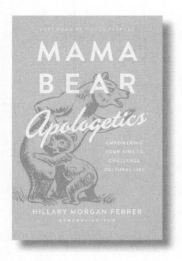

Mama Bear Apologetics

From a group of everyday Christian moms comes *Mama Bear Apologetics*®. This book equips you to teach your kids how to form their beliefs about what is true and what is false. Join bestselling author Hillary Morgan Ferrer in the Mama Bear movement—when you mess with our kids, we will demolish your arguments!

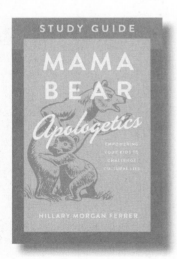

Mama Bear Apologetics Study Guide

When your kids come home from school asking questions about everything from moral relativity to cultural Marxism to whether God even exists, you need to be prepared with biblically sound answers. With this user-friendly companion to the bestselling book *Mama Bear Apologetics*®, you'll understand the secular worldviews your children face every day and build the foundation of faith and knowledge you need to equip them to respond to culture's lies.

For a list of recommended resources for further study, visit
www.mamabearapologetics.com/reources

To learn more about Harvest House books and
to read sample chapters, visit our website:

www.harvesthousepublishers.com

HARVEST HOUSE PUBLISHERS
EUGENE, OREGON